I0128385

Emery Alexander Storrs, Isaac E Adams

Political Oratory of Emery A. Storrs

Emery Alexander Storrs, Isaac E Adams

Political Oratory of Emery A. Storrs

ISBN/EAN: 9783337068691

Printed in Europe, USA, Canada, Australia, Japan

Cover: Foto ©Suzi / pixelio.de

More available books at **www.hansebooks.com**

EMERY A. STORRS.

POLITICAL ORATORY

OF

EMERY A. STORRS.

FROM LINCOLN TO GARFIELD.

BY

ISAAC E. ADAMS.

"IN ORATORY THE ESSENTIAL SECRET IS A GIFT OF GOD."

CHICAGO, NEW YORK, SAN FRANCISCO:

BELFORD, CLARKE & CO.

1888.

TABLE OF CONTENTS.

VI.

THE CAMPAIGN OF 1876.

VII.

THE CAMPAIGN OF 1880.

VIII.

THE CAMPAIGN OF 1884.

IX.

THE TARIFF ISSUE.

INTRODUCTORY CHAPTER.

POLITICAL ORATORY.

Rarity of Eminent Examples of Political Orators
or Oratory—Framework of Mr. Storrs' Life—
Unique Career—Comparison of Fame of Choate
and Sumner—Personal Appearance and Charac-
teristics—Remarkable Illustrations of Wonderful
Memory and Extempore Powers—Nature of Work.

FEW examples of political oratory have been embalmed in literature. Men, too, remembered for
oratorical power are easily reckoned, and tower conspicuously along the shores of time. There was once a
Demosthenes, once a Cicero, once a Burke. The time will
come when, looking back upon the centuries of American
history, it will be said there was, also, once a Webster
and once a Lincoln. Around each of these political suns
may swing, here and there in unshrouding space, a glowing light; but the lesser luminaries pale and eventually
become lost to the mind's sight with the receding
years. Moreover, the exceptional oratorical efforts —
politically—of even these preëminent ones in the world's
annals, are few in number, and come to active mankind
but as memories of droning school elocution. Attempt
to recollect the orators of the past, and their efforts, and
it must be said with Cicero that the orator is a rarer
product of nature than the poet. Demosthenes has
been named — he was partly the born and partly the

made orator, and his speeches are as few as the digits
upon the hand; Burke, whose orations are the greatest
in the English language, himself esteemed highly but
two of his speeches, and it is true, that, while he began
by surprising Parliament as a prodigy, he ended by
emptying the house. Mirabeau, ranking in the annals
of his country as the most famous, fiery and effective of
French orators, is scarcely known. Lord Chesterfield,
Lord Chatham, the Foxes — who can recall more than
the fleeting phrase from their many utterances? Almost
of yesterday were Tyng, Bethune, Chapin, McClintock,
Cheever, Starr King, Cuyler, Milburn, Bellows, Thompson — some of them as eloquent as any men in our history — but they are already engulphed in almost total
oblivion. Wendell Phillips, silvery as the tinkle of an
Alpine bell; Kossuth, the soul of mingled fun and
pathos; Gough, who for a score of years held, upon his
reels and staggers and mimicry, weeping and laughing
crowds — are sure to speedily be but traditions — so with
Beecher, so with Spurgeon. To change the use of an
old figure, it matters not whether the eloquence of
the orator, during his day, is like a summer shower,
lightning striking, passing on; or whether like a storm
at sea, rising lowly, with hazy sun, with threatening
clouds, with awesome thunder — it prevails over all — in
every case, Time obscures its path. Oratory of all
kinds is, has been, and will be scarce. Therefore, at
any time, and especially upon the eve of a national
campaign, no excuse can be needed for presenting to
the thinking, reading and speaking public some selections from one who deservedly ranked as one of the
greatest political orators of his day — a day embracing

a period of remarkable internecine war and subsequent equally remarkable prosperity; and nowhere is extant a volume of equal size containing so splendid examples of perfect argument, bristling with satire, and embellished by all the magnificence of genuine eloquence.

* * *

The framework of the life of Emery A. Storrs was simple:

Born August 12, 1835, he lived fifty years, dying September 12, 1885. Thirty years — two at Buffalo, N. Y., and twenty-eight at Chicago — as a lawyer he occupied the front rank at the American bar. He never held public office. He never received any remunera. tion for his political achievements. He was content to be a great orator.

With no pedestal of high office, with no monument of some permanent creation in literature, Mr. Storrs may be ephemeral in American fame. The hand of forgetting Fate may relentlessly thrust him altogether from even the vestibule of that temple within which stand eternally the Lincoln and the Grant of the great rebellion. If Choate and Sumner are surely sinking into oblivion, little more can be hoped for one who, it has been said, possessed the endowments of both — the tirelessness in preparation, the nervous, magnetic energy in execution, and the fidelity in trying emergencies of the one, and the convincing logic, the impressiveness of style, and the persuasive richness of the other. But, he was an ornament to his day and generation. The public speaker can well afford to study Emery A. Storrs' orations as models in oratory.

In appearance, he was not unusual. Physically, he

was small, not weighing over one hundred and twenty avoirdupois; owing to inherited weakness, he was wont to stoop slightly, except when engaged in public speaking, and then he always stood erect, firm and straight as an Indian. His voice was rich, deep, full as an organ note — extraordinary in its sweetness, and rounded intoning. There was something singularly fascinating in his style and manner of speaking. His custom was to begin every argument or any oratorical effort in slow, measured tones, sinking at times almost into a whisper, but always clear and clean-cut, so that unto the remotest listener every inflection would come distinct as though thundered. Gradually his voice would rise and strengthen, until the words poured forth a fiery flood of irresistible argument, gleaming with sharp invective and brillian wit. His dialect was simple, pure, and direct. He employed judiciously the graces of imagination. He was totally devoid of theatricalism in elocution, gesture, and personal bearing, but would sometimes resort to the most intense dramatic effects, while his wondrous wit, rarely, if ever, surpassed on the rostra or in the forum, could break, at his will, into a terribly biting whirlwind of raillery and jest, before which show men and tinsel appearances were swept into a sea of ridiculousness. Yet, this splendid wit of Mr. Storrs — this merry and ridiculing laugh, so to speak, of his intellect — was not his real temper. He prided himself more upon the thoroughness with which he mastered facts and upon the surpassing skill with which he added them to great truths and broad principles.

His mind was stored to overflowing with the

treasures of literature, ever ready to be uttered. No one of that vast audience which had gathered upon the shores of Lake Michigan that autumn day to listen to Mr. Storrs speak, can ever forget the marvelous appropriateness with which he interweaved into the panegyric he suddenly pronounced upon the dead Garfield — the news of whose death came with the moment to the orator — the veriest gems of literature. Take but one short paragraph of that tender, beautiful eulogy, pronounced impromptu, but which in the language of a contemporary "moved the multitude to tears and left an impression ineffaceable during life."

"Our departed Garfield wisely said that God reigns; and in the presence of that great national calamity and bereavement, the martyrdom of Lincoln, he declared 'God reigns, and the government at Washington still lives.' The life of man is but a few short years. This nation is immortal. Its life is indestructible. No bullet was ever cast or ever will be that can reach its heart. No assassin can ever shatter it, and it is for us to take up the thread of this noble life, so untimely and tragically closed, and carry on our shoulders, inspired by his example, the country which he had done so much to honor and to save, forward on the great and lofty mission which he had again and again pointed out for it. He would have it march in the pathway of noble resolve and spotless honor, and so will we. He would have its pathway marked by the skeleton of no broken engagements or violated promises. Nor will we. He would leave behind it no desolated homes, but would have in its career smiling villages, prospering towns, fields of waving grain, golden harvest, contented and prospering homes, and the hum of busy cities greeting it everywhere. So will we. On its banners he would have no stain, no spot or blemish, or any such thing. Nor will we. And the most touching tributes that we can pay to the memory of our dead President and friend will not be the flowers we may cast upon his grave, but they will be a steady striving toward the example of his pure and spotless life. For these, after all, are the patriotic harmonies which the solemn dirges that fill the air over all the continent carry with them.

"It is to such music, sad, solemn, but lofty as this, that the funeral processions throughout the continent, and all but a part of that sad procession which to-day follows the remains of our dead President to their last resting place, are marching.

"Our sweetest songs are those that tell of saddest thought.

"And there are no harmonies so grand as those which come from high hearts, beating in unison a lofty and patriotic purpose. Thus honoring and thus loving him, we commit our great Chief Magistrate to his final resting-place—

"His body to that blessed country's earth,
And his pure soul unto his Captain, Christ,
Under whose colors he had fought so long.

"The lesson of his life was:

"Be just and fear not,
Let all the ends thou aim'st at be thy country's,
Thy God's, and truth's,
Then, if thou fallest, thou fallest a blessed martyr

"Sadly, with our eyes blinded with bitter tears, we gather around that open grave. The flowers which we heap about it are not those of forgetfulness. As the green grasses shall grow above it at the first quick flush of the opening spring, as the flowers shall bloom over it through all the long summer days, so from that poor shattered and coffined body shall the noble spirit rise, living, immortal, a tender memory and a holy inspiration."

Emery A. Storrs had, moreover, a power of extempore oratory in no wise dependent upon his remarkable retentiveness of memory. While in St. Louis, as leading counsel for the defense in the famous Babcock trial, he exhibited his readiness in marshalling thoughts and his amazing command of language in a wonderful instance. His great cause had been won; his client had been honorably acquitted; and there gathered around Mr. Storrs at the Lindell Hotel a congratulating circle, including many eminent members of the St. Louis bar. Some of these were disposed to celebrate the occasion by conviviality, but Mr. Storrs could not be induced to join in their potations, though he sat smiling by, drinking lemonade. One of his legal brethren suggested that he surely never had gone through the fatigues of such a trial without some stronger stimulus than lemonade; he doubted its power of inspiration, and challenged Mr. Storrs to make an off-hand temperance speech. The challenge was promptly accepted, and a short-hand reporter who was present took notes of what he said, and published the speech from his notes after Mr. Storrs' death. Although modeled on John B. Gough's well-known apostrophe to water — which, in its turn, was said to have been original with Lorenzo Dow — the speech which follows is so thoroughly characteristic in ideas and method of expression as to be altogether and most brilliantly Mr. Storrs' own brain-child:

"How do you expect to improve upon the beverage furnished by nature? Here it is — Adam's ale — about the only gift that has descended undefiled from the garden of

Eden! Nature's common carrier — not created in the rottenness of fermentation, not distilled over guilty fires! Virtues and not vices are its companions. Does it cause drunkenness, disease, death, cruelty to women and children? Will it place rags on the person, mortgages on the stock, farm, and furniture? Will it consume wages and income in advance and ruin men in business? No! But it floats in white gossamer clouds far up in the quiet summer sky, and hovers in dreamy mist over the merry faces of all our sparkling lakes. It veils the woods and hills of earth's landscapes in a purple haze, where filmy lights and shadows drift hour after hour. It piles itself in tumbled masses of cloud-domes and thunderheads, draws the electric flash from its mysterious hiding-places, and seams and shocks the wide air with vivid lines of fire. It is carried by kind winds, and falls in rustling curtains of liquid drapery over all the thirsty woods and fields, and fixes in God's mystic eastern heavens His beautiful bow of promise, glorified with a radiance that seems reflected out of heaven itself. It gleams in the frost crystals of the mountain tops and the dews of the valleys. It silently creeps up to each leaf in the myriad forests of the world and tints each fruit and flower. It is here in the grass-blades of the meadows, and there where the corn waves its tassels and the wheat is billowing! It gems the depths of the desert with the glad, green oasis, winds itself in oceans round the whole earth, and roars its hoarse, eternal anthems on a hundred thousand miles of coast! It claps its hands in the flashing wave-crests of the sea, laughs in the little rapids of the brooks, kisses the dripping, moss-covered, old oaken well-buckets in a countless host of happy homes! See these pieces of cracked ice, full of prismatic colors, clear as diamonds! Listen to their fairy tinkle against the brimming glass, that sweetest music in all the world to one half-fainting with thirst! And so, in the language of that grand old man, Gough, I ask you, Brothers all, would you exchange that sparkling glass of water for alcohol, the drink of the very Devil himself?"

* * *

This little work, although especially planned for a presentation of the fullness of Mr. Storrs' rich and peerless political argument and for a showing of the massiveness and the incisiveness of his logic, may not be unhappily introduced further by one chapter devoted to illustrations of some of his witty and eloquent characterizations of persons and parties, as gathered from some of his forensic victories. The work, however, as its title implies, treats, through Mr. Storrs' great speeches, of the Kansas troubles of 1858; it covers the agitating questions of the campaigns of 1860, 1868, 1872, 1876, 1880 and 1884. There is, also, an exposition of Mr. Storrs' free-trade sentiments in 1870, when he discussed the high tariff as a war measure and claimed that the farmers of the West needed to be protected against protection; — together with an exposition of how, in 1882, he became an ardent protectionist. In these later chapters, more particularly, the reader is invited to selections from most impressive arguments, brightened by felicitous wit and all the graces of magnificent oratory. It is the work of Mr. Storrs. The diction, the beauties of expression, above all the keen-edged logic, are suggested as worthy the study of all thinkers.

II.

ILLUSTRATIONS OF WIT AND WISDOM.

EVIDENCE OF AN ORATOR'S POWER—DEMOCRATIC CHARAC-
TERIZATIONS—THE MODERNIZED PRODIGAL SON—FUN
WITH SEYMOUR—TILDEN WRITES A LETTER—BRAVES
WHO REMAINED AT HOME—CHARACTER OF CHARLES
SUMNER—VARIOUS TYPES OF ELOQUENCE.

IT will some time be regarded as a remarkable fact
that a political orator of the days of the Rebellion,
and immediately afterwards, should indulge in such
ardent displays of partisanship and personality, and yet
hold — as did always Mr. Storrs — the unanimous and
enthusiastic sympathy of his vast audiences. All classes,
the high and the low, the rich and the poor, the intellectual and the dullard, Democrat and Republican, helped
fill to overflowing the auditorium or public square whenever it was announced that Emery A. Storrs was to be
the orator of the occasion. There seemed to be a sort
of witchery about his name, or a spell of magic about
his utterances. The laugh at his lanced personal dia-
tribes, the cheer at his party eulogiums, and the storm
of vehement applause at his floods of brilliant eloquence,
were ever as from one man. To this fact, the thousands
living can bear witness — for Mr. Storrs was of yesterday. Yet no man, perhaps, ever swayed an audience
who was so radical, so extreme in all his portraitures of
men and measures. It is true, doubtless, that one chief
reason for what will in the days to come be considered

14

somewhat in the light of an anomaly, is due to the times in which Mr. Storrs lived and participated; for he began his career in the season of war, and he passed away not long after the cannon had ceased its wonderful music. The chiefest reason, though, in the case of Mr. Storrs, rested in the fact that he was "the orator born." The sensorium of mortals seems to yield to the natural genius of oratory. It is, as of old, a music which thrills. The vibration of thought, of voice, of action — all conquered, and foe and friend roared or maintained silence at his wish. The doubter is referred to those living who have heard Mr. Storrs speak, or, indeed, to the columns of the contemporary press, studded with parenthetic [cheers], [applause].

He did, though, say many severe things of his opponents. His comparison of the record of the Democratic party will not soon be forgotten. "The Democratic party is like a mule: it has neither pride of ancestry nor hope of posterity." "There are millions," he said, " better than the party, and none worse." "The Democratic party cannot be compared to sin, but only because it is sin itself." It will be remembered, too, what he said of Democratic assurances:

" We are satisfied that any policy, particularly any Republican policy, based upon Democratic promises, is resting upon a foundation so frail and insecure that it must ultimately perish. London is proverbially foggy. The fog there, at times, is said to be so dense that it is actually palpable to the touch. An honest and enterprising British carpenter, shingling his house on one foggy day, was surprised to find, when the day's work was concluded, that he had shingled out about three feet on to the fog. My good,

timorous Republican friends, for God's sake don't let us
shingle on to the fog.   One day of fair weather destroys
that unsubstantial foundation, and you might as well
attempt to build out on to a fog as to establish any policy
from which the country is to derive substantial and continuous peace or quiet, upon any assurance of the Democratic
party as such."

And none can ever forget his comparison of the
Democratic party to the prodigal son.   He said :

" It takes but a very few days' contact with the Democracy to stain the white and spotless garment of Republicanism. They mistake a great Scriptural story.   Mr.
Chairman, the air is full of devotion.   I feel a good deal
like talking Scripture myself. They are misled by the
story of the prodigal son. They seem to think that that
parable was told as an invitation for young men to go off
and be prodigals.   It was not told for any such purpose.
The prodigal made nothing whatever out of the experiment.
He took what money belonged to him and went away fool-
ishly, as other young men have done.   He fell among the
Democrats, and was naturally cleaned out.   And when his
money was gone, and his clothes gone, and his credit gone,
the Democrats of that day had no further use for him.   He
went into the swine business, Mr. Chairman, as I read it.
He went to feed swine, and the swine were discouraged ;
and then he went feeding with swine, and they turned him
out, and it was hard times with the poor, young independent prodigal.   And without clothes enough on him to wad
a gun, he started for home.   The point comes right here :
How much did the prodigal make out of that enterprise ?
The dear old father looking down that dusty turnpike
expecting the boy back ultimately, and seeing him coming,
went out and threw himself around his neck and welcomed

him. And what did he give him? He did not give him
back any of the farm; he did not give him an office — no,
not the smell of an office. The prodigal had too much
good sense to ask for one. All he cared for was to be taken
in as a hired servant. And what that father gave him was
a new suit of clothes and a ring on his finger, and a veal
dinner. A fatted calf. That contribution has always
been over-estimated. Everybody was engaged in raising
calves. There was no market for calves — calves were
"long." And the boy who stayed at home did not quite
relish this uproar, on account of this sore-eyed prodigal,
and he turned to his father with some complaint; but his
father said, " Don't complain, son, you are always with
me; all that I have is thine." Not a cent of money, not a
foot of ground, not an office was given to the prodigal;
but the boy who staid at home had it all. Now I do hope
that my Independent friends won't wait — that they won't
tarry. My good friends down there in New York, you
can never occupy a mansion that is so spacious and so splendid. You will never again be so honorably and comfortably housed. Come back to the great mansion, the dome
of which glistens with stars and is as broad as the very
heavens. Come back to the old mansion. It is capable of
entertaining the fifty millions of good, earnest, patriotic
people of this nation. Come back to it. After all the
decayed timbers of human chattelhood have been removed,
and we have supplied their places with the everlasting
granite of universal freedom, come back to it — with its
glorious inscriptions written and emblazoned upon its walls,
no longer devastated by the fugitive slave law; no longer
befouled and besmirched by the inscriptions of the Dred
Scott case. Come back with the Fourteenth and Fifteenth
Amendments that glimmer like shining planets from its
white and stainless walls."

More dignified, but more terrible was his arraignment of the same party when replying to an opponent who had alluded to the history of the Democratic party.

"Its history," said he, "is made up of great, ghostly scars inflicted upon the nation, of cemeteries filled with noble men who have fallen victims to its doctrines. Its history can be traced on bloody battle-fields, where citizens of the same nationality have been arrayed against each other because of Democratic heresies. Its history is found in desolated homes and speaks through mourning weeds, orphan children and widowed wives, made so through a causeless, cruel, wicked war. Its history is found also in the gigantic national debt, created to save a nation which its heresies came very near destroying. Every one-legged soldier furnished a bit of history of Democratic doctrine; the black stain of repudiation fastened upon the Southern states remains there to-day as proof of Democratic doctrine, eternally ineffaceable — and there is no tradition about it, for the creditors still live and they know they have been plundered. The mellow light of tradition does not rest upon Democratic political crimes; it is the ghastly light of to-day which discloses their political offenses in all their hideous deformities.

"It is difficult to restrain one's self so as to talk composedly of this Democratic party when we reflect that it undertook to fasten the blighting, blistering curse of African chattelhood upon the great, verdant territories of the West, which the Republican party has made free states and saved to be splendid homes for free men. It is difficult to speak quietly and patiently of a party which, being defeated in the execution of such a gigantic crime against the civilization of the age and against common humanity, hurried and forced a great republic into a rebellion the most causeless and the most wicked that history has recorded. A party which would thus imperil the success of the experiment of self-government inaugurated upon this continent, imperil that great experiment to promote a cause so indescribably wicked as that of African slavery, can hardly look for gingerly treatment or language of courtesy when its career and history are under discussion. But this party, which for twenty-five years has been political crime and lust for power, organized with faults that disprove all protestations of good conduct for the future on its lips, comes to our people and has the audacity — I say *audacity:* it is so when we consider what its past doctrines and traditions have been — to employ this language: 'We pledge ourselves anew to the constitutional doctrines and traditions of the Democratic party, as illustrated by the teachings and example of a long line of Democratic statesmen and patriots.' The line of Democratic statesmen and patriots here referred to practically begins with Franklin Pierce. It was continued by James Buchanan, and while the line was somewhat interrupted thereafter, Jefferson Davis, Horatio Seymour, Wade Hampton, Senator Hendricks, Robert Toombs, Ben Butler, Ben Hill, Governor English have been and are still leaders of the Democratic party north and south, and a part of the long line to which this platform refers. Its long lines of doctrines and traditions began with its attempt to steal the territories from freedom and to dedicate them to slavery, supplemented by an attempt to steal the island of Cuba for the same purpose. In 1856 the Democratic party, in national convention assembled, denied the power of the general government to charter a national bank, pledged itself to resist all attempts in Congress or out of it to agitate the slavery question, and resolved that the party would faithfully abide by and uphold the principles laid down in the celebrated secession Kentucky and Virginia resolutions of 1798. It adopted those principles as constituting one of the main foundations of its political creed, and resolved to carry them out; and in 1880 the same party declares: ' We pledge ourselves anew to the constitutional doctrines and traditions of the Democratic party.' "

Campaign listeners of the days of 1868 will recall many of Mr. Storrs' droll hits at Governor Seymour, the candidate for Democratic presidency. It will be remembered how in October of that year, the Governor had visited Chicago and addressed a meeting in the old Court House square, and how Mr. Storrs reviewed him at Library Hall a few days later.

"About six years ago," said Mr. Storrs, " I was riding through Greenwood cemetery, and I observed a venerable looking person apparently examining a monument not yet entirely constructed. Being somewhat curious in the matter, I asked the person in charge of the grounds who that old man was that was bossing the tombstone. He told me that it was the owner of the tombstone, and that he was fixing it up for his own accommodation. It appeared to me to be a melancholy kind of amusement; but I was satisfied last Saturday night that that venerable old gentleman was not the only man engaged in the same kind of business. For I saw, standing on the steps of the north door of the Court House, surrounded by his friends, some of whom he had brought with him from the city of New York, a gentleman observing the preparations for his own funeral, and with a melancholy kind of jocularity engaging in them. Horatio Seymour has been here. Horatio Seymour has gone. 'Why should we mourn departed friends?' "

The Governor in one of his speeches had said that

Grant and Colfax were in full retreat and he had brought them in as captives.

"It is," said Mr. Storrs, "a good deal such a capture as was accomplished by the hunter on the plains when h was sent out at night to shoot a buffalo for his friends. He hit the buffalo, and just barely hit him, and maddened him. The old beast started for the hunter, who was on horseback, and went vigorously for him. The dust flew in large quantities, and the hunter made for the camp immediately. They arrived in sight of it, and he, in order to keep up his reputation for courage, took off his hat and valiantly swung it, and hardly able to keep away from the enraged buffalo, shouted, ' Here we come ! You sent me after a buffalo, and I will bring it to you alive !'"

The same Democratic favorite after having been nominated, declined three or four times before he would stand as a candidate.

"And now," said his ridiculer, "that the New York *World* and other papers think that he had better quit, he seems as resolutely disposed not to quit as he was resolutely disposed not to run. In that particular he is a good deal like Sam Casey's calf. Sam said he had to pull his ears off to get him to suck, and then to pull his tail off to get him to quit."

Criticising Mr. Seymour's speech upon the issues of the campaign, Mr. Storrs remarked :

"He said not a word about his own platform, and he thereby admits that it is indefensible. He has not said a word against our platform, and thereby he admits that it is unassailable. He stands in the position of the ox just half jumped over the fence, utterly worthless either for aggressive or defensive purposes."

But Mr. Storrs could be terribly bitter in his treatment of even such political opponents to his party as

was Horatio Seymour.   His thrilling comparison of the
two letters which passed between Seymour and Lincoln
in the Rebellion times — the one letter imprudently
demanding that the draft should be suspended until the
constitutionality of the law should be tested by the
courts, and the other promptly replying that the time
allowed no delay, that a nation's life was imperiled —
can never be forgotten by those who listened to the
speaker as with trumpet tones, he exclaimed :

"As thoroughly as I dislike the record which Horatio
Seymour has made, as malignant and as dangerous as I
deem it to be, as great as I conceive the punishment for
those offenses ought to be, yet I could ask that no severer
punishment be visited upon him than that the spirit of
those two letters, taking visible shape, should march down
the aisles of history together.   How, as we stood upon some
elevated table land, where we could watch their progress,
would, as the distance lengthened out, the spirit of Horatio Seymour's letter warp, and dwindle, and halt, and
wither, while that of our grand old patriotic President,
growing greater and greater as the years receded, swelling
into loftier and grander proportions as the mist of prejudice and passion cleared away from it, disclosing in its out-
lines the perfect symmetry of patriotic, high-hearted faith
in the great cause for which he died, would challenge the
admiration of all the ages, reaching at last the highest
summits of historic renown.   We would all find that as we
gazed upon it we stood in the presence of a great character.
Before it we would, with uncovered head, reverently bow.
We would hail and salute it.   Thus would the muse of history, making up the records of human achievements,
address it : 'Stand up, Abraham Lincoln, among the
greatest and the noblest, and the best of this world's his-

tory.' And, looking about, discovering the halting spirit of Horatio Seymour had, in some mysterious way, corkscrewed itself into that glorious company where it did not belong, it would address him, saying: 'Stand down, Horatio Seymour, among the falterers, and sneaks, and cowards, and doubters, and those who sought to obstruct the march of a great nation, as it was resolutely treading the road which led to the clear atmospheres of freedom.'"

The power possessed by Mr. Storrs for holding up to the ridicule of laughing auditors, the unfortunate blunders and utterances of some candidate, was exerted against Mr. Tilden in a way which can never be separated from that really great statesman's career. To the well-informed political student a half-sad laugh must ever, unfortunately perhaps, be linked with the political utterances of "Sammy J." Take, for instance, Mr. Storrs' fun with him, in a Cincinnati speech, over his letter of declination:

"When the Democratic party becomes sentimental, it is time for those whose digestion operates in the ordinary way to become alarmed. Their sentiment is Mr. Tilden; and at the expense of being somewhat tedious, I wish to read to you quite briefly one of the most tender, one of the most pathetic, and one of the most tearful contributions to political literature — his recent letter of declination. Here I intend to be fair, absolutely fair. Last week, in the city of Chicago, I did a great injustice. I intimated in a speech, which it was my good fortune there to deliver, that his intellect was impaired, and that his sagacity had become enfeebled. I was mistaken; I am mistaken; and no better proof of my mistake can be furnished than the fact that within three days after the nomination of Blaine and Logan he sent in his letter of declination. All this demonstrates that Samuel J. Tilden is just as keen, and sharp, and far-sighted as he has ever been. He has taken, Mr. Chairman, to his earthworks and fortifications early. He has seen the storm coming up from the West. And Samuel J. Tilden is in out of the rain. I shall not read all his letter. The life of man is limited to about seventy years, ordinarily, and you cannot expect me to consume all that time in reading a tearful, sobbing epistle from the great railroad wrecker of the continent, who is the spirit of the present Democratic party manifest in the flesh ; and whoever is nominated will be but the reflection of Samuel J. Tilden. Just one sentence, and then I am going to ask who wrote this :

" 'Twenty years of continuous maladministration, under the demoralizing influences of intestine war and of bad finance, have infected the whole governmental system of the United States with the cancerous growths of false constructions and corrupt practices.'

"I have a right, every human being in this country, proud of what it is and hopeful of what it is to be, has a right to denounce that as a wicked and malicious slander upon the most glorious period in our history or in the history of the world. I don't take to this kindly. What has been the history of that twenty years ; that this man, whom I will not now further attempt to characterize, denounces as 'cancerous maladministration ?' In that twenty years this great party, for which this imperial state speaks to-night, in that time it has crowded a thousand years of the most glorious history that this world has ever witnessed. Within that twenty years Abraham Lincoln has been elected. Within that twenty years this party of 'maladministration' has lifted four millions of human beings from the night and savagery and barbarism of chattelhood into the clear, bracing and elevated air of American citizenship. And yet with such an achievement, that shines with the light of planets against the sky, a railroad wrecker, embodying the sentiments of his party, speaks of it as a career of 'maladministration.' Within that time this 'intestine war' to which he refers—this intestine war which, in 1864, he declared was a failure, was waged — a Union has been saved and the greatest achievement ever recorded in history, passed to the credit of the Republican party, represented here to-night. Within that twenty years, in that splendid, that glorious twenty years, the national honor has been saved against the assaults of his own party, who sought to destroy it. In that twenty years the national credit has been maintained, when he and his party would have debauched our honor by the repudiation of our public debt. Within that length of time this administration, which he characterizes as 'maladministration,' has taken a newly-made citizen by the hand, has made him a citizen, has given him the right of suffrage, has embodied that right in the constitution, and, by the grace and help of God, means to secure him in its full enjoyment.

"That is the 'maladministration' of which Mr. Samuel J. Tilden speaks. This glorious apostle of our history closes with this tender and touching appeal which I shall have occasion to say to you has made the eyes of Democrats suffuse with tears, choked their utterance, and has almost smothered them with sobs:

"'Having given to their welfare whatever of health and strength I possessed, or could borrow from the future, and having reached the term of my capacity for such labors as their welfare now demands, I but submit to the will of God in deeming my public career for ever closed. SAMUEL J. TILDEN.'

"That letter was written in the mansion made famous by receipts of cipher dispatches, upon the walls of which hung

the skeletons of wrecked railroads and other corporations!
Samuel J. Tilden, with his hand on the bung of his barrel,
ecorously submits himself to the will of God.

"'That is very kind of Mr. Tilden. This tender epistle
goes all over the country. The distinguished mayor of
Chicago reads it—and he is a distinguished man; he is a
genuine, straight-forward Democrat. I supposed him to
be over and above the sympathetic. But it goes right to
the tender heart of Chicago's mayor, and he says: 'As I
read it my eyes were dimmed with tears, my utterance was
choked, my heart filled with sobs, and a great grief over-
came me.' This is the sentiment and the sympathy of the
Democratic party. 'Willie, we have missed you.' I am
anxious to see that party turned into a purely emotional
and sympathetic entertainment. I am anxious to see the
club of 'rounders' in New York; the representatives of
the horny-handed and the hard-fisted, who have made night
hideous with their yells in many campaigns; I am anxious
to see the belligerent Democrats of our great cities whose
ears have been bit off in some joint debate, whose noses
have been broken in some election contest, gather unto the
shadow of weeping willows, marching to funeral music in
a great sympathetic campaign. Why, think of the old
party? Think of its universal crookedness — a party that
never did a right thing in its whole life! As I see it to-day
weaving and winding out on the tariff question, Mr. Chairman, I am reminded of the experience of the boy in that
good old county Cattaraugus, in the state of New York,
where I was born. Our mothers were good, prudent,
thrifty women. When our trousers were worn one side
they were turned the other way, so that when you watched
a tow-headed boy you could not tell whether he was going
to school or coming home. It's the same with the Democratic party. Watch this Democratic party with its politi-

cal feet cross-eyed, with its right political foot on its left
political leg. Take the tariff question, take the question
of the support of the public-credit, take the subject of the
vindication of the public honor — in favor, they say, of
preserving and maintaining the national dignity ; and yet
voting appropriations of money to build gunboats, and then
refusing to vote an appropriation of money to supply the
guns."

The foregoing are types of the lighter side of Mr.
Storrs' intellect. They occur all through his speeches,
but not more frequently than such splendid passages as :

"I like sometimes to figure in my imagination our
nation taking a physical form and shape. How great, how
radiant, how transcendent seems to be the genius of our
institutions ! How much grander than on any other occasion does she appear when descending from her radiant
throne she takes the trembling citizen, white or black,
native or foreign born, by the hand, and covering him with
her shield leads him safely to the polls, and protects him
there until he casts a free and unconstrained ballot. That
is justice."

Nor do jibes appear in his efforts as frequently as
such beautiful sentiments as :

"I love to talk to young men, and to this young and
giant West. I believe in the dreams that young men
dream, and in the visions that young men see, and in the
castles that young men build. For where without the
dreams of the young men, lighting up the future with
human possibilities, would be the deeds of the old men,
dignifying the past with heroic achievements. Young
men of this district, be brave, be hopeful, be true. Believing always more in the goodness of God than in the dexterity of the devil, rest assured that in the long run the

right side is the strong side, and no expediency can finally succeed which has not justice for its foundation. Let your courage increase as dangers thicken, and as difficulties multiply. Be not disheartened by long delay, nor elated by hopes of too easy success. The providence of God rules this world, and the nations thereof, and, true to Him and to yourselves, our country may yet become the incarnation of all that is wise and just in human government, and the lighted torch which she carries shall bring health and healing to all the nations."

Describing the sweep of an on-coming Republican storm of victory at the polls, he exclaimed:

"Gentlemen, the first-heard patterings of the coming storm are here. The great droppings are beginning to fall on the far Pacific coast. It gathers volume as it moves west. The roar of the advancing multitudes fills all the sky, and the gleam of their fires on every hill fills the whole heavens with flame.

"When the mighty storm, gathering force and volume as it proceeds, strikes those eastern states, then there will be a deluge that will bury in one common watery, dishonorable grave Democrat and Independent alike."

Himself, on account of physical weakness, never in the army, at a grand soldiers' banquet, at which he was called upon for a toast, he pled forcibly for the brave ones who remained at home, and said among other things in fine antithesis:

"Not alone to the soldier does the glory of the great triumph belong. Every single citizen who cast even the measure of his influence on the right side is entitled to share in this common glory. History will inscribe, in making up her final and impartial judgments, on parallel lines, the solid heroism and sturdy sense of Grant, and the patient, long-suffering loyalty of Lincoln; the grand strategy of Sherman, and the wise counsels of Seward; the dashing and intrepid valor of Sheridan, and the devoted love of country of Richard Yates; the fiery energy and splendid generalship of Logan, and the wise statesmanship of Morton; the dauntless courage of fighting Joe Hooker, and the resolute and uncomprising patriotism and sense of justice of Zachariah Chandler. Upon these imperishable records there will be inscribed not only the names of the great leaders in the great cause, but the humblest worker in its behalf will find his name upon its pages. Bright and shining on those resplendent annals shall appear the names of those thousands of noble, heroic and self-sacrificing women who organized and carried forward to triumphant success a colossal sanitary and charitable scheme, the like of which, in nobility of conception and perfectness of execution, the world has never before witnessed, and which carried all around the globe the fame and the name of the women of America. From camp to camp, from battle-field to battle-field, through the long and toilsome march, by day and by night, these sacred charities followed, and the prayers of the devoted and the true were ceaselessly with you. Leagues and leagues separated you from home, but the blessings there invoked upon you hovered over and around you, and sweetened your sleep like angels' visits. While the boy soldier slept by his camp fire at night and dreamed of home, and what his valor would achieve for his country, uttered in his dreams prayers for the loved ones who had made that home so dear to him, the mother dreaming of her son breathed at the same time prayers for his safety and for the triumph of his cause. The prayers and blessings of mother and son, borne heavenward, met in the bosom of their common God and Father."

This classical and Periclean style of oratory of Mr.

Storrs, occurring so frequently in his preserved literary remains, is perhaps nowhere better shown than in his eulogy upon Charles Sumner, uttered by him just after that prominent American's death in 1875, during a Decoration address. He said of him:

"A deed of patriotic heroism is in its effects eternal. It possesses an indestructible vitality. The heroic deeds of which blind old Homer sung, have come down to us across the chasm of thousands of years, and to-day inspire the farmer boy upon the hillside and the prairie with high and noble resolve. Great deeds and great men make great nations. The Greece of to-day has the same hills and the same valleys that it had two thousand years ago — the same sky bends over it to-day that canopied it then; but Pericles and Phidias, Plato, Demosthenes, and the great men who made Athens the seat of culture and philosophy, are no more, and Greece — *the* Greece — lives no longer. And so our country, young as it is, is the country which our great and patriotic men have made it. Into the current of our national history the heroic deeds of the Union soldier have passed. Their names 'history will never willingly permit to die.'

"We speak a few weak words; but the great heart's gone to God.
  They have fought with their swords, won our battles, red, wet-shod!
  While we sat at home new laurels for our land they went to win,
  And with smiles Valhalla lightens as our heroes enter in.
  They bore our banners fearless to the death as to the fight,
  They raised our nation peerless to the old heroic height.
  We weep not for the heroes whom we never more shall see,
  We weep we were not with them in their ruddy revelry.

"But not alone in the rude shock of battle were the great results to which I have referred accomplished. The rebellion was a contest between opposing ideas, and long before they flamed out into war had they been brooded over by the thinker, urged upon the platform, proclaimed through the press, declaimed upon the stump, debated in Congress, discussed and argued in the courts. The great champion of the cause for which the soldier died, lived to see its complete triumph — and then he passed away.

"From his boyhood, through obloquy and abuse, Charles Sumner stood forth the unflinching, unswerving champion of the rights of man. It would ill become me to attempt to pronounce a eulogy upon Charles Sumner. That work has been so well, so beautifully, so feelingly and truthfully done already in every city in the country that it would be an impertinence in me to undertake the task. But the great leading features of Mr. Sumner's character, intellectual and moral, were of such transcendent merit, that surely it will be well if his example is constantly kept before us, and our public men. A man of the broadest culture, and the largest literary acquirements, he never employed them for the promotion of his own personal ends, nor for any purpose of self-aggrandizement. He never used his vast learning to tickle the ears of the multitude, nor were his literary quotations, numerous and beautiful as they were, ever employed to gild an unworthy purpose. His intellectual fiber was of the most perfect rectitude. He could no more take a position that he did not believe to be right than he could change his nature. He made up his mind that the institution of slavery was a blistering shame to our civilization, that it was a relic of barbarism; and thus believing, he so declared, when to make the declaration brought upon him not only frowns from, and alienation of, old friends, but personal violence, from the effects of which he never recovered. In the midst of the tempest which surrounded him, he stood unmoved and immovable.

"Those perilous times came when, cringing beneath the threats of the slave power, bent on destroying the

Union, the cry of compromise filled the air, and frightened politicians hastened to abandon the professions of a lifetime ; hastened to give back to the slave power all that years of manly struggle had wrested from it ; hastened to renounce every principle secured by the election of Abraham Lincoln, in order — vain hope — to appease their Southern brethren, and to persuade them not to leave us. Not so Charles Sumner.   Upon the eternal rocks had he planted his feet, and there was he determined that they should remain, and they did remain.   How splendidly he stands out to-day as he then stood, now that the mists of passion and prejudice have cleared away and revealed his true position to us.

"The war came : it was inevitable.   We all remember how reluctantly we accepted the conclusion; how for weeks and dreary months we dallied and toyed with the slave, fearing to touch the question, and even returning the slave to his rebel master, hoping still to appease him and persuade him back.   But Charles Sumner knew that there could be no reconciliation until one or the other of the opposing ideas, freedom or slavery, perished.   Years before in his college halls, he had chosen under which banner he would be found.   His splendid rhetoric, now persuading and now denouncing ; his powerful logic was day and night, in season and out of season, employed to press upon the government the necessity of making the issue direct, offering the slave his freedom, and using his services as a Union soldier.   The proclamation of Emancipation came.   I do not attribute this result solely to Mr. Sumner, nor do I say that Mr. Lincoln did not see its necessity quite as clearly as did Mr. Sumner.   Their positions were entirely different.   Their responsibilities were different.   The merit of this great measure can be attributed to no one man.

"But as the war progressed — defeat following defeat in swift and sickening succession — Charles Sumner was found the earnest advocate of every measure by which our soldiers could be sustained in the field and the great contest finally pushed through to success. During all these years Charles Sumner never for one moment lost sight of that down-trodden race in whose cause he had, when a boy, enlisted. When the war closed the question faced the country and could not be avoided, 'What shall be done with the negro?' The slave-holder thought in the pacificating policy pursued by Andrew Johnson, that he saw an opportunity to still retain the old power over the slave; penal codes were adopted by the seceding states, the effect of which would have been to reduce the negro to substantially his old condition. The people were wearied with the slave question, wearied of the war, anxious at once to heal the breaches which it had made, and disposed to be careless as to the means. The danger was imminent. Faithful through the years which have since passed, Charles Sumner stood sentinel, and never rested his labors until the negro was not only a freeman but a citizen.

"The last crowning glory of his life, his 'Civil Rights' bill, has just ripened into law, and by it every vestige of the old slave system is wiped away. His 'works did follow him,' and almost his last words were 'take care of my Civil Rights bill.'

"And thus his career ended. Where shall we find a nobler, a more patriotic, a more lofty one? But one great feature which distinguishes his career I have not yet noted. The negro having secured the privileges of citizenship, Charles Sumner showed to the world that the warfare which he had waged in his behalf was based upon no mean considerations of personal hatred toward the master. Accordingly the great heart that bled for the slave, when he was in the agony of his bondage, after his release, sorrowed for the master in the trouble which environed him. The great purpose of his life had been accomplished, and he turned his mind to relieving the oppressed whites of the South. His idea of human rights knew no distinction of color or of creed; and Charles Sumner, he who but ten short years ago, had he then died, would have been execrated by the entire South, to-day finds the old slave-holder and the old slave alike sincere mourners at his grave, both feeling that they have lost a friend whom money could not buy, whom power and threats could not coerce. Over the grave of this great moral and intellectual hero we drop the tear of affection and reverence. It, too, shall we clothe with flowers, for in that grave rests all that is mortal of a states-man as pure in heart, and lofty and patriotic in purpose, as ever brightened the pages of history.

"His spirit stands to-day face to face with the soldier of the Union whose cause he so valiantly maintained. The Confederate who once deemed him his bitterest enemy, now knows that he was his friend. Around the grave of such a man, all citizens of a restored Union can meet. In that solemn presence all bitterness is vanished. Adapting to my purpose the language of a great master of English literature, I would say to North and South, black and white alike: 'Oh, brothers, enemies no more, let us take a mournful hand together, as we stand over his grave, and call a truce to battle. Hush, strife and quarrel, over the the solemn grave. Sound, trumpets, a mournful march. Fall, dark curtain,' upon a life thus gloriously closed."

Such was his estimate of a great patriot, while of patriotism itself he said:

"Patriotism knows neither latitude nor longitude. It is not climatic. It thrives on the cold and rugged mountain tops of our extremest East; it flourishes on the fertile field and abounding prairies of the West; it flowers out and blossoms into splendid fruitage on the plantations of the South. Think of your country and live for your children. It is worthy of it all. Young man, never fall into the error of supposing that interest in these great questions must be beneath you. It cannot. The man who thinks himself above politics is making a double mistake. He is over-estimating himself, and is underestimating all that magnificent science which should determine how best the interests of 50,000,000 of people might be promoted. Young men, I honor your ambitions, and I honor all your dreams. I honor every vision that you see in the greatness of our country in the future, and your honorable and distinguished part in it. I am a young man myself and always shall be. I believe in the visions that young men see. I believe in the reality of the castles that they build. I believe in the fruition and performance of these splendid dreams. For all those golden visions, all those glittering dreams, are but the promises of the future. 'For where, where, without the dreams of the young men lighting up all the future and making it radiant and splendid with human possibilities, would be the deeds of the old men glorifying the past with human achievements?''

His close to a grand oration upon the struggle between the North and South can well end this chapter of general illustrations.

"The inevitable end came, the triumph of right over wrong, of justice over injustice, and the rebellion fell in utter wreck, with a resounding crash that was heard by all nations. The great cause of the Union, with spotless robes, with shining face and majestic form, came forth to meet and receive the surrender of her adversary. From

murky battle-cloud, from stifling slave pen, the dark spirit
of secession and slavery emerged; her garments stained
with the blood of the slave, her brow in gloom, the lust of
power and pride of empire in her eyes.   Forth she came,
and prostrating herself before the majestic presence in which
she stood, surrendered herself, the guilty cause of a wicked
rebellion."

III.

EARLY POLITICAL SPEECHES.

THE KANSAS TROUBLES — '58 — DOWNFALL OF THE DEMO-
CRATIC MISRULE FORETOLD — FOURTH OF JULY, 1854—
OUR NATION'S FUTURE — LINCOLN'S EMANCIPATION
PROCLAMATION — JOHNSON'S SOUTHERN POLICY.

"I HAVE always been a Republican," said Mr. Storrs
in a speech delivered in Horticultural Hall, Philadelphia, in the fall of 1880. "The Lord was very good
to me, and postponed my birth so late that I never had
occasion to vote the Democratic ticket. I voted first
for John C. Fremont. I kept straight at it ever since,
voting the Republican ticket."

Two years after he cast his first vote, Mr. Storrs
addressed a mass meeting at Ellicottsville, Cattaraugus
county, New York state, October 19, 1858, in behalf of
the Republican candidates at the state election. In that
speech he reviewed the questions at issue between Republicans and Democrats, which finally culminated in open
war, and particularly the dispute on the admission of Kansas as a state under Buchanan's administration, which
at that time was agitating the whole country. His
first political address of which there is any record is
characterized by the same maturity of thought, the
same clear logic, and the same pointed wit that marked
the best efforts of his later life.

In those days the Democratic party assumed to be
the sole friends and guardians of the Union, and every

37

attempt to impose restrictions upon the slave-holding power was met by clamorous protestations, that unless the slave-holders were allowed to have their own way, the Union would be broken up. In a few trenchant words Mr. Storrs disposed of these hypocritical pretentions:

"Every Democratic platform has a peculiar, distinguishing mark, by which it can everywhere be recognized. There are some men whose business is advertised in their countenances. We can always recognize a quack doctor, a Jew peddler, and a Democratic member of assembly at first sight. Our Democratic friends seem to derive great consolation from the reflection that they are conservative; but that is not what ails them. 'A great many good people,' said that brilliant and witty English divine, Sydney Smith, 'think they are pious, when they are only bilious. Many a young gentleman turns down his shirt collar, retires from the world in disgust, reposes himself on the banks of some murmuring stream, and thinks that he is a misanthrope and a poet, when his stomach is only out of order. Many a man thinks he is inspired when he is simply dyspeptic, and many a worthy old gentleman puts his hands loftily under his coat tails, spreads out his feet, stands with his back to the fire, and thinks he is a conservative when he is only a flunkey.' We have a large number of these illustrious ghosts, long since politically entombed by the people, whose principle business seems to be that of saving the Union ! Every question of interest to them seems bristling with danger. They have any number of medicines and prescriptions for it they sit up with it nights, preserve it by Union-saving committees, and are constantly on the ground with their glue-pots at Mason and Dixon's line to stick the Union together. Whenever any question having the remotest relation to the institution of slavery is broached, these solemn old doctors are clamorous in their cries of danger to the Union; and when, at the ensuing session of Congress, Kansas shall knock at the door of the confederacy and demand admission as a free state, you will see them running for their medicaments, and their cordials, their paregoric and catnip, their laudanum and pennyroyal; a nigger will be in the question, and the Union in danger!"

His conclusion was prophetic:

"We are asked where we are coming out. That is not a question for us to answer; it is sufficient for us to go in right, and trust in a good Providence to bring us out right. When a man goes in at the wrong gate, it is asking altogether too much of Providence by some special interposition to bring him out at the right. 'I will,' said the Mussulman, 'unloose my camel, and commit him to God.' 'First hitch your camel,' said Mahomet, 'and then commit him to God.'

"The Democratic party seems to have a holy horror of agitation. What other or better way is there for a free people to arrive at correct conclusions on any given subject, than by a full discussion of it? Agitation is as neccesary in the political as in the moral or physical world. The darkest periods in this world's history are those in which free discussion was prevented. No great reform has ever yet been effected without it, and it sometimes requires the earthquake to upheave to the surface the ores of truth from under the layers of ignorance and falsehood which had covered them. When the atmosphere in our still and sultry summer days is charged with malaria and pestilence, the Almighty sends the thunder-storm, and the rain, and the whirlwind, and in the commotion of the elements which follows, the air is cleansed and purified, and we can breathe again with safety. If necessary, by such means

must our present choked and pestilential political atmosphere be purified; and as a free people, wherever there is
a wrong to right, or a great truth to be asserted and
advanced, we shall claim and assert the right of the freest
discussion.

"The days of democratic misrule are numbered.
From the waving prairies of Iowa to the coal and iron fields
of Pennsylvania, the shouts of victory are sweeping over
the land. Indiana and Ohio are swelling in grand chorus
the glad song of triumph. They have nobly wheeled into
the republican line, and are proudly keeping step to the
music of freedom. And New York is unworthy of her
high position if she does not drive Lecomptonism from her
borders, to the cypress and willow swamps of Carolina.
Upon congressional action this winter depends the freedom of Kansas; and as far as your member of congress is
concerned, his past record is clear, consistent and unflinching in opposition to the extension of slavery. Put in nomination by the soundest men in your county, always having
been true to the principles we advocate, honest, faithful,
capable, he will receive the vote of every good Republican
in the district who desires the success of the republican
doctrines. A political party is something more than a
debating society. If it proposes to accomplish any practical results, it must have organization, and its candidates
must be supported. The only question we, as Republicans,
are to ask is, — is the candidate honest, capable and faithful to the principles of the party? This answered in the
affirmative, there is but one course for every true Republican, and that is to give to those candidates a hearty and
vigorous support. A democratic convention is a poor place
for a man to get his republicanism indorsed; 'and if I
desired to travel on the strength of my republicanism, I
should not go to a democratic convention for my creden-

tials. The victories of 1856 were but beginnings, in the contest to follow. Soon are we to reap the practical results of those victories. Let every man feel that upon himself personally rests the responsibility. There is yet nerve and muscle enough left in the popular arm to shatter the democracy to atoms; and when at last, one after another, those magnificent Western empires shall take positions in the line of states, joining in the march of advancing civilization, with the song of Freedom on their lips, and its bright star glittering full upon their foreheads, we will join in that grand festival in which the North and the South, the East and the West, shall strike hands in a common brotherhood of interests, whose high purpose it shall be to extend all over this vast continent republican doctrines, and establish upon it, for all time to come, republican institutions."

Six years later, while the ultimate issue of the war was yet undetermined, Mr. Storrs delivered in Chicago a Fourth of July oration, choosing for his subject "Our National Future." He spoke substantially as follows:

"Never since governments existed among men has a mightier question been presented, nor one in which mankind everywhere, to-day and for all time to come, have a deeper interest.

"The purpose of a nation is to train men ; that nation which trains the best men is the best nation ; and that nation which gives to human thought its largest scope and freest range ; which without shackles or hinderances places in every man's hands the implements by which he is to work out his own success ; which makes of each individual the architect of his own fortunes, and which limits the range of human thought and human enterprise, only within the boundaries of absolute right and justice ; — that nation trains the best men and is therefore the best nation.

"And so, embodied in this question,—' What shall be our national future ?'— is not merely whether Jefferson Davis shall fail or succeed, whether the boundaries of the United States of America shall by rebellious bayonets be crowded from the gulf to the very gates of our national capital; but what is of vastly more consequence than these even, whether the experiment of self-government so magnificently inaugurated upon this continent shall be a final success, gladdening the hearts of good men everywhere through all the ages to come, or whether disastrous defeat shall overtake its champions, and it be pronounced a failure for evermore. For this sublime experiment failing here *does* fail for evermore.

"Upon the triumph of the national arms depends not only all that we have of material and physical consequence, but disaster to the mighty cause is ruin to all the glorious promises of our ideal future as well. It has been defended as never cause was defended before. With a zeal loftier and holier than that which fired the hearts of the followers of the hermit to rescue from the profanation of infidel presence the tomb of the Lord, have the millions of this great republic lavished blood and treasure to rescue from the profanation of rebel hands the sacred depository of human freedom. We fight then for *the nation*, and this includes not merely the territory which makes up its physical extent, but the idea which is embodied in it. Our nation is not simply thirty-four states, but it is all the glory of our past, all the hope and promise of the future. We are the trustees of this continent not for our own interests alone but for mankind everywhere. We have been fighting now for nearly three years to save this nation, not for the value of its cotton, and wheat, and corn, and manufactures, but for the value of the hope, the ideas, the aspirations, the tendencies which it embodies and of which it is

the divinely chosen champion.   To-day the nation for
whose salvation we are fighting is the embodied spirit of
the great departed ones who have contributed to its glory.
Our nation is the wise forecast of Washington ; the sturdy
patriotism of Adams ; the earnest philosophic love of equal
rights of Jefferson ; the clear and penetrating vision of
Hamilton ; the fiery zeal of Clay ; the intellectual grandeur
of Webster ; the indomitable honesty of purpose of Jackson.   Every great man or woman who has ever lived in it
and contributed to its growth has infused the ideas which
have constituted that greatness into the national life, and
thus has each one become a part of the nation.

   " The nation which we now fight to save is all the heroic
endurance, lofty fortitude, patient, uncomplaining patriotism of the revolutionary fathers, the broad and world
embracing enterprise, the marvelous activity, the wonderful progressiveness of their children, knit indissolubly
together by that divine idea of self-government which
inspired the fathers through the bloody toils of its creation
and which, if faithfully adhered to, will crown with triumphant glory the efforts of their children for its everlasting perpetuation.

   " This *nation* then, is, so to speak, the spirit of representative government made manifest in the flesh of its
people.   The grand old puritan poet, John Milton, who
although he saw not with earthly vision, did see with the
infinitely clearer perception of an earnest, holy and exalted
vision, said :   ' Better kill a man than a good book.   Who
kills a man kills a reasonable creature, God's image ; but
who kills a good book kills the image of God as it were in
the eye.'   And so I say better that our darlings should all
perish in this mighty struggle than that it be not prosecuted to success.   They are, it is true, God's noblest
images ; but who kills this nation, the embodiment of all

these heaven-born aspirations, these grand ideas, kills the image of God as it were in the eye. For this nation is the precious life-blood of all these master spirits embalmed and treasured up on purpose for a life beyond life. We are here in this mighty Northwest from every portion of the country; from every quarter of the globe. The spirit of our institutions, now imperiled, and which we now fight to save, has drawn us hither. We come from the shadows of the old South Church, baptized as it has been in the waters of a religious faith; from the fields of Lexington and Concord where the first shot of a farmer soldier was fired, a shot which was heard all around the globe; from the grand old Empire state, with its long line of noble names and its long list of heroic achievements, with its colossal commerce, the fibers of which intertwine the fate of kingdoms and which stands like the angel of the Apocalypse, one foot resting on the sea and the other upon the land, and mistress of both; from the old Keystone, glorified by the greatness of Penn and Franklin, and whose reddened fields at Gettysburg are sanctified by the blood of heroes dying to save the cause, for which Penn and Franklin lived and died before them; from the old world, too, with its noble traditions and with its noble names, — are we here as well. All these memories, all these exalted deeds, have we brought hither with us, the idea of free government crystallizing them all about. These—these thus fused together, thus working out their colossal results through us on these fruitful plans — are our *nation's,* and how worthily that nation has been defended by her northwestern sons history has already recorded.

"I speak to you this night the language of exultant hope: hope for the great nation we love so justly and so much, hope for our country's future; hope for ourselves and for our **children.** And even now, wandering in the thin uncertain light which I take to be the promise of a rapidly approaching and glorious dawn ;— as with eager eyes we watch the moving clouds that yet overspread the sky;—as we ask of the watchmen stationed upon the watch-towers and citadels of the Union, ' Watchman, what of the night ? '— the answer comes back to us, strong and clear, and full of assuring hope, 'All is well.' And despite our early disasters and defeat, despite the long and wearisome and sometimes almost disheartening delay, despite the gloom that has overspread us—the cause of the Union, the cause of good government everywhere, upheld by the strong arms of the stalwart sons of the Northwest, thank God, moves gloriously and nobly on.

"I have then no doubt as to the result of this mighty contest—and who can have ? I have no doubt but that the power of our government will assert itself in triumph. I have no doubt but that this, the most wicked rebellion which has ever blackened the annals of history, will be ground to powder. I have no doubt but that our national integrity will be preserved. I have no doubt but that the union of these states will be restored and that the nation will emerge from the fiery trial through which it has passed brighter and better and stronger than it has ever been before. It would be impossible, however, that a conflict mighty as that from which we are now I trust emerging, should not leave its deep and permanent impress upon our future national character. It will give tone to our politics, our literature, and our feelings as a people for ages to come. A nation saved at such a tremendous expenditure of life and treasure, whose title to the claims of nationality is written all over with the blood of heroes, will think more highly of the privileges which it confers than it ever thought before. Purchased at a price so dear, and rescued from destruction at a cost so fearful, it will be valued accordingly, and preserve through all the future the name and privilege of an American citizen. Knowing how much they have cost, they will be prized and cherished as they have always deserved to be—but as they have never been. And so it will come to pass, that for the times to come, the *people*, who make this nation's greatness and who served it in its trial, will watch its interests with jealous eyes, and guard its honor with an earnest and a lofty zeal. Then it will come to pass that the mere politician shall no more trifle with its glory, trade away its honor, or sacrifice its interests for the advancement of his selfish ends. I am not claiming that scoundrelism in politics will cease altogether at the close of the war. So thoroughly chronic have scoundrelism and base selfishness become with some of those who have hitherto disgraced the name of politics by calling themselves politicians, that I fear the disease is altogether ineradicable in them. What I do mean to say is this : that the people have always appreciated the greatness of our nation and its value infinitely better than politicians as a class have done ; that had its salvation been entrusted to politicians alone it would have miserably perished the first year of the rebellion ; that the loyal hearts and strong arms and earnest will of the people have saved it, and that in the future they will watch the management of our national affairs, and the conduct of our public men, with a vigilance so keen as to be a continuing terror to the demagogue and the mere partisan. Straightforward honesty of purpose in the management of public affairs the people of this country have always appreciated and always rewarded. Still more will they do so in the future. I do not mean to say but that swindlers will yet ask for place, nor that scoundrels will not occasionally steal into office. Hereafter, however, this will be the exception. Our public men will be inspired by higher motives. The people themselves will realize more completely than they have ever done before the value of this Union. There will be greater care exercised in framing laws, and they will be more scrupulously obeyed.

"Not less marked or decided in character will be the impress which will be left upon our national literature and our habits of thought. The meditations of the philosopher, the dreams of the poet the fancies of the romancer will all, years and years hence, be colored by it and draw their inspiration from it. Literature, whether it be in the tomes of the philosopher or in the song of the poet, has always, since the world began, drawn its holiest inspiration and its clearest expression from patriotic feelings and impulses. Since the blind old poet sang the contests between Hector and Achilles, down to this very moment, that literature which will live—because it is the expression of the human heart wherever it may be—is that which clothes one's country with all the beauties which the lover sees in the mistress whom he adores, and which ranks the heroes of the native land among the good and great of the world. This love of country is one of the loftiest virtues which the Almighty has planted in the human heart, and so treason against it has been considered among the most damning sins. The history of the world teaches us that every great convulsion like that through which we are now passing has given new life and stimulus to intellectual exertion. Such wars as these tear up old formulas by the roots and scatter the fetters which have bound the human mind in special ruts and channels to the winds. The chariot wheels of war break down most mercilessly old barriers; and the thunder of battles, and the bugle blast, summon from the deepest recesses of the human heart its deepest feelings and emotions, and give to them an intensity and vigor of expression which the summer days of peace may never know. Who when he thinks of this our native land, of its glorious past, so brief yet so marvelously great, with its history thronging with names that have honored human nature and added to the dignity of our common manhood; of its mighty physical resources; of its vast territorial extent; of its sublime present and the promise of its future, but that feels the heart throb with quicker beat; the blood run with swifter course; the feeling of inspiration changing our every nature almost and lifting us far above the dull level of our ordinary thought? And when added to that history of the past, and adding new luster to the promise of the future is the record of this mighty rebellion crushed; who can doubt but that the literature of our country, embodying this grand and ennobling experience, will in the years to come grow broader, higher, and weightier,— the expression of a nation which has left behind the period of joyous infancy, and attained through fierce tribulation the dignity and gravity of a noble manhood? I look for all these results, and many more, to the great crisis which our nation is now passing through; and I look to its future with confident hope and expectations."

President Lincoln's emancipation proclamation having been denounced by the copperhead element at the North as unconstitutional, Mr. Storrs, in September, 1863, made a zealous defense of it in a speech at Sycamore, Illinois. He discussed from a legal standpoint the leading measures of the administration, including the emancipation proclamation, the military arrests of Confederate sympathizers at the North, the conscription law, and the use of negroes as soldiers. He argued that the constitution having given Congress power to declare war and suppress insurrection, and constituted the President commander-in-chief of the army and navy, the President had the right to use all the means at his command to weaken the enemy and strengthen the government.

"Who then is to judge of the necessity? Is it Lincoln or Vallandigham? Upon the President of the United States, as commander-in-chief of the army and navy, devolves the especial duty to protect and defend the constitution of the United States ; as the head of our forces, on him devolves the responsibility of so using them, of furnishing them with such means, of so augmenting their strength, of so weakening the hands of the enemy whom they shall be compelled to meet, that they may be successful in overcoming all resistance to the enforcement of the laws, and all attempts to overthrow the government. It will require no argument to show that he upon whom the responsibility and duty of accomplishing a particular end is devolved, is also clothed with full power to select such means as to him may seem necessary to the accomplishment of that end. Plain, however, as this proposition is, we are not left without authority. The Supreme Court of the United States, as well as many of the most eminent statesmen of our earlier history, have repeatedly declared the rule in substance as I have stated it. The President, then, must have the right to determine whether the liberation of the slaves is one of the necessary means for the successful prosecution of the war. This right, established as well by our own judicial decisions as by the law of nations, must also be regarded as a part of the constitution. Hence, in issuing that proclamation, the President did not suspend the constitution, but called into life its powers against those in arms seeking to overthrow it.

"But can we not see that the means was necessary and proper? Pollard, writing the southern view of the rebellion, in his history of the first year of the war, concludes by way of encouragement to rebels by saying that thus **far** the war has proved that the system of slavery has been an element of strength to the South, a faithful ally to their armies; the slave has tilled their fields while his master has fought. It is probable that Mr. Pollard is quite as well advised upon that subject as his Copperhead friends in the North, and understands the subject quite as well as they. If it has, then, been an element of strength to the South, why not weaken or altogether destroy that element of their strength? If the slave has tilled while the master has fought, tilling is as necessary as fighting, and the slave has thereby been made as efficient an enemy to the government as his master; and if we have a right to kill the fighting master, we have the same right to appropriate the services of the equally efficient tilling slave. If the slave has hitherto been a faithful ally to the South, the government surely has the right to break, if possible, the alliance, and I think to enter into the same alliance itself. Even a Copperhead will probably not deny that if it is constitutional for the South to form an alliance with the slave for the purpose of destroying the government, it is equally competent for the government to form an alliance with the slave for the purpose of saving itself."

If, as the Supreme Court decision in the Dred Scott case affirmed, the negroes were the property of their masters, Mr. Storrs contended that the Federal armies had as good a right to confiscate them as any other species of property.

"It must be remembered in this connection that the government has the right to demand the service of all its subjects for its own preservation. The law of self-preservation, says Vattel, applies as well to nations as to individuals. It is the duty of the government to protect all its citizens in the enjoyment of their rights; it is equally the duty of the citizen to protect the government when its rights or existence are threatened or imperiled. There can be no doubt but that the government could enforce the service of the indentured apprentice, or of any person bound to service for any period of time. If it have this right—and it cannot be disputed that it has—the length of serving can make no difference with its exercise. It would have the right to draft into the armies men bound to service for ten years as well as those bound for five. It could, therefore, annul a contract requiring service for life, as well as for a certain number of years. In other words, it could declare the relation of master and slave at an end as well as the relation of master and apprentice. To deny the conclusion would be to say that the government is at liberty to annul contracts between its own citizens when the safety of the state demands it but cannot thus affect its enemies under a like emergency.

"In short, if slaves are to be regarded as property, then the right of the government to take them, and the right of the commander-in-chief to order them to be taken, are undisputed. If not property, then the South has no right to complain. If the slave is not the property of the master, then the master has no right to his services, and the commander-in-chief must clearly have the right to prevent those services being in any way used either to strengthen the hands of the rebellion or to resist the armies of which the commander-in-chief is the head."

On the subject of military arrests, it was claimed by the opponents of Mr. Lincoln's administration that neither the President nor Congress had any constitutional right to suspend the writ of habeas corpus unless the public safety required it, and that the courts were the proper judges of such necessity.

"It would be absurd," argued Mr. Storrs, "to insist that the right to suspend the privilege of the writ of *habeas corpus* should be exercised either by Congress or by the President, but that the time when it should be done should be submitted to the judiciary. Clearly enough, in clothing Congress or the President with the right to suspend the privilege of the writ when its suspension becomes necessary for the preservation of the public safety, the right of determining the existence of that necessity must also rest either in Congress or the President. To say that the Supreme Court has a supervisory control over the exercise of this discretion is to deny its existence altogether elsewhere; for if, when the President exercises his discretion as to the necessity, the courts may supervise it, then it becomes not the President's discretion, but the discretion of the court; and the constitution would be made to read thus: 'The writ of *habeas corpus* may be suspended by Congress or the President in cases of rebellion or invasion, whenever the Supreme Court shall deem such suspension necessary for the preservation of the public safety.'

"It is alleged, however, that the arrests made by the government have been an unconstitutional interference with the rights of the citizens, and that no such arrests can be made in a community professedly loyal without the process of law. The liberty of speech and the freedom of the press, we are told, have been invaded and trampled upon without justification or necessity. The arrest of Vallandigham has excited more discussion than any other, and upon that a direct issue has been made with the administration. This arrest is denounced on the ground that Vallandigham was not connected either with the army or navy; that Ohio is a loyal state, and that war does not prevail there; that no military operations were being actively carried on there; and that consequently martial law could

not be declared, nor could the laws of war be applied to
any of its citizens not actively engaged in the military
service.   But it is not true that the operations of this war
are confined to the immediate territory in which battles are
fought and armies are moved.   There is war as well in
Ohio as in Virginia.   Wherever there is any of the slightest
opposition to the government in the prosecution of the
war, or the slightest assistance rendered to the rebellion in
its efforts to overthrow the government, there is war.   In
some portions of the country, loyalty dominates and controls society.   In others, rebellion controls and dominates.
There is no place so dark but that some prayer is offered
for the success of our cause ; there is no place so light but
that lurking treason may be found.

"The agencies invoked by this rebellion to its support
are multiform.   The means which it uses to accomplish
success are various.   The rebellion demands not only soldiers and cannon, and the ordinary implements of war, but
sympathy and argument to support its cause at home, to
weaken its enemies, and to give it dignity and support
abroad.   Whoever aids the rebellion in either of these particulars ; whoever, by speech or writing, contributes to the
unity of its people, to the weakening of our own, to the
undermining of public confidence in our eventful success,
to the withholding of troops from the service, to their
desertion when once engaged in the service,—is as much an
enemy to the government and as much at war with it as he
who carries arms in his hands.   Wherever such a condition of things exists there is insurrection — there is war.
Whoever engages in such an enterprise is an insurgent.
All these are the means which the rebellion calls to its aid ;
these are the elements which it enlists in its behalf ; these
are the instruments by means of which, as well as by
armies, it wages war against the nation.   All these helps

combine to make up the strength and power of the insurrection ; and we, therefore, while at war with the insurrection, are at war with every part of it.   Our purpose is
to cripple and destroy every element of its strength ; to
meet and overcome every means which it uses for the
furtherance of its designs.   If armies are arrayed against
the government, we meet and crush them.   If the institution of slavery is used against the national life, we meet
and crush it.   If seditious speech and seditious writing are
used to weaken our own strength and encourage and
embolden the adversary, we meet and crush that as well.
All these agencies are parts of the insurrection, and we are
at war with every part of it.   Whatever strengthens rebels
weakens us ; whatever encourages and emboldens them
dispirits and disheartens us.   Wherever any of these
means are used against us, there is insurrection ; and
wherever there is insurrection there is war.   It would be
strange indeed if rebels should have greater rights against
the government than the government possesses for its own
defense.

" To me it appears that the right of the military power
to arrest and punish the citizen depends not upon the
place where the alleged offense is committed, but upon
the nature of the offense.   If Vallandigham, at Dayton,
discourages enlistments, encourages desertions, creates dis-
satisfaction and excites discontent in the army, I can see no
good reason why he has not made himself as amenable to
military trial and punishment as if the same offense had
been committed at Vicksburg or Chattanooga.   The freedom of speech and of the press are indeed the highest
privileges, but when these are used to overthrow the very
government under which they are enjoyed, then they cease
to be rights, but are wrongs which assume the largest proportions and are fruitful of the most alarming conse-

quences. When Vallandigham roams about the country, seeking by every means to excite popular discontent; to impair and weaken the efficiency of our arms ; to discourage enlistments ; to encourage desertions; to weaken ourselves and to strengthen the rebellion, he is simply turning against the government the very privileges which he derives from the government. I fail to see that Vallandigham possesses any greater rights to stir up sedition among us here than he would have to work to the same end were he in the rebel states. If Vallandigham should, as a citizen of Virginia, endeavor to weaken our strength by speeches and by publications, no one would doubt the right of the government to stop his speaking whenever it could lay its hands upon him. I cannot understand how it is that he has larger privileges in Ohio than in Virginia. I fail to see that seditious speeches or conduct is any the less an offense when perpetrated in Ohio, which is confessedly loyal, than when perpetrated in South Carolina, which is confessedly disloyal ; and hence I say that in spouting sedition in a loyal community, where converts to such sedition may be made, Vallandigham is as guilty in fact and inflicts greater damage than he would by seditious talk in a disloyal community, where no converts were to be made. The military power being employed for the preservation of the nation, and Vallandigham for its destruction, they met as inevitably as the army of Pemberton met that of Grant at Vicksburg, and with like results. If Mr. Vallandigham and his followers do not like the use of military force against them, they had better not array themselves against military force ; and whenever they choose to do so, they may be prepared to take the consequences.

" An opposition to the government as bitter and malignant as that which proceeds from any other source is made on the ground of the employment of negroes as soldiers.

I am unable to see why it is not infinitely better that the
negro should fight for, rather than against us. There certainly can be no legal objection to it, for, if we have the
right to deprive the master of the services of the negro,
we clearly have as much right to require the services of
the negro in our own behalf as we have to command the
services of white men. I am not prepared to admit that
the negro is relieved from his responsibilities to aid the
government because of his color. I know of no provision
in the constitution which declares of what color our armies
shall be constituted. There being, then, no legal objection,
it becomes a question of policy merely, and to the past
history of the nation I appeal for the determination of
that question. When I remember that the first blood shed
in the revolution was the blood of a negro, Crispus Attucks;
that at Bunker Hill negroes fought side by side with white
men, and that among the heroes of that day is Peter
Salem, the negro; that in Massachusetts, negroes, bond
and free, were enlisted in the continental armies; that
Connecticut passed laws for that very purpose, giving as the
reward of such service, freedom to the slave; that Rhode
Island sent its negro brigade, which fought under the eyes
of Washington and Lafayette, and always with credit; that
more negroes were in the service of the country, enlisted
from the New England states, than there were white soldiers from Georgia and South Carolina; that the legis-
latures of Maryland, New York, Pennsylvania and Virginia authorized the enlistment of negroes, bond and free,
with the approbation of every general in our armies; that
by direction of Congress Henry Laurens went to Georgia
and South Carolina, with all the aid which Washington
could render him, to enlist negroes there in the service of
the country,—a step made necessary because neither
Georgia nor South Carolina had contributed their quota of

troops ; that of the army of Washington at Monmonth 755 were negroes; that during our last war with Great Britain the services of the negro were again invoked ; that one-fourth of Perry's force at Lake Erie were negroes ; that Jackson enlisted them at New Orleans, promised them their freedom for their services, and faithfully kept his promise good ; and when, added to all these teachings of our past history, I remember the services of the slaves at Milliken's Bend, Port Hudson, and Fort Wagner, I prefer to base my judgment as to the expediency and policy of this measure rather upon the records of our history, the teachings of our experience, and the united testimony of the great men and the great events of our national career, · than upon the carping criticisms of the mere politicians, or the elegant conservatism of Governor Seymour and 'his friends.' Washington, Jefferson, Adams, Laurens, Greene, Lafayette, Hamilton, Jay, Knox, and Henry, of our revolutionary history,— Jackson, Perry, Scott, and Van Rensselaer, in our more modern history,— judged it wise to use the negro as a soldier, and acted upon that judgment. Seymour, Vallandigham, Voorhees and Singleton think otherwise. I have no difficulty in making choice as to whom I shall follow. I have already made my choice. I prefer the precedents of our early history, and the teachings of the wise and great men who have made that history glorious, to the sophisms of Seymour and his associates. I shall act upon that preference in the future ; and I doubt not that the great mass of the people will also."

The course of President Johnson towards the Southern states, which resulted in his impeachment, was discussed by Mr. Storrs in an exhaustive speech at Ottawa, Ill., in September, 1866. The Chicago *Tribune* reported it in full, and editorially characterized it as

"Websterian in logical reasoning, in purity of diction, and in force and clearness of statement." He began by saying:

"The political issues involved in the pending elections are but a continuation of those that have been before us for the past five years. During all that period of time the Republican party has urged a vigorous prosecution of war against a rebellion in arms. The political issues were those which naturally grew out of the war. They involved questions of policy as to the manner in which it should be conducted and the purpose for which it should be waged. The continued and triumphant supremacy of the Republican party was evidence of the resolute will of the people to suppress rebellion, to crush out treason, to punish traitors, and so thoroughly preserve our national integrity as to remove all the causes which had given rise to the war. We were at war with the rebellion in its every part; at war as well with the ideas to carry out which rebellion was inaugurated as with the armies which were marshaled for the support of those ideas,— for the armies of the rebellion were but the physical expression of the political principles to sustain which these armies were organized. Every battle fought by Southern armies, every shot fired by Southern traitors, was in behalf of the right of secession, the political power of slavery, and the Calhoun doctrine of state sovereignty. In contending with Southern armies we contended with these political principles. When their armies were defeated the principles for which those armies fought were defeated also. When their armies surrendered to ours, they surrendered not only the guns with which they fought, but the principles for which they fought. For if, after fighting traitors in the field and vanquishing them, we fail to vanquish also the treason for which they fought, the war has been a failure infinitely more ignominious and disgraceful than it would have been had the Democratic platform of 1864 been true when it was written. The question now is, as it then was, Is the war a failure?

"If after the sacrifice of three hundred thousand lives, and an expenditure of almost countless millions of money in conquering the military power of the rebellion, the only result has been to restore at once subjugated rebels to a place in our national councils, to a voice in national legislation without adequate guarantees that the political heresies which gave life to treason, and inspired its exertion, shall not flame out anew into the horrors of civil war ; then is the war a failure indeed, then treason meets with no punishment, and patriotism has no rewards. For, refine and reason upon it as we may, the question of the hour is, Shall the fruits of Union victories be gathered and secured?"

Scouting the idea that this could be done by an unconditional restoration of yet disloyal states to a share in the national councils, he traced the course of Johnson point by point, showing that each of his executive acts "in behalf of treason and against loyalty" had been in violation of the constitution.

"He found these states without governors, and he appointed governors. He found them without a constituency entitled to vote, and he straightway created a constituency. He found them without political power, and he clothed them with it, and so it was that the strange spectacle was presented of rebels again exercising political power. The result of the elections for delegates was such as might well have been expected. The conventions were as much rebel conventions as those which the fortunes of war had just dissolved. With the advice and under the direction of Andrew Johnson, constitutions were framed and declared to be the law of the land. These constitutions were as much the work of the President, as were the governors themselves the creatures of his authority.

"The new Moses seems to be laboring under the impression that the exercise of political privileges and the enjoyment of political rights rest solely and altogether upon his decision. He says that the people of the seceded states are all loyal, and that they have organized state governments, and elected members of congress who are at once entitled to admission. I, for one, desire better evidence of a man's loyalty than Andrew Johnson's indorsement of it. The President cannot change *facts* by *assertions.* He cannot make a treasonable people loyal by declaring that they are loyal, any more than he can swing around the circle, and by hammering at the other end make the great loyal North disloyal by drunken and mendacious charges that they are traitors."

He argued that Congress alone had the power to determine upon what conditons the rebel states should be re-admitted to the Union, and placed the issue before his audience in his wonted terse and pithy form:

"The policy of Andrew Johnson and his supporters is the immediate restoration of southern states to power irrespective of their present loyalty or disloyalty, without guarantees for the future, and without punishment for the past. The policy of Congress is to restore southern people and states to their original relations with the Union upon their adopting the constitutional amendment agreed upon by Congress. Nothing more, nothing less, is required of the South than this."

The negro, he contended, must be protected in all his rights of citizenship, and this ought to be guaranteed by legislation in every rebel state as a condition of their restoration to the political privileges they had forfeited.

"The Republican platform of 1864 declares of slavery, that 'justice and the national safety *demand its utter and complete extirpation* from the soil of the Republic. But it is proposed by the author of that resolution and by the party in whose employ he now is, and whose addresses, manifestoes and declarations he writes, that the main structure of the institution may be destroyed, but that its scaffolding and supports shall still be left to offend the eye and disfigure the landscape. The work of extirpation is not completed until every statute which recognized it, every benefit to the master which grew out of it, every constitutional provision which secured and guarded it, every political power or privilege which resulted from it, is *rooted out* with slavery itself. For all these were but parts of the system, the limbs, the heart of slavery, and they are all foredoomed to 'extirpation from the soil of the Republic.' This great crime which, like a poisonous plant, grew upon the soil of the Republic, carefully watched and tended by zealous friends, grew with ominous rapidity, until its far-reaching branches, lengthening day by day, threw their shadows all over the land; its roots struck deep and widespreading into earth; from these the parent trunk sent forth its supports, and the odors of its blossomings lulled to sleep the patriotic vigilance of a nation, and numbed its conscience. The war waged against this gigantic crime by the Republican party is not ended until the poisonous thing is utterly and completely extirpated. So long as a root, or limb, or fiber remains, our work is incomplete."

He ridiculed Johnson's idea that the rebel states had a right to a voice and vote in proposing amendments to the constitution. This claim for the rebel states was put forward on the ground that as these states had no legal right to secede, therefore they had never been out of the Union.

"A state cannot secede, in the same sense that a man cannot steal. It cannot legally, although it may in fact secede, and a man cannot legally, but the records of our courts show that many men do in fact steal. And so a state like Virginia is in the Union, in the same sense that the convicted thief is in Illinois. He is in Illinois, but he is also in the penitentiary. While there he has his rights, but they are the rights of a thief and not of a law-abiding citizen; and so Virginia, a rebel state, has its rights, but they are the rights of a rebel state, and not of a loyal one. The thief must serve his time out 'before he can be restored to his proper practical relations' with the people whose laws he has offended,—and so must Virginia. The thief so long as he sees no chance for a pardon, or for an escape, 'accepts the situation' for the most excellent of reasons,—he can't help it. Virginia accepts the situation for the same reason. But because the thief gave up the stolen property when the officers of the law by force took it away from him, he does not thereby escape punishment for the crime, although, in the language of Andrew Johnson, the larceny was utterly 'null and void,' any more than Virginia does when she surrenders the forts and arms that she has stolen, because she was compelled by force to do so. Nor when the thief is brought to trial is he permitted to have a voice or a vote in proposing what his punishment shall be, nor in 'ratifying the same.' Nor will Virginia, while she is on trial at the bar of the country, be permitted to say upon what condition her guilt shall be washed away and what securities shall be demanded for the future.

"If, however, when Andrew Johnson was occupying the bench, a thief should be brought to trial before him, he would insist that it was a clear case of taxation without representation; that the criminal was taxed to pay the expenses of the jury while he was not represented upon it, and that therefore twelve thieves should at once sit with the twelve honest men in proposing measures of punishment and security, and thus taxation and representation would go hand in hand; there would be harmony and fraternal feeling; thirty-six stars on the flag, a copy of the constitution at every railroad crossing, and a magic circle in every family.

"Slavery, we are told, is abolished, and the negro is free. But until the seed is so thoroughly destroyed that it may never again grow into life and be re-established, until the negro is not only free, but the enjoyment of that freedom is secured to him against all invasion in the future, slavery is not abolished, nor is the negro free, in the full measure which the nation requires.

"Like the fabled monster Briareus, slavery has an hundred arms, and like Proteus, may assume almost innumerable forms. With every hand it works mischief, and in every form that it assumes it is dangerous. Every law which deprives the negro of the enjoyment of any of the rights of a citizen, or interferes with him in the enjoyment of any one of those rights, is the handiwork of slavery, is one of the forms which it assumes.

"Until the negro is free, not only in the ownership of himself, but free to work for whom he pleases, free to have a voice in the making of his own contracts, free in the enjoyment of the proceeds of his own labor, free to invoke all the agencies of the law for the redress of his wrongs or the defense or enforcement of his rights, free to educate himself and his children, free to think as he pleases and to speak what he thinks, free as you and I are free, and certain that no power shall deprive him of it, the magnificent promise, made in our platform in 1864, that slavery should be extirpated from the soil of the Republic, remains unfulfilled.

" If we fall short in either of these things, and while we have relieved the slave from one form of bondage, suffer his old master to reduce him to another, we are false to our high pledges.   The slave and all the world may then well say of us —

> " And be these juggling fiends no more believ'd
> That palter with us in a double sense ;
> That keep the word of promise to our ear
> And break it to our hope.'

"Slavery is not yet abolished.   The negro is not yet free.   For, if to-day we adopt the policy of Andrew Johnson, to-morrow every rebellious state has it within its power to annul all its previous action, and by such hampering legislation as their ingenuity would readily devise, reduce the negro to a condition of slavery *in fact*, whatever it might be in name."

If the Southern States desired in good faith to accept the results of the war, he saw no reason why they should not " prove their faith by their works," by putting on record their ratification of the constitutional amendments, and taking legislative measures to enforce them. He concluded with a scathing review of Johnson's record, especially denouncing the part he took in connection with the massacre of Union men at New Orleans.

" He declared that treason was a crime, and should be punished, while hardly a loyal man fills an office in the South, and the punishment of rebels is by taking them into his confidence.   He declared that they should be impoverished, and fills the promise by placing it within the power of unrepentant rebels to persecute Union men and drive them from their midst.   He declared that treason was a crime, and should be so treated, and proves the sincerity of his professions, by aiding with his sympathy, and with his power as commander-in-chief of the army, the traitors and convicted murderers of New Orleans in the cold-blooded slaughter of faithful and long-tried Union men, while in convention peaceably assembled. He declared that in the work of reconstruction none but loyal men should participate, while in the reorganization of these state governments loyal men have no share, and in the administration of their affairs are premitted to take no part. Elevated to power by the Republican party, he spurns the counsels of its leaders, and defiantly seeks to defeat the measures adopted by the representatives of that party and of the people. Not satisfied with this, he seeks its overthrow by the organization of a new party in the country, which derives all its strength from rebels at the South and Copperheads at the North, and which he essays to build up by the distributions of official patronage, by removing from office, without cause, tried and trusted Union men, and putting in their places pliant tools of his own, or those who have always been bitterly hostile to the party by whom he was elected and to the principles which it has always espoused. He has deserted all his old friends, who were the friends of the Union and the country. for new ones who have always been the enemies of both.

"The man guilty of all these crimes is to-day President of the United States. This is his policy. With the blood of the slaughtered Union men of New Orleans upon his hands, he makes the tour of the loyal North, insults its sentiment, defies its representatives, and threatens more violence in the future.

"He knows the people but poorly. They are as resolutely resolved to save this Union to-day as they ever have been. That purpose, rest assured, will be achieved, and whoever stands in the way of its accomplishment will be crushed finer than powder."

IV.

THE CAMPAIGN OF 1868.

THE foregoing speeches of Mr. Storrs have been
deemed worthy of preservation for their historical
interest, as presenting in a lucid and forcible manner the
issues which absorbed public attention in this country
thirty years ago. It was not until the Presidential
campaign of 1868, that Mr. Storrs achieved a national
reputation as a political orator. By a singular coinci-
dence, the State where he first won the distinction as a
stump speaker which continued to grow and brighten
to the close of his life, was also the scene of his last
oratorical triumphs. The fame he won by his speeches
in Maine during the campaign of 1868, brought him
prominently before the country, and inspired that
demand for his services in other states, through subsequent campaigns, which never ceased until his death ;
and it was in Maine, standing on the edge of Lake
Maranacook by the side of James G. Blaine, that he
made his crowning effort in the campaign of 1884, the
last in which he was destined to take a part. He had
gone to Maine in 1868 for a summer vacation, and
letters from the West to prominent Republicans there
spoke of him in such glowing terms, that he was sought

out and invited to speak at Portland along with Hon. George S. Boutwell, of Massachusetts. The Maine and Boston papers were enthusiastic in their praise of his eloquence, and on his return to Chicago he was requested to address meetings in this city and other parts of the State. The following speech was delivered at St. Charles, Illinois, in the fall of that year:

"In 1860 the Democratic party forfeited public confidence and was driven from power. In 1864 it demanded that it should receive from the people the confidence it had forfeited four years before, and asked to be restored to power. The nation answered this demand, and with overwhelming majorities declared that it was not entitled to public confidence, and that the reasons which had induced the people to drive it from power in 1860 had been intensified and multiplied. Two years later, in 1866, they again went before the people, their claims were re-examined and, with increased emphasis, rejected. To-day, the same party again appeals to the country and again asks that the interests of the nation be intrusted to its keeping. It is our business to inquire: first, whether the three verdicts given against the Democratic party were righteous verdicts; and second, if they were, what they have done since then to restore confidence in them. That the verdict rendered against the Democratic party in 1860 was a righteous one, I will not attempt to prove to you here. That party sought to fasten the institution of slavery upon free territories. It sought to protect it there by all the powers of the general government. It appealed to the people for aid in this wicked purpose, and the people righteously refused it. Nor need I spend much time in demonstrating that the verdict of 1864 was warranted by all the facts in the case. It then declared the war an experiment, and the experiment a failure; demanded that hostilities should cease, which would have resulted in the immediate recognition of the independence of the southern confederacy by every foreign power. The righteousness of the popular verdict rendered in 1866 was equally clear to us. The rebellion having been crushed by force of arms, the Democratic party insisted that neither rebel state nor rebel citizen had lost anything by his crime; that he should be permitted to dictate the terms of his re-admission to the Union which he had sought to destroy, and should be made the custodian of the interests of a nation which he had wickedly sought to overthrow.

"Assuredly, then, the Democratic party cannot successfully ask us to restore them to power, on the ground that our former judgments against it have been erroneous, nor can it ask us to reverse the decisions delivered by the people in 1860, 1864 and 1866. Their claims for support must rest, not upon the ground that they were innocent of the crimes of which the people convicted them at those great public trials, but that, confessing their guilt, they have atoned for it by public services since rendered, of a character sufficiently important to entitle them to a full and complete pardon from the people against whom they had offended. And hence it is that the demand made by the Democratic party to-day for power cannot be entertained, unless it has either an entirely new set of leaders, or different views upon the questions which have divided the country for the past eight years, from those which it has held for the past eight years, or unless all those questions have passed out of political controversy, and have been replaced by entirely new issues.

"That the leaders of the Democratic party are the same they have been for the past eight years, every one knows. Seymour and Vallandigham, Pendleton and Belmont, Henry Clay Dean and Brick Pomeroy were leaders in the

Democratic party in 1864 and they are leaders in the same party in 1868. Wade Hampton and Toombs, Fort Pillow Forrest and Beauregard, were leaders in the Democratic party in 1860; their operations North were suspended by four years of war, at the close of which they promptly fill their old positions as leaders in the Democratic party of the nation.

"Not only has there been no change of leaders, but there has been no abandonment of the position which the party has held on political issues. They denounce coercion as unconstitutional. We have yet to learn that their opinions have met with any change on that point. They opposed every measure adopted by the administration for the prosecution of the war. They denounced the first call for troops as unauthorized. They denounced the proclamation of emancipation as unconstitutional. They opposed the means adopted by Congress for raising money, as unconstitutional. They claimed that the conscription law was revolutionary, unconstitutional and void, and sought to prevent its execution by force. They declared the war a failure. We have yet to learn that they do not hold these opinions still. These were questions which we discussed up to the close of the war. With reference to them, the position of the Democratic party is unchanged, and our verdict must be the same that it has always been.

"It is true that they have assumed a somewhat different form, but in substance there has been no change. They are the same to-day as when the rebellion began and closed. In his last message to Congress, James Buchanan, the last Democratic President, declared that the government had no authority to coerce a state. The limit of national authority, he said, was to assist the judges and the marshals, and they having all resigned in the seceding states, there was nobody to assist and consequently nothing

could be done. James Buchanan died a Democrat. The
Attorney-General, Jeremiah S. Black, wrote a long opinion
holding the same doctrine. Horatio Seymour declared
that an attempt at coercion was no less revolutionary than
secession. This, at the outbreak of the war, was the
position of what then remained of the Democratic party as
a political organization. But the people believed that the
government could coerce a state, and the attempt was
made. Three years afterwards, and in 1864, the Democratic party declared the attempt a failure. In other
words they said: 'We told in 1861 you could not coerce a
state. You have tried and you have failed. Your failure
proves that you cannot coerce those states.' Up to that
time certainly the issues were the same. But the surrender
of Lee having demonstrated that a rebellious state and its
people could be coerced as a matter of fact, because they
had been and were coerced, the same question again arose
when the nation proposed to reconstruct and rehabilitate
those states. Having defeated the rebellion in arms, over-
turned their entire political system, and conquered the
people of the rebellious states, we insisted in 1866 that
they must recognize the validity of the national debt contracted to suppress the rebellion, that the freedmen should
be entitled to citizenship, and that slavery, to perpetuate
which the rebellion was inaugurated, must be abolished.
We insisted in 1866 that upon the recognition of these
ideas, and their incorporation into the organic law,
depended a return to them of the full enjoyment of political privileges within the Union. Our right to make these
demands was denied. The Democratic party claimed that
those rebellious states, immediately at the close of the war,
occupied a position of entire equality with the loyal states,
and that the government had no right to coerce them into
a delivery into the hands of the nation of the results and

fruits of the victories which the nation had achieved over them.

"The people, however, decided, in 1866, that they had the right to dictate terms to a conquered rebellion, and demand that their representatives in Congress should exercise that right. Refusing to accept the constitutional amendments proffered by Congress, that body undertook by a series of measures called the reconstruction acts, to enforce substantially those terms upon the South; in other words, to coerce them into yielding up to the nation the fruits of the victories which it had achieved. As a result of these measures, what has been known as the Fourteenth Constitutional Amendment has been adopted. Under these measures eight of the seceding states have been readmitted, they having paid the price of their admission by the ratification of this amendment to the constitution. This, indeed, looked like coercion. It was as complete a coercion of rebel political ideas and principles as the overthrow of Lee's army, and its forced surrender was a coercion of the military power of the southern states.

"True to the old instincts—preferring that the old issues should still be kept alive and the old questions still be agitated—the Democratic party met in national convention at the city of New York, on the 4th day of July, 1868, and solemnly declared that the reconstruction measures of Congress were usurpations---revolutionary, unconstitutional and void. If that declaration be true, and such be the opinion of the people, as a matter of course the fourteenth amendment falls with those measures of which it is the offspring. The state governments organized under it also fall, and it will indeed be true that the general government has no power to coerce a state in rebellion against its authority. It may conquer by mere force its armies, but all such measures as it may see fit to

adopt to secure the results of its victories will be 'usurpations — revolutionary, unconstitutional and void.' Whether
this nation has a right to coerce a state in rebellion against
its authority into obedience to its authority, and whether
to render that coercion effectual it may demand guarantees
for future peace, is the distinct question put to the people
by the Democratic party in its platform. It is the same
question which we have thrice settled at the ballot box
within the last eight years. The position of the Democratic party on that question is unchanged. And so I
confidently believe the position of the people on that question is unchanged and unchangeabl

"The Democratic platform not only denounces the
reconstruction measures in the general language which I
have quoted, but it takes direct issue with almost every
provision of the fourteenth amendment. It denies to the
freedmen one of the highest attributes of citizenship, the
right of suffrage, and demands that the exercise of that
right shall be regulated by the citizens of rebellious states,
who were the nation's enemies against the freedmen, who
were the nation's friends. It demands that the national
debt created to crush the rebellion shall be paid in an irredeemable promise, thus destroying its validity declared in
the fourteenth amendment, and adding to the crime of
repudiation all the calamities of a worthless currency, or
the imposition of onerous and unendurable taxation. It
demands the taxation of the Government bonds, none of
which being held in the rebellious states, would devolve
additional burdens upon the loyal people of the country.
It demands the immediate restoration of all the states, of
course without condition. Such a declaration of principles
opens every question which the war settled. It renders
our victories valueless; for if the seceding states are to
return to the Union in precisely the same position they

left it — which would be the case were tne reconstruction measures of Congress declared by the voice of the people revolutionary, unconstitutional and void—the war is a failure. Five hundred thousand lives have been sacrificed, and three thousand millions of dollars expended in vain.

"And yet with such a platform of principles, and with candidates upon it who propose to carry it out by force, we are constantly told that all discussion of the war and its results is the discussion of a dead issue. They entreat us to 'let bygones be bygones,' and to 'let the dead past bury its dead.' With a platform that would upset all that the war has accomplished, we are asked to say nothing about the war. With a platform which thrusts into our very faces every issue that the war settled, and demands that even by violence those issues must be resettled, and in another way, which demands that we shall repudiate every vote we have given for the last eight years, we are asked to forget the past. Wade Hampton, with the smoke of burning loyal homes still clinging to his garments, whose hands are red with the blood of our brothers and our sons, and Forrest, fresh from the atrocities of Fort Pillow, demanded that the states which they carried into and aided in rebellion, shall suffer nothing for their great crime, and beseechingly entreat us to let bygones be bygones. If a forcible attempt is made to despoil you of your property and destroy your homes, you can hardly regard such an attempt as a bygone, until it is adequately protected against all future attacks of the same character. But it would be quite in keeping with this Democratic platform for the robber and the incendiary yet hovering around your home, kept at a respectful distance by barricades which you had erected, and watchmen whom you had placed about it for its protection, to denounce those barricades and watchmen as revolutionary, unconstitutional and void, and whenever you referred to the old robberies and burnings, to entreat you to let bygones be bygones. I apprehend that, coming from the old robber and the old incendiary, you would regard a proposition to remove your watchmen and barricades as a renewal of an attempt to despoil your property and burn your home, and as, substantially, the same old question. Such a barricade, guarding for the future the results of our victories, protecting us against rebellion in the future, is the fourteenth constitutional amendment. It is demanded, by those who sought to destroy the nation that that barrier be removed. It is the same old question. I make the same old answer — No.

"The Democratic party having done nothing to win back your confidence, has the Republican party been guilty of any acts which would justify the withdrawal of public confidence from it? Mr. Pendleton, in his speech at Springfield, arraigns the Republican party before the people, and proposes that it be tried and convicted on its history. By its history we are quite willing that it should be tried. By that test let it stand or fall. If within the comparatively short period of its existence it has achieved nothing for the cause of humanity and the interests of good government; if under its sway freedom has made no progress, and the nation itself no advancement, it deserves to forfeit public confidence; it deserves removal from power.

"In detailing the history of the Republican party, Mr. Pendleton in his speech at Springfield, said: 'The Republican party, on the other hand, is not of long duration. It was founded in 1856, upon the ruins of the old Whig party. But all who were sectional, all who were fanatical, all who hated the constitution, all who hated the Union, all who were dissatisfied, went into the Republican organization, and they carried with them many dissatisfied Democrats. I need not tell you that the infancy of this party was marked by the bloody troubles in Kansas, and by the invasion of Virginia by John Brown of Ossawatomie. I need not tell you that its advent to power in 1860 was marked by the destruction of the harmony which up to that time had existed among the people; that it was marked by an attempt at dissolution of the ties which bound our states together; that it was marked by the sorrows and miseries of the greatest civil war of which history has given us any record. But these parties — the Republican party and Democratic party — to-day stand where they stood in the beginning, carrying out to their logical conclusions the principles upon which they were founded.'

"It is not of decisive consequence in determining the merits of the Republican party from its history to know how its infancy was marked, nor by what events its advent was marked. It is true that its infancy was marked by the bloody troubles in Kansas; but it is equally true that those bloody marks upon the infancy of the Republican party, and upon the history of the nation, were all made by Democratic hands, and all bear the impress of Democratic fingers. The question is not so much what were the marks, but who made the marks? The bloody troubles in Kansas were the outgrowth of a wicked attempt of the Democratic party and a Democratic administration to force upon that territory, against the will of its people, by violence and fraud and bloodshed, the blithing curse of slavery. It is equally true that during the infancy of the Republican party, John Brown with thirteen men invaded Virginia. For an attempt to liberate the slave he was tried and hung. That the Republican party was responsible for John Brown's raid Mr. Pendleton dare not assert. The men who hung John Brown were Democrats. The body of the old hero was hardly cold in its grave before his executioners had kindled the flames of civil war, had been guilty of the vilest treason against the nation, and are now demanding the overthrow of those laws enacted to prevent another rebellion. The memory of John Brown's executioners will be handed to infamy. But though 'John Brown's body lies moldering in the grave, his soul goes marching on.'

"The advent of the Republican party to power was, Mr. Pendleton informs us, marked 'by the destruction of the harmony which up to that time had existed among the people.' It was a curious kind of harmony which existed during the administration of Pierce and Buchanan. 'Order,' it was once said, 'reigns in Warsaw.' The Poles had all been slaughtered. It was the order which despotism brings about, by the destruction of those who chafe under it. It was the quiet of death. The Poles all massacred, order reigned in Warsaw. The voice of freedom having been hushed, and her slightest utterance choked, harmony prevailed, for the slave-driver had everything his own way. We are also told that the advent of the Republican party was marked 'by an attempt at dissolution of the ties which bound our states together.' That is true, but the truth of the statement is the everlasting disgrace of the Democratic party. The attempt at dissolution was made by the Democratic party, for no other reason than that Abraham Lincoln was elected President of the United States. It was an attempt of measureless wickedness and causelessness which Mr. Pendleton did not attempt to prevent, but rather urged on by saying to those actively engaged in it, 'I would mark their departure with tokens of affection; I would bid them adieu so tenderly that their hearts would be touched by the recollection of it.' For the wickedness of this attempt and for the attempt itself, Mr. Pendleton and the Democratic party are alone responsible. They made no effort to prevent the attempt being made; they put forth no exertion to prevent it succeeding. The infamy of this attempt rests alone upon the shoulders of the Democratic party. The humiliations and disasters of its defeat should be borne by them alone, and the glory of its overthrow belongs alone to the great loyal people, who proved themselves as able to meet and overcome the Democratic party in the field, as at the ballot box. Mr. Pendleton also graciously assures the liberty-loving men of this country that their advent to power was ' marked by the sorrows and miseries of the greatest civil war of which history has given us any record.' This is true again, and it is also true that for that war, and all the sorrows and miseries which it entailed, the Democratic party is alone responsible. These sorrows and miseries are indeed marked deeply upon the history of the country, and their guilty authors will not soon be forgotten. The responsibility for that gigantic crime, and the griefs resulting from it, as a part of the burdens which the Democratic party must carry down with it through all history, is engraved upon the heart of every mother whose boy died in the great cause; it is witnessed by the tear of every widowed wife whose husband fell from Southern bullets, or perished ultimately in a Southern prison-pen. There is not a desolate home in all the land, nor a deserted fireside, made so by this wicked rebellion, that does not bear eloquent testimony that all those marks of desolating grief were made by Democratic hands. And all the countless graves of the slain heroes of the republic are marks of misery and suffering made by Democratic rebels, not only on the peaceful advent of a great party to power, but upon the pages of our country's and the world's history. All these ' marks' which Mr. Pendleton flourishingly parcels, were made by the Democratic party. When the burglar can safely denounce the merchant, because his advent to a prosperous business was marked by a robbery of his substance; when the incendiary can denounce his

victim because his advent to his new home was marked by
its conflagration, then let the Democratic party, North and
South, denounce the Republicans because their advent to
power was marked by the miseries of a war which Democrats began by an attempt at dissolution, in which they
alone engaged. We gladly accept Mr. Pendleton's challenge,
and will test the claims of the Republicans by what the
Republican party has achieved.

'It entered the field in 1856, a protest of the best
thought, the highest culture and the soundest heart of the
country, against the aggressions of the slave power. On
behalf of the dignity of free labor, free speech and free
thought, it appealed to the highest motives, and its appeal
was nobly answered.

"Its first great achievement, resulting from the election of Abraham Lincoln, was the rescue of our vast western territories from the grasp of slavery, and from its
blighting effects upon the interests and dignity of labor,
and the dedication of those territories, now prosperous
states, to free labor, and to free men. Against this great
achievement, up to this time the grandest event in American history, the Democratic party rebelled. Having saved
the territories to freedom, the Republican party entered on
the second stage of its career, and its second achievement,
wrought out with more than one-half the Democratic
party of the nation in open arms against it, and the other
half in covert opposition, was the salvation of this nation,
for all peoples and to all ages, as the sacred custodian of
the priceless treasure of free government. Its great career
was not ended. Having crushed the rebellion, it determined to rid the country of the evil out of which rebellion
grew, and the nation of the foulest stain resting upon its
fair fame. It entered at once upon the third stage of its
career, and for its third achievement in the interests of

humanity, for the cause of good government and in behalf of the downtrodden and the oppressed, declared that 'neither slavery nor involuntary servitude, except as a punishment for crime, whereof the party shall have been duly convicted, shall exist within the United States, or any place subject to their jurisdiction.' And yet its work is not finished. It is now closing the fourth period of its history, and preparing finally to consummate its fourth achievement.

"The salvation of the nation, wrought out through the perils of the mightiest rebellion which history records, involved the building of great fleets, the raising and equipping of gigantic armies. For these purposes a great national debt was incurred. And that debt the Republican party proposes to pay.

"It entered upon the great contest with four millions of slaves in the rebellious states, who, during the entire period of the war, were our friends, and hundreds and thousands of whom fought for us. It found those slaves at the close of the war free men. It proposes to make them citizens, and protect them in the full enjoyment of their rights as citizens Having crushed the rebellion, it proposes to protect the nation against its recurrence, and to withhold from those who sought the destruction of the national life any share in the control of our national destinies until they have furnished us the surest evidences that the national interests can be safely intrusted to their hands.

"Thus having carried the nation safely through the perils of the rebellion, it proposes to gather the fruits of all its triumphs, and imbed them in the constitution of the United States, secure for all the future in the fourteenth amendment to the constitution, wherein are secured national honor, the freedom of the slave, and national

security for the future, as a fitting consummation of the
great work of the Republican party, for the people and for
the world.   The same opposition which it has encountered
at every period of its progress it now encounters.   The
Democratic party, which opposed it in its efforts to give
the territories to freedom, which rebelled when the effort
proved a success, which opposed it in its great effort to
preserve the national integrity, which opposed it when it
gave freedom, opposes it now, when it seeks to embody all
these results in the organic law, and threatens to tear
down the sanctuary in which they are enshrined, and
denounces the great measure by which these results have
all been gathered together as usurpations revolutionary,
unconstitutional and void.

   " These are the great events in the history of the Republican party.   Considering the mighty consequence of what
it has accomplished, it would seem that it has crowded a
thousand years of history into eight short years of time.
It found our territories in the clutch of slavery; it broke
its hold and dedicated them to freedom.   It found the
nation beset by spies and encompassed by treason, trembling upon the very brink of ruin; it rescued it from danger.   It saved the only free government on earth.   It
found four millions of human beings slaves; it gave them
freedom.   It has lifted four millions of chattels out of the
night and barbarism of slavery into the clear pure air of
American citizenship.   It has for the first time made
American citizenship a living reality — has made citizenship broader than the mere boundaries of a state; has made
it in its privileges coextensive with the whole nation.   It
has vindicated the national faith, and if the people permit,
will secure to all the future domestic prosperity and tranquility, honor and respect, abroad.   It has vindicated the
capacity of men for self government, and a united Italy

and a united Germany follow closely upon and result from
the example of a united nationality in this great republic.
All these mighty results, the most cheering for our hopes
of humanity, has the Republican party accomplished in
eight short years. Test it by its history. Judge it by what
has been done, and when you have found that all the
parties of which history gives us any record can produce
nothing to compare with these results, you will decide as
you have decided, that whatever mistakes of detail it may
have committed it is still entitled to the largest measure
of our confidence; that we are prepared to say to it, ' Well
done, good and faithful servant.'

" Besides the general charges which Mr. Pendleton
makes against the Republican party, and to which I have
already alluded, he makes several specific allegations against
it, the most important of which seems to relate to the constitutional amendments.   Mr. Pendleton professes an
almost idolatrous admiration of the constitution, insists
that our fathers who made it were wise men, and he said
in his speech at Springfield, speaking of the constitution:
' I charge upon you who are Democrats .   .   .   do not
seek to amend it, do not seek to change it.'   We yield
nothing to Mr. Pendleton in admiration of the constitution.   We appreciate as fully as he does the wisdom of our
fathers who made it.   But we admire it not alone for its
' checks and balances,' of which he has so much to say.
We do not regard it as a mere political ' teeter.'   We
admire it among other reasons because it was made by the
people of the United States in order to form a more perfect union, establish justice, insure domestic tranquility,
provide for the common defense, promote the general welfare, and secure the blessings of liberty to ourselves and
our posterity.'   We admire it for the ample shield of protection which it throws about the citizen in time of peace.

We admire it for the tremendous armory of power which it
furnishes the nation in time of war. We think its framers
were wise men, and they exhibited their wisdom by embodying in the constitution provisions for its amendment.

" This nervous anxiety about amendments to the constitution is a new thing with the Democratic party. When,
in 1860, Mr. Chittenden, for the purpose of coaxing the
South back into the Union which they had determined to
destroy, proposed amendments to the constitution dedicat-
ing vast tracts of free territory to slavery, and pledging it
the protection of the nation, even against the will of the
people of those territories, no Democrat opposed such an
amendment. They not only did not oppose it, but, Mr. Pendleton among the number, gave it most hearty and cordial
support. Again, when that distinguished Democrat, Mr.
Vallandigham, proposed such an amendment of the constitution as worked a radical change in the very structure
of our government, by having two presidents, one from
the North and one from the South, Democratic objectors
were silent. Again, when Horatio Seymour proposed a
very essential amendment to the constitution, which was
nothing less than the substitution of the Montgomery
Confederate constitution in the place of our own, Democrats did not seem to be particularly alarmed, nor were
they entreatingly besought to take the constitution home
with them and place it on the family altar next the Bible,
where they might watch it in the intervals of their slumbers, and dream of it when sleep oppressed their eye-lids.

" This new-born anxiety in the Democratic mind about
amending the constitution springs from the fact that the
thirteenth and fourteenth amendments are in the interests
of freedom, while the others proposed were additional
guarantees for slavery.

" Mr. Pendleton in his speech at Portland, delivered on

the 23d day of August, emphasizes his attack upon the Republican party, and reiterates it by declaring, as one of the crimes of which the Republican party has been guilty against the South, that ' it has destroyed their labor system ; it has converted three million of industrious negroes into very bad politicians.' The labor system to which Mr. Pendleton alludes is the institution of slavery. One of the peculiarities of the system was that it was all work and no pay. Mr. Pendleton complains that this system has been abolished, hopes for its return, and, to bring his hopes to fruition, demands that the Republican shall be driven from power. He might as well attempt to set time back, to roll the tides back upon the sea as they flow upon the land. But the exhibition of such an intense Bourbonism as this may well make us despair of ever having any new issues with the Democratic party. Mr. Pendleton is kind enough to furnish us the reason why he should not give political power to the negro. In his speech at Portland, he said, in speaking of the negro : 'I would not admit him to political power because I believe he is of a different race from ourselves. I am in favor of maintaining this a white man's government.' A discussion of such a topic as the origin of our species, the diversity of races, and whether the Almighty made of one flesh all the nations of the earth, perplexes political controversy. Without going very deeply into that subject, the Republican party contents itself that all human beings are entitled to human rights, and that all the citizens of the republic should stand on a footing of political equality. The questions of intellectual and social equality it leaves to be determined by what each man may do for himself, believing that every man should have the largest liberty in doing for himself in the way of social or intellectual development all that he can do. But it seems that our Democratic friends propose to determine a citi-

zen's right to vote by physiological, anatomical, ethnolog-
ical and purely scientific tests.   For this purpose we may
expect the endowment of a university, headed by Mr. Pendleton, assisted by those able *savants*, Messrs. Morrissey,
Rynders, Dean and Pomeroy, and before whom the negro's
right of suffrage shall be subjected to the just, but nevertheless stern and relentless, tests of science.   Before such
an able body of professors, I think I see as students the
earnest searchers after truth from the sixth ward in the
city of New York, numerously appearing, armed with a
copy of Cuvier's 'Animal Kingdom' under one arm, the
'Vestiges of Creation' under the other, and in their pocket
a copy of the Democratic platform.   Upon comparing the
astragalus of a negro with the *astragalus* of a white man, it
may be found that they differ.   From this important fact
will be deduced the conclusion that they are of different
race, and denial of political rights to the negro would follow
as a natural consequence, not from prejudice against the
negro, but out of glory to science.   What the result might
be, if it were found that the same difference in the *astragalus* existed between different white men, I cannot undertake
to say ; and the results which might flow from the adoption
of the theory of the growth of human beings from oysters
up to monkeys and through successive stages of development
until creation flowered and blossomed out into the perfect
Democrat, are fearful to contemplate.

"Ages of slavery are not likely to develop great intellectual activity, and, to a certain extent at least, may the
negro's want of intelligence be ascribed to the condition of
bondage in which he has been kept.   A slave no longer,
the problem is, how he may be made sufficiently intelligent to discharge all the duties and exercise all the privileges of a citizen wisely and well.   It is very clear that to
limit his opportunities for self-improvement would not

result in a satisfactory solution of this problem. Mr. Pendleton seems to belong to that class of politicians who are in the habit of laying it down as a self-evident proposition, that no people ought to be free till they are fit to use their freedom. 'If men are to wait for liberty until they become wise and good in slavery, they may indeed wait forever.' It may be that there are evils resulting from the newly acquired freedom of the slave. But as Macaulay has well said, 'There is only one cure for the evils which newly-acquired freedom produces — and that cure is freedom!' When a prisoner leaves his cell he cannot bear the light of day; he is unable to discriminate colors or recognize faces. But the remedy is not to remand him into his dungeon, but to accustom him to the rays of the sun. The blaze of truth and liberty may at first dazzle and bewilder nations which have become half blind in the house of bondage. But let them gaze on and they will soon be able to bear it.

"Mr. Pendleton demands that this shall be a white man's government. Whether he intends to exclude from the privileges of this free government all men who are not white, he does not clearly set forth. If this demand means anything, however, it means that none but white men shall be permitted to be citizens. For if negroes, under any circumstances, are permitted to become citizens, this certainly would not be exclusively a white man's government. The result of this doctrine clearly would be to deprive the freedman of his newly-acquired citizenship, and that such is the purpose of the Democratic party, appears not only from their platform denouncing the legislation by which that citizenship is declared and secured as unconstitutional, revolutionary and void, but from the exposition of that platform by the leading members of the party, Mr. Pendleton among the number.

"It is insisted, however, that the questions of citizen-

ship and suffrage should be left exclusively to the states.
Under ordinary circumstances this would be so. But for
the nation to have submitted the absolute dominion over
our friends in the seceding and conquered states to our
enemies in those states, would have been an act of injustice
so outrageous and so gross as justly to have called down
upon us the reproaches of every nation on the face of the
globe. In the process of reconstruction the injustice of
submitting to the rebel the decision of the extent of the
rights of the freedman is too obvious to admit of comment.
When the Democratic party insists that the people of the
rebellious states shall decide who shall be citizens and who
shall be voters in those states, they do not mean what they
say, for by the people they mean, not the negro, who has
achieved his citizenship by his loyalty, but the rebel, who
has forfeited his privileges by his treason. And hence in
the decision of this question the freedman, who is especially
interested, shall have nothing to say, while the rebel shall
have everything to say. If the citizenship of the negro in
the rebellious states is to be recognized as a matter of
fact, it would seem clear that the enjoyment of the privileges of civilization should be secured and guaranteed him.
If to protect him in the full and complete enjoyment of
those rights the ballot is necessary, I for one would confer
it upon him. I would make the gift no idle one. I would
have it real and substantial. I believe that in the states
covered by the reconstruction measures the ballot is absolutely necessary to protect the negro in his newly acquired
rights, and, believing that, I would give him the ballot,
feeling well assured that he who had sufficient intelligence
to throw the weight of his influence in favor of the nation
in its struggle for its existence, and sufficient courage and
patriotism to peril his life in the nation's defense, would
be quite as likely to use the ballot wisely and well as he who

waged for four years a rebellious war against the nation.

"The denial of the right of Congress to legislate upon these questions proceeds upon the assumption that the seceding states and the people thereof lost nothing by their rebellion. Mr. Pendleton in his speech at Bangor declares, with reference to the seceding states, that their state governments 'were in full vigor and operation before and during and after the war.' With reference to the vigor of those state governments before the war, no question is made. But that they were in full vigor as state governments within the Union during the war we deny. We recognized their vigor as state governments during the war. They vigorously raised troops and vigorously carried on war against the nation. They did these things as state governments outside the Union, and as members of the Southern Confederacy, and it seems somewhat curious that such exhibitions of vigor which we finally succeeded in pulling down should be adduced as reasons why we have no control over them now. Had there been during the war less vigor of this kind there would have been less cause of complaint on our part. Had there been more vigor the nation would have been destroyed. Had there been no vigor, such as was exhibited by the Confederate state governments, there would have been no war. That those state governments had during the war no vigor within the Union which they were seeking to destroy, is a fact which cannot be upset by any amount of plausible theory. If during that time they were as a matter of fact state governments within the Southern Confederacy, they were not within the Union. They could not be within both the Confederacy and the Union at the same time. The task of showing that during the rebellion the South- ern states were not, as a matter of fact, members of the Southern Confederacy may safely be left to Democratic

orators and statesmen. If they could have been argued
out of the Confederacy and into the Union, that remedy
would certainly have been employed during the war. If
it could have been made efficacious, its cheapness compared
with the vast armies which we were, as we supposed,
obliged to employ to effect that object would certainly
have been a great recommendation in its favor.

"Nearly two hundred years ago the British nation was
called upon to face very much such a theory as the one
now insisted upon by Mr. Pendleton and the Democratic
party. King James II. was a model conservative. His
character bears many striking resemblances to that of
Andrew Johnson. It is said of him by an eminent historian, 'The obstinate and imperious nature of the king gave
great advantages to those who advised him to be firm to
yield nothing, and to make himself feared. One state
maxim had taken possession of his small understanding
and was not to be dislodged by reason. His mode of
arguing, if it is to be so called, was one not uncommon
among dull and stubborn persons who are accustomed to
be surrounded by their inferiors. He asserted a proposition; and as often as wiser people ventured respectfully to
show that it was erroneous, he asserted it again in exactly
the same words, and conceived that by doing so he at once
disposed of all objections.' By various acts of parliament,
penalties had been imposed and tests applied against particular individuals, depriving them of office, and James proposed to exercise the dispensing power so as substantially
to annul those acts of Parliament. This he called 'my
policy.' Finding Parliament refractory, he determined to
call together a new Parliament, and in doing so employed
precisely the same agencies to secure a Parliament favor-
able to his purposes, as were resorted to by Andrew Johnson in 1866. Returning officers were appointed, directed

to avail themselves of the slightest pretense to declare the
king's friends duly elected. Every placeman, from the
highest to the lowest, was made to understand that if he
wished to retain his office, he must support the throne by
his vote and interest. A proclamation appeared in the
Gazette, announcing that the king had determined to
revive the commissions of peace and of lieutenancy, and to
retain in public employment only such gentlemen as should
be disposed to support his policy. The commissioners of
custom and excise were ordered to attend his Majesty at
the treasury. There he demanded from them a promise
to support his policy, and directed them to require a similar
promise from all their subordinates. One custom house
officer notified his submission to the royal will by saying
that he had fourteen reasons for obeying his Majesty's
commands,—a wife and thirteen young children. But
with all these precautions, James failed, as Andrew failed.
The new Parliament were more stubborn and refractory
than the old had been, and finally James fled the country,.
took his son with him and went to France. And there
the question arose whether the states were out of the
Union. At once there arose in Great Britain a party who
insisted upon the theory that there could be no vacancy in
the throne; that James not being dead, the throne was not
vacant, and that, accordingly, writs must run in his name.
Acts of Parliament must be still called from the years of
his reign, but that the administration must nevertheless be
confided to a regent. Macaulay says that 'it seems incred-
ible that any man should really have been imposed upon
by such nonsense.' And yet it had great weight with the
whole Tory party. The difficulty was solved by the
British people, very much as the loyal people of the
country have answered the Democratic theory. 'We
recognize,' said the British people, 'the general correctness

of the theory, as a legal proposition, that the throne cannot be vacant. But whatever the theory may be, we look at the throne, and see that as a matter of fact no one occupies it. It is vacant.' They accordingly declared the fact as they saw it — that the throne was vacant — and, being vacant, they proceeded to fill it. And they did fill it in a way which secured constitutional liberty to the British nation down to this day. And so the people of this country recognize the fact that for four years the rebellious states were out of the Union; that they did establish and sought to perpetuate an independent government; that their places in the Union were vacant; that their seats in Congress were vacant. That they had no right thus to rebel we well knew; that the right to exercise national authority over them was never destroyed we also well knew. That their secession did not impair the rights of the nation over them we perfectly well understood; but that it did impair their rights within the nation we believe was equally clear. Their argument is based upon their own wrong, and they claim that they lost no political rights by rebellion because they had no right to rebel.

"The position of the Confederate states during the war was defined to the entire satisfaction of the loyal people of the country by Mr. Lincoln in his amnesty proclamation, December 8, 1863. He there declares that by the rebellion the loyal state governments of several states ' have for a long time been subverted;' that the national authority has been suspended; that we are to reconstruct and re-establish loyal state governments, and that the concessions demanded by him were in return for pardon and restoration of forfeited rights. The work of reconstruction has been based upon this theory and upon the facts. As a consequence of the rebellion, the national authority over the rebellious states was superseded, to be assumed when it achieved the power to do so, the state governments of those states were subverted, overthrown to be reëstablished when we had the physical power to do so. Remembering in the language of Mr. Lincoln that an 'attempt to guarantee and protect a revived state government, constructed in whole or in preponderating part from the very element against whose hostility and violence it is to be protected, is simply absurd. There must be a test by which to separate the opposing elements so as to build only from the sound; the political rights of the people of those states had been forfeited,' to be restored only upon such terms as the nation might see fit to impose.

"Such being the condition of the seceded states and people during the war, how was any change effected in their condition by the defeat of their armies? Our rights over them when their armies surrendered were certainly as great as when they kept the field against us. Our power over them was greater. Clearly the Southern Confederacy could achieve no rights which they had not during the war, merely because their armies had been defeated by ours, and they were unable further to prosecute the war. The defeat of a rebellion cannot enlarge its rights. During the war, we had, as against the South, the rights to say the least which any nation would have in waging war, or which we would have had in waging war against any other nation. We had the rights of war because we were at war, and when the war closed, we victorious and the Southern Confederacy conquered, we had the rights which the position gave to us, namely, the rights of a conqueror, and they had the rights which their position gave them, namely, the rights of a conquered people. To what extent we should exercise those rights was another question. But to say that at the close of a long war the rights of the conqueror and the conquered are equal is an absurdity and an impossibility. If it required four years of war, five hundred thousand lives and the expenditure of three thousand millions of money to conquer the seceding states down to a condition of equality with us, they must certainly have been our superiors when the war began. It must be remembered, too, that we conquered not only the armies of the rebellion, but the entire structure of government, state and national, which rebellion organized and to maintain which its armies fought. And when the Confederate flag went down in final defeat at Appomattox courthouse, the Southern Confederacy and every state government organized under it went down with it. The results of these victories are gathered in the fourteenth constitutional amendment. We intend they shall remain there.

" It is not strange that the Democratic party, having opposed every measure resorted to by the administration for the prosecution of the war, and denounced the Republican party as guilty of gross usurpation of power in the means which it employed to crush out rebellion, should look with exceeding disfavor upon the debt which the nation was compelled to contract in order to furnish for its defense men and munitions of war. The staple charge made against the Republican party by Democratic orators is that it has left a legacy of $2,700,000,000 of debt to the people. It is hardly worth while to discuss the question as to where the responsibility of this great debt properly belongs. If the Democratic party and the South are responsible for the war, then are they responsible for the debt, and that they are so responsible the people of this country have repeatedly decided and still firmly believe. The debt was created in order to crush rebellion, and now that the active leaders and fomentors of that rebellion of the South, with their sympathizers at the North, should charge upon the people whose government they undertook to destroy the responsibility of the debt, is an exhibition of impudence to which history furnishes no parallel. They may feel thankful that they are not compelled alone to bear its burdens. But assume that this debt is to be charged up against the Republican party, how then would the account stand? In the national ledger we might find the party charged with twenty-seven hundred millions of dollars loaned to it by the people; but we would find it credited, if the accounts were correctly kept, with a nation saved. In whose favor the balance would be could be quite easily determined; for to this nation—the only sanctuary of free government on earth—no value can be set. Its value is incalculable.

"We propose to pay our national debt in money. Of that debt $356,000,000 are in promises of the government long since past due, and which as yet the government has been unable to pay. This debt is owing to the people, for a loan which at an early stage of the war the government forced the people to make to it. Every holder of a greenback is a government creditor, and has a right to demand payment before the holder of any bond shall be paid, because the greenback is due and the bond is not. It is our policy, and it is wise policy, to pay this past due indebtedness at the earliest possible moment. We all desire a resumption of specie payments as early as possible, and that, it would seem, is the duty which first presses upon us. The stability of business, every interest indeed, demands an early resumption of specie payments, or, in other words, the payment of the $356,000,000 of its indebtedness represented by greenbacks. So far as I have been able to learn from reading its speeches, the Democratic party also professes to desire that specie payments may be soon resumed. But the general method which it recommends for the treatment of the national debt would not only indefinitely postpone specie payments, but would render it impossible. It is easy to see that if an individual was desirous of extricating himself from his indebtedness he would first direct his attention to the payment of that which was first due, and attend to the balance of his indebtedness in the order of its maturity. If such a man were owing $5,000 of indebtedness past due, and which he was still unable to pay, and $25,000 of indebtedness to mature at some future period, and bearing interest, he would not be considered a very wise financier if he were to insist that his paper should all be made due at once in order to save interest. In other words, a man's ability to pay his debts is not advanced by doubling the amount of his present liabilities. In addition to the greenback debt, the government owes $160,000,000 of indebtedness, represented by what are known as the 5-20 bonds, bearing interest at six per cent, and due in about twenty years. This debt the Democratic party proposes shall be paid in greenbacks and that it shall be immediately paid. This would, of course, involve the necessity of the issuance of that amount of greenbacks in addition to the amount already in circulation. If we are yet unable to resume specie payments, it is not very difficult to see that by making our demand debt five times larger than it now is, what is now difficult would become impossible, and we could expect nothing but an eternity of irredeemable and depreciated paper currency. And thus the immediate results of the adoption of the Democratic policy would be to eternally dishonor the payment of the indebtedness owing by the government to the people. The proposition to pay the 5-20 bonds in greenbacks amounts to nothing, unless we understand when payment is to be made in that way. If we await the maturity of these bonds, and greenbacks have, in the meantime, so appreciated that they are at par with gold, the question as to whether payment shall

be made in gold or greenbacks has not the slightest consequence, and any human being accountable to his Maker
for the proper use of his time could find no justification in
spending any portion of it in the discussion of such a question. If it is intended, however, that the debts shall be
paid in greenbacks now, inflation is a necessity, for the
greenbacks can be had in no other way. That such is the
intention of the Democratic party, is clearly shown by the
reasons which they urge in support of that scheme. They
allege that the people are burdened with taxation, and that
this taxation results from the necessity of paying the interest upon the public debt, and that by the payment of the
principal this burden will be removed. If they mean what
they say, when they assert that their purpose is at once to
relieve the people from the burdens of taxation, then they
can mean nothing else than that they intend to accomplish
that end by an immediate payment, as they call it, of the
national debt in greenbacks. Mr. Pendleton, generally,
has the credit of organizing this scheme, and he clearly
fixes the time when he proposes that payment shall be
made. In his speech at Centralia he said, 'I would inflate
if we were driven to it, just as much as is necessary to pay
these 5-20 bonds in greenbacks. And I say it is the duty
of the government, in one way or another, either out of its
savings, out of the destruction of the national bank system, or out of inflation, to pay these bonds just as soon as,
under the law, the government can pay them to save the
interest.' The government has the right, under the law,
to pay one-third of those bonds now, and accordingly Mr.
Pendleton means that they shall be paid now. It is only
by inflation to the amount of these bonds that they can
now be paid, and hence inflation would be a necessity.
But Mr. Pendleton suggests two or three methods, one of
which is payment out of the government savings. But the

Democratic party proposes to raise no more money than is absolutely necessary to pay the ordinary expenses of government, and under that theory it would have no savings. These savings, whatever they might be, can be produced only by taxes, and the Democratic party proposes very materially to reduce them. It charges that the present revenues of the government are largely in excess of its needs, and proposes to reduce them. In short, the plan of paying the national debt out of our surplus revenues involves the necessity of increasing taxation. It is the policy of the Republican party to diminish it.

"Another scheme suggested by Mr. Pendleton is the payment of the national debt out of the destruction of the national bank system. When we consider the taxes imposed upon the shares of those banks and the federal taxes which they pay, but about $3,000,000 per year would be saved by this operation, and whether that would compensate for the panics created by sudden contraction and calling in of loans, which the destruction of those banks would involve, is a question about which there may well be grave doubts. It is not, however, a party issue, and it is enough to say that the payment of $3,000,000 per year of the national debt would be a very slow way of extinguishing it, and would hardly be a payment now, which Mr. Pendleton demands. Thus these two schemes are evidently impracticable, and so Mr. Pendleton evidently considers them, for he frankly says that he would inflate if we were driven to it, just as much as is necessary to pay those 5-20 bonds in greenbacks.

"We have already seen that his plan involves the practical repudiation of the greenbacks, and accordingly the practical repudiation of the bonds. For the proposition simply amounts to this—a pretended payment by the government of one debt, by the creation of another debt,

which by the very act of its creation is made worthless.
By such an inflation, the government renders its own promises worthless, compels its creditor to take that promise
which it has of its own act made valueless, and calls that
payment. I need not dwell upon the ingenuity of this
proceeding, nor the effect which it must have upon the
future credit of the country. I need not repeat here that
when those bonds were issued, the government through its
agents, represented that they were to be paid in coin, and
that when the law authorizing the issuance of those bonds
was under discussion, every one who had anything to say
upon the subject insisted that the fact that they were to
be paid in coin was one of the great reasons recommending
them to popular favor ; that the provision requiring the
payment of the interest in coin was placed in the law to
guard against any possibility of misconstruction which
might arise from the fact that interest would mature before
the resumption of specie payments, a contingency which
no one contemplated with reference to the principal, and,
therefore, no such provision was deemed necessary as to it.

" Nor need I enlarge upon the calamities which would
inevitably follow such a vast inflation. The whole body of
our currency would be rendered comparatively worthless,
gold would be drawn from the country by such a vast body
of irredeemable currency, and values not only unsettled
but substantially destroyed.

"This would work not merely a burden upon the
interests of labor, but would be the destruction of those
interests — the paralyzation of trade, the overthrow of commerce, industry palsied, enterprise deadened, — these would
be among the first fruits of the inflation policy, and which
would grow worse as the years rolled on.

" Added to this would be the utter loss of national
honor, the complete destruction of national credit. Thus

situated, without the ability to borrow a dollar in money, for any purpose, either to enable us to punish our enemies or to defend ourselves against foreign or domestic foes, the Democratic programme of overthrowing the state governments organized under the reconstruction measures of Congress, which they denounce as revolutionary, unconstitutional and void, could be easily and would be readily carried into execution.

"The scheme of taking government bonds is equally wicked, equally impracticable, and a part of the same general scheme of running the national credit.

"That the state cannot tax those bonds every one knows. That Congress cannot confer the power upon the states to tax them is authoritatively settled. All this Mr. Pendleton has been forced to admit, and yet he thinks that in some way or other, which he does not attempt to point out, some man with a ' clear head and an honest purpose' may be able to devise some scheme by which the law with reference to the taxation of the national securities may be evaded.

"To retain from the foreign bondholder a portion of his interest is not taxation. That is repudiation. The Republican party proposes such a policy as will result in improving the national credit, thereby enabling it to borrow money at lower rates than it is obliged to pay. This done, the road out of our difficulties is easy and honorable. Our ability to pay our national debt is settled. Our willingness now alone remains to be decided. That question decided, as it will be by the election of Grant and Colfax, in the affirmative, our credit is safe, and the adjustment of our national debt easy.

"In the presence of such an attack upon the national life and honor, preserved at so vast a cost, who is there that does not say, in the language of our great captain,

'Let us have peace,'—the peace that comes from good government, the peace that comes from equality of political privileges, the peace that follows a vindication of national honor, and the assertion of the national credit ; the peace which will come when rebellion, in all its shapes, is conquered and all its heresies extirpated ; the peace which a careful preservation of the fruits of our great victories will insure ; the peace which will come when we are secured against future attacks upon the national life. A peace thus secured is full of glory for the future. Such a peace is solid and enduring, and its green and sunny slopes stretch out in infinite distances before us. For such a peace all generations of time will thank us. The widowed wife of the soldier will thank us for it ; the bereaved mother whose boy died that he might have such a peace, will thank us for it ; and ringing through the very arches of Heaven, will come the thanks of the spirits of the slain heroes of the republic, that we have secured the peace for which they died."

CHAPTER V.

IN 1872 the Republican party had not only to contend with its recognized Democratic opponents, but with a discontented band within its own ranks, led by Carl Schurz, whose great cry was for civil service reform, but who also disapproved of the reconstruction measures of General Grant's administration as too radical and repressive towards the rebel element of the South. The doings of the " Ku-Klux " had made military interference necessary, and General Grant had not hesitated to put down their lawless organization by military force. Mr. Storrs thoroughly believed that any truckling to the ruffians who drove negroes from the polls, and shot down white men suspected of sympathy with the negro in respect to his civil rights, was mere cowardice, and sure to end in defeating the action of Congress on behalf of that oppressed race. He was, moreover, an ardent admirer of the strong soldier President. He therefore threw himself into the campaign of 1872 with all his characteristic energy and enthusiasm as an advocate of the reëlection of President Grant.

The disaffected Republicans, arrogating to themselves the title of " liberal " Republicans, were joined by some who had become Democrats after the impeachment of Andrew Johnson, and held a convention at Cincinnati in May, where they nominated Horace Greeley for President. The Republican convention of the state of Illinois met at Springfield toward the end of May, and Mr. Storrs, who was there as a delegate, addressed a mass-meeting in the hall of the House of Representatives the night before its session was formally opened. The first sentences that he uttered evoked an enthusiasm which was sustained to the end. He began by saying:

"It is quite evident from what I see before me here to-night that the Republicans of the state of Illinois have but little thought of abandoning their party colors, or of deserting that glorious political organization which for fifteen years of our past history has represented the purest patriotism, the best thought and the highest impulses of the country. Coming together from every portion of the state to take counsel with each other, we have found, I have been delighted to note, that in our ranks there is no faltering, and that no appeals to merely personal prejudices, no platforms which have their foundation on mere personal grievances, can swerve the old party of the Union a hair's-breadth from its course.

" A year ago the Democratic party, tired and heart-sick at over ten years of continuous defeats, took what they called 'a new departure.' How dismal a failure they made of it I will not distress them nor weary you by repeating. We have had for several years in our own party many very excellent gentlemen who, wearied with success, and finding that the Democratic ' new departure ' was a failure, have undertaken to get up one of their own, and ask the Republican party to join with them. The experiment which the Democracy tried was an entirely safe one, for however it might result, it was impossible that their condition should be any worse than it was. They could lose nothing by failure, and therefore it was entirely safe to try. But we are very differently situated. It is very doubtful whether our condition could be improved by the success of such an experiment, while it is entirely cer-

tain that it would be seriously damaged by a failure.   As a
matter of common prudence, I object to any Republican
new departure.   We started right at the outset.   We
have been going right ever since.   We have reached the
haven of success and victory at the end of each trip.   A
new departure would probably land us in another port, and
whoever leaves our craft, to adopt the Democratic style of
navigation, will wind up by becoming one of them, for new
departure will land him where theirs landed them: on the
bleak and desolate shores of political defeat and disappointment.

"I fail see any good reason why I should leave the
Republican party.   I fail to see why the party itself should
be dissolved.   If for nothing more than what it has done,
we should be loth to desert it, and least of all should we
leave it until we can find some organization which will suit
us better."

He then appealed to the past record of the Republican party, and contended that the interests of the country would be safest in their hands.

"But complaint is made that it has no new policy to
propose; that the country requires, now that the war has
ended, a line of policy looking solely to the conditions of
peace, and that the Republican party has failed to furnish
it.   On this basis a new party has been organized, called
the Liberal Republicans.   Why they are thus called I
shall presently undertake to show.   We are all invited to
abandon the old organization, to throw General Grant
overboard; but before accepting such invitation, I desire
to know what new line of policy this new party proposes;
what measures it favors which are not already adopted by
the Republican party."

He proceeded to review the issues upon which the
Cincinnati party based their platform.   In his last mes-

sage, President Grant had recommended the removal of the disabilities imposed by the fourteenth amendment, and Congress had taken action on the subject, so that "general amnesty" was likely soon to be made a dead issue.

On the question of civil service reform, about which a great clamor was made at Cincinnati, Mr. Storrs again referred to the message of President Grant, advising a reform of the civil service and announcing that he had appointed a commission to devise rules and regulations for the purpose. "Their labors," said General Grant, "are not yet complete; but it is believed that they will succeed in devising a plan that can be adopted, to the great relief of the executive, the heads of depart-ments, and members of congress, and which will re-dound to the true interest of the public service. At all events the experiment shall have a fair trial."

" He appointed on that commission Joseph Medill, one of the editors of the Chicago *Tribune*, when the Chicago *Tribune* was a republican paper — a true and able man; Geo. W. Curtis; one of the most cultivated and trustworthy men in the country; ex-Senator Cattell, of New Jersey, and a Southern gentleman of equal prominence. His desire to give this civil service reform a fair trial was demonstrated by the character of the men whom he appointed, each and every one of whom was known to be in favor of the experiment. Rules were established by those commissioners. The President has acted in hearty accord with them, and Congress has appropriated $25,000 — all that was asked by the commissioners — for the purpose of carrying their schemes into operation."

What more did the new party want?

"Is it revenue reform? They have just nominated

for president the most bigoted, insane and absurd protectionist in the country, and have openly and conspicuously abandoned that question as an issue in national politics by remitting it to the people of the congressional districts. Is it a reduction of the tariff which they desire? We need organize no new party on that basis, for Congress is now reducing the tariff at least fifty millions of dollars. Is it the payment of the national debt? The Republican party is paying it at the rate of one hundred millions of dollars per year. Do they wish it paid more rapidly? They dare not say so. Is it the resumption of specie payments? We are all in favor of that, and only differ in the manner in which specie payments shall be resumed. Greeley says, 'The way to resume is to resume.' Is that the policy of the Liberal party? They have no plan. They dare not name one· Are they for the continuance of the national banks or against them? They have not answered; they dare not answer. Is it for the further reduction of the army and navy? They have not said. Our army is not now a decent police force. Our navy is notoriously inadequate to the wants of the government. Do they propose to reduce them still further? They dare not say so, and the people demand an increase rather than a diminution of our naval strength. Is the new party founded upon the ground of opposition to land grants to railroad companies? On this question they occupy the same ground that we do, and Greeley has always been the advocate of these grants. Is it for settling our foreign quarrels by peaceful arbitration? This is precisely what, for the first time in the history of our politics, we are doing. The Alabama claims we propose to settle by arbitration. We shall thus settle them. Before the election has arrived they will be a 'dead issue.'"

The proceedings of the Cincinnati convention were subjected to a scathing criticism.

" The shame of that convention was in this : they were harmonious on questions of principle on which their differences were irreconcilable, and they were irreconcilable on mere questions of personal preferment which involved no principles whatever.

" They were agreed where agreement was shameful. They differed where differences were contemptible. Thus, Greeley and Horace White agreed on the tariff — where it was impossible that they should honestly agree. They differed as to candidates, where, if their party has been organized on principle, a disagreement would have been equally shameful. They surrendered principles to which they should have unfalteringly adhered, irrespective of men or personal prejudices. They clung to personal prejudices, which they should have at once surrendered if their party had been one of principle. Their harmony was disgraceful, because it was the price of the surrender of principle. Their differences were contemptible, because they were quarrels merely about *men*. It is the first instance in the history of our politics, where a *new party* signalizes its entry into public life by the open and undisguised sale and abandonment of the idea which called it into being.

" But this convention met. It fairly organized on Sunday. If it had carried no other baggage than its *principles* it would have been the most harmonious convention that the world has ever seen. For on that first day of conference, protectionists avowed their willingness to go for free trade, and revenue reformers avowed their willingness to go for protection — all in the interests of *reform*. When Horace Greeley and David A. Wells met harmoniously on the question of the tariff we might well expect that the lion and the lamb were prepared to lie down together.

"The convention declared against the course of Congress in its legislation against the South. Yet Horace

Greeley always has been, and is to-day, the steady advocate of Ku-Klux legislation.   The platform and their candidate are irreconcilable.   One nullifies the other, and
this convention, while seeking to organize a new party,
barters its principles at the outset, claims the support of
Republicans for the only man in their party who has ever
openly advocated the right of secession, and slanders the
memory of one dear to the heart of every true Republican—Abraham Lincoln.

 " Bitterly opposed to a protective tariff, the Liberal Republicans, so self-styled, have selected as their standard-
bearer and their leader the most prominent and conspicuous opponent of their doctrine in the whole country.   Opposed, or professing to be, with equal bitterness to the legislation of Congress with regard to the Ku-Klux, they have
nominated the principal leader of the movement in favor
of that legislation."

Speaking of Ottawa, Ill., in the last week of June,
from the bench of the circuit court, Mr. Storrs humor-
ously alluded to his occupying there for the first time
something like a judicial position.   He said:—

 "I have always spoken here as an advocate.   I have
addressed the great constituency of big-hearted, broad-
browed Republicans of La Salle county as an advocate ; as
the advocate of a great party, which it is pretty well demonstrated is as strong to-day as it has ever been ; a party
whose fires are burning as brightly, whose spirit is just as
high, and whose purpose is just as resolute, as when in
1854 it first grappled with the aggressions of the slave
power, and when, in 1860, it triumphed upon the election
of Abraham Lincoln to the Presidency.   It has a future
before it, I think, just as proud and noble as the past of
its career and history.   It is a party which, if there was
nothing more to be said about it than what it has done in

the interests of good government and of this people, I should feel very loth to desert; and least of all can I come to the conclusion that it is worth while for me to abandon the Republican party because I find here and there a few men — men with grievances, men 'with a mission,' men who call themselves self-appointed leaders of this great movement.

"Mr. Sumner, in a recent speech which he made in the Senate of the United States, declares substantially that he was the father of this great party, that the credit of its paternity belongs to him, and that its cradle was in the city of Boston. I have this to say with regard to our party that is peculiar to it, in the fullest sense of that term, the Republican party never had a leader; it has not got a leader to-day; it will never have a leader. The Republican party was made up from the start of independent men, thinking each man for himself; and the rank and file of the party never followed one single step after the leadership of any man, where that man, essaying to be its leader, did not go in the direction which the Republican party desired to go. It has never had a series of platforms written for it and dictated to it by a convention; the platforms of the Republican party have always been written in the hearts of the rank and file long before they had been inscribed upon the records of the convention. The rank and file have given law to conventions, and they have never received the law from conventions. Republicans can go to sleep at night perfectly well assured of what their principles will be the next night, although a convention should in the meantime assemble. But how has it been,— how is it to-day,— with the Democratic party of the country? The Democrat goes to bed to-night in favor of revenue reform; and he retires to bed to-morrow night in favor of a high protective tariff. He does it because he has found in

the meantime a convention has assembled, which tells him
what he must believe, and what he must not believe. Mr.
Sumner talks about the leaders of this great party. I say
this to Mr. Sumner upon that point, that if he has any
doubt about it, I would like to have him and any other
ambitious man look up and down that great track of light
which the pathway of the Republican party makes all
across this continent, and he will see all along the line of
its march that its course is strewn with the carcasses
of its self-appointed leaders. We have thrown them
overboard, one after another, and one after another,
regretting, perhaps, the necessity of our doing so, but
at the same time, that fact, that we have disposed
of a leader, never has for a single instant impeded
the progress of that great political organization. I recollect, in 1866, when I had the honor of addressing the
Republicans of La Salle county in this place, that we had
thrown overboard a whole cargo of leaders, a president and
cabinet ; and it operated upon the party like a tonic, and
we were stronger and clearer-headed for the exercise. I tell
Mr. Sumner — and as speaking for the rank and file we
may all tell him, and all others similarly disposed — that
the will of that great party is infinitely stronger than all
the influence that all its leaders ever exercised. It is a
vain thing, and a weak and idle thing for them to attempt
to resist it. Mr. Sumner claims its paternity. It was an
old doctrine of the heathen that the father should have the
right under the law to kill his children ; perhaps it is on
this basis that Mr. Sumner claims the fathership of the
Republican party. My fellow citizens, no man was the
father of the Republican party. No set of men were the
fathers of the Republican party. The Republican party,
like Topsy, 'bore itself.' It was the result of circumstances. All the leaders in the country could not have

hurried its birth one single instant. All the politicians on the top of God's green earth could not have retarded it one single moment. Slavery had made aggressions on our territory; the Democratic party were in favor of it, and the old Whigs did not oppose it; therefore the people, finding in the existing parties no expressions of their sentiments, organized a party for themselves. You might as well say that when the earth has been parched and dry for weeks, and we see great black clouds moving up in the west, coming speedier and speedier toward the zenith, suppose that Mr. Charles Sumner should stand off, just as the cloud reaches us, and say, 'I order it to rain;' and afterwards it does rain; and ten years after, when we are felicitating ourselves on the refreshing effects of that shower, Charles Sumner says, 'I was the author of that rain; I was the father of that shower! I told you, didn't I say, Let it rain, and didn't it rain?' 'Oh,' we say back to Mr. Sumner, 'the cloud was rising, and your little hand could not stop it; it was charged with moisture; the earth was dry; and God Almighty, that made great natural laws, made it rain, and you are altogether an insignificant trifle in his hands.' Mr. Sumner bring on that tremendous storm that in 1854 swept over this whole country like a whirlwind! Why, he would have been borne on the wings of that wind as easily as ever a feather was floated on the breeze. If he or anybody else had undertaken to stop it, they had better have been in a boat of stone, with sails of lead, and oars of iron, the wrath of God for a gale, and hell the nearest port!

"He the father of the Republican party! He has given his dates, and says the 19th of September, 1854, he christened it, at Boston. He quotes his words, where he used the word 'Republican' as applying to this great organization, and claims that that was the first instance where it was used

"If any place was the cradle of the Republican party, that place was Ottawa, Ill. If any man was the father of the Republican party, that man was E. S. Leland, for sixty days before Charles Sumner made his speech in Boston, Judge E. S. Leland made a speech from these very steps, and introduced a series of resolutions in which he proclaimed the will of the people of Illinois, and named that great organization the Republican party of America. If the honor is anywhere, that is where it belongs. If we are to have history of this business, let history tell the truth. I do not know whether Judge Leland was ahead of everybody else or not. He was two months ahead of Charles Sumner; and in the meantime the party had grown so strong and so powerful that the uses and purposes of Charles Sumner, even as wet nurse, might with entire safety have been dispensed with.

He then answered the "liberal" objections to the administration of affairs by the Republican party, as he had done in his Springfield speech, and proceeded to dispose of Mr. Sumner's objections to General Grant:

"Great objections were made to General Grant, but I prefer going to the people— to the rank and file—and judging General Grant precisely according to the results and what he has achieved. Men come to me with pallid faces and with trembling nerves and say, 'Great God, this country is all going to pieces!' Says I, 'What's the matter?' 'Why, Grant has been four weeks at Long Branch!' Perhaps he has; I am disposed to be candid; he has been there; but, my fellow-citizens, let us treat Grant as we treat everybody else, not better, and no worse. Give him credit for what he has done, and charge him for his defaults. Keep the books as you please, either in double or single entry, and how will it figure up? Charge him with four weeks at Long Branch, but give him credit for four weeks at Vicksburg. Charge him with three days behind a trotting horse at Central Park, but give him credit for a week at Chattanooga. Charge him with a week at Chicago, but give him credit for a week a Fort Donelson. Charge him with a trip into Pennsylvania, but give him credit for Appomattox. Go and charge it all up; there is enough of patriotic achievement still left to the credit of General Grant to stop the mouths of all the liberal parties that the sun will ever shine upon.

"Mr. Sumner, in his essay in the Senate, says that a military man never has made a successful civilian. He cites history to prove it; and if Charles is great in anything, he is great in his history. He cites the cases of Frederick the Great, the Duke of Marlborough, and the Duke of Wellington. His proposition is that a great military chieftan must of necessity and for that reason be a failure in civil life; and he cites these three cases. In the first place, suppose I admit his instances are in point, his logic is bad. The instances are not sufficiently numerous; you cannot prove a general rule by three instances. I put against him William the Silent, Oliver Cromwell, and George Washington and Charles Sumner's illustrations are all gone to pieces. My illustrations are as many as his, and prove just as much as his do. But they are not in point. Frederick the Great was the greatest civil leader the Prussian nation ever had; it is to him their system of education is due. What was the matter with the Duke of Marlborough? A great military chieftain, it is true; a wonderful success in that capacity, and a failure as a civilian. Why? Did he fail as a civilian because he was a great military man? No; he failed as a civilian because he could not stop in one party thirty days at a time; because he was more like a 'Liberal Republican' than any man that lived in the British Empire; because in the morning he attended a convention to keep

in the reigning dynasty, and the same evening he attended
another convention to bring over the pretender. Marlborough was great as a military man because he was like
Grant; he was a fizzle and a dead failure as a civilian
because he was like Schurz; he was a failure as a civilian because nobody could trust him and nobody would trust him.
The proposition amounts to this, that a great military man
and a brave man is a poor President, and therefore the
converse of the proposition must be true—that a poor
general and a coward must be a good President. Therefore I suppose they have nominated Horace Greeley. If
that is so, he fills the whole bill and has all the accom-
plishments.

"It is insisted that Grant can't make a speech. I
think he can; for I think the speeches that are going to
be remembered in the history of this world are not the
mere words which we utter in halls like this, not the mere
essays which we write, but after all they are the deeds
which men do. The world, three thousand years ago, had
forgotten all that the old Egyptians had ever written about
architecture, and all that the old Egyptians had ever said;
but there, on those desert plains of Egypt, stand those
mighty pyramids, witnesses for all time to come of what
the old Egyptains accomplished. We have all forgotten
what John Brown said; who remembers what John Brown
wrote? Who will ever forget what John Brown did? And
while John Brown's body lies moldering in the ground,
isn't his soul a-marching on? You may take, if you please,
or let Mr. Sumner and Mr. Schurz select for themselves,
the greatest speeches that either of them has ever made,
write them in letters of living flame right against the whole
sky, and put by the side of them the single word 'Appomattox,' and behold, how in that magnificent presence the
flame of Charles Sumner's speech will pale their inef-

fectual fires. The world will never forget what U. S. Grant has done; the world will soon cease to remember what Charles Sumner has said. I would detract nothing from the merits of that accomplished statesman; I concede his magnificent endowments; I concede his wonderful acquirements; but this great party of ours, which has, as I believe, the custody of the interests of good government for all the years to come in its hands, is infinitely better, and holier, and greater, and more valuable, than any man; and much as I revere the name of Charles Sumner, I would see him sink out of sight into utter forgetfulness, into the deepest oblivion, rather than I would see one single star on the banner of this great party pale its fires. For, think what it has done. In twelve short years of time it has eclipsed a thousand years of the most magnificent history that this world has ever seen. It has taken four millions of chattels, and lifted them from the night and barbarism of slavery into the clear, pure atmosphere of American citizenship. It has taken a chattel and made him a senator. It has taken personal property and made it members of congress. It is the great, progressive party of mankind. I cannot but sometimes sympathize with that conservative spirit that looks lovingly and affectionately back upon the past; but while I sympathize with it I cannot go with it. I know the picture that it has presented of the good old times when the slaveholder ruled is a pretty one; the slaveholder sitting like a patriarch, as they used to tell us, with his broad-brim out on his piazza, and his little chattels, male and female, dancing on the green before him. It is a pretty picture; but this is the one which the Republican party draws — no longer chattels, male or female; nothing, thank God, on this continent but free men and free women; by the mighty exertions of this great party, the architects of their own fortunes. You see no longer

the negro child, boy and girl, dancing upon the green; you
see them at the school-house, at the workshop, at the bench,
on the farm, each, thank God, his own master, each carv-
ing out his own fortune for the future. There may be less
poetry in it, but how much more magnificent it is in the
story it tells for our common humanity? How much more
magnificent it is in the exalted and lofty patriotism which
it typifies!

Grant cannot speak; he is no orator, as Brutus was;
and he has appointed his relatives to office. I suppose it
was necessary for him to appoint somebody's relatives. I
do not care who he makes collector of customs, nor who
he appoints assessor; it is somebody's relative; and by and
by, when the history of this great captain comes to be
written, let us think what history will say. I suppose
that history will tell us nothing about how he started from
Galena to fight at Fort Donelson, about how he took these
great western armies swinging around from Cairo to the
sea; and how that great, silent soldier saved the nation the
priceless treasure of free government for all ages to come.
Perhaps the historian will say nothing about that. He
will omit Appomattox, he will omit Spotsylvania; he will
omit the bloody record of the days in the wilderness in
what he has to say; but he will tell you how this man
found his old father a postmaster when he was elected,
and kept him there; he will tell he was at Long Branch
four weeks; he will tell you that somebody complained that
he received a gift. Stop and think how mean, how trivial,
how utterly and altogether unworthy in the record which
history shall make up, when the mists of passion and prejudice shall have cleared away, will all these things seem to
be! They are just as small, and just as trivial, and just
as mean, and just as ungrateful, and just as dirty to-day
as they will be a hundred years hence; but in the light of

history, how small, will be more clearly apparent, perhaps, than to-day. But when the record of his name comes to be written, when the great journey of that silent soldier is completed, he will march down the aisles of time hand in hand with our great martyred President, Abraham Lincoln; and, standing on the highest summit of earthly eminence and heroic achievement, the whole world will hail and salute him."

Mr. Greeley's record was reviewed as follows:

"Opposed to him is Horace Greeley. Now, we all know Horace Greeley. We all know what he has been in politics, and we all know what he is in politics to-day. I have no terms of opprobrium to apply to him; no denunciating epithets to use against him. I appeal hurriedly and briefly to his record, and let his record speak; and his record is all the more damaging, and his unfitness for the great place for which he is nominated all the more conspicuous, when I concede, as for the purpose of the argument I will do, that he is honest.

"In 1858 he signalized himself in this state by interfering in our senatorial election, and attempting to dictate to the Republicans of the state of Illinois that they should throw Abraham Lincoln overboard and return Stephen A. Douglas to the United States senate. In 1860 he made his advent in Chicago as a delegate to the National Convention from the state of Oregon. He came there, not for the purpose of fulfilling any great mission, but he came there to gratify a spite which he entertained against William H. Seward, for whom his whole state was unanimous, and voted $48\frac{1}{2}$ times for Edward Bates as President of the United States. We all know how, through those days which preceded the war, how vigorously, bravely and courageously he talked, how he denounced the accursed slave-power; how he urged all young men to war to the

knife against it, if need be; but when the final hour of
need came, when, having urged it on the stump, in
Congress, and at the polls, then, when the supreme moment
of trial came, and the question was submitted to the last
court to which these questions are ever taken — the arbitrament of war, when our ranks were being filled up, and
we looked around for the great leader whose clarion voice
had for ten years shouted us on, where did we find him ?
Was Horace Greeley there ? We saw him, with tail down
and ears pinned back, cutting for the brush, and the first
thing that Horace Greeley recommended when the hour
of trouble finally reached us was that our 'Southern sisters
should be permitted to depart in peace.'   I shall not stop
here to read extracts; I shall not stop to discuss whether
the advice was wise or unwise ; but suppose that we had
taken Horace Greeley's advice.   Suppose that in 1860 his
advice had been followed, and Bates had been nominated
for President instead of Abraham Lincoln ; suppose his
advice had been taken at the outbreak of the war, when the
clouds began for the first time to roll threateningly up in
the sky; if we had taken Horace Greeley's advice at that
moment we would have been to-day a disgraced, broken,
shamed and humilated nation.

   'I will follow him a little further.   There was different stuff, thank God, in this people than in Horace
Greeley.   They resolved that what he had said on the
stump, and what they had declared at the polls, should be
carried out, and that this nation, which was worth talking
for, was worth fighting for.   They fought for it, and they
saved it.   Finding that his advice was not taken, you all
remember how he wrote his most intemperate 'On to
Richmond' call, and finally, after our arms had been
defeated at Bull Run, he penned at the top of an article,
'Just This Once,' and begged pardon of the people, whom

he was afraid he had betrayed, and promised never to do so any more. By and by he got courageous again, and before the proper moment had arrived, he insisted in an impudent letter to Abraham Lincoln that the slaves must be all at once emancipated. You remember how Lincoln answered that letter. Down in the mouth again, he insisted that if Lee watered his horses in the river Delaware we should cry quits, and give up the contest; surrender our national integrity, and recognize the independence of the Southern Confederacy. We didn't do it. Lee did water his horses in the waters of the Delaware, and the silent soldier who makes no speeches answered that piece of southern bravado on the 4th of July, 1863, by sending us the intelligence that he had taken the stronghold of Vicksburg, captured 30,000 rebel prisoners of war, and opened the Mississippi from St. Paul to the Gulf. On that same day, on the blood-stained field of Gettysburg, Lee, who had watered his horses in the river Delaware, was driven back defeated and discomfited, the backbone of the rebellion was broken, and a check put upon its career from which it never recovered.

"That is not all. A call was made for troops, and, of course, Greeley flunked again. In 1864 he inaugurated peace negotiations — with whom ? With Colorado Jewett, probably the champion free-lunch eater of the American continent; a man known all over the country as a chronic dead-beat. He was the negotiator with whom Horace Greeley opened negotiations for the purpose of securing peace; and after letters had passed between him and Jewett, he writes to the President, calling his attention to the fact, and using this expression: — ' Mr. President, I venture to remind you that our broken, bleeding, dying, and almost bankrupt country cries for peace.' Lincoln at once upon the reception of that letter, wrote him back that if there

was anybody anxious to treat for peace on the basis of a
restored Union and the abandonment of slavery, to send
him or bring him to him, and he was ready to treat upon
that basis. You remember the course which the negotiations took. It turned out that the commissioners were not
authorized. Finally Greeley wrote a letter to the President stating that these men in Canada were not authorized
to treat, but they thought they might get somebody
who would be, and, accordingly, the President wrote that
famous ' To Whom it May Concern ' paper, stating precisely
the same terms embraced in the first letter he addressed to
Greeley. Greeley withheld from the 'rebel commissioners
that the President had in the first instance made that the
only basis on which negotiations could be conducted ; and
when Clay and Holcombe made a complaint that the President had seduced them into the belief that the negotiations
might be made freely and without terms, Greeley joined
with them and said the negotiations had been brought to
an end because the President had abandoned the basis on
which they had been inaugurated. Now, I do not care so
much that in the course of these negotiations he recommended that $400,000,000 be paid for the slaves ; I do not
care so much that he blundered in opening them with
Colorado Jewett ; I do not care so much that he misled the
rebel commissioners themselves ; but I do care, as it
behooves every Illinoisan who holds the good name and
memory of Abraham Lincoln dear in his heart, — I do care
that on that occasion Horace Greeley joined with the rebel
commissioners and placed Abraham Lincoln in a false
position before the country. Abraham Lincoln had made
no change of base; the first letter he sent announced the
only basis on which these negotiations could be conducted;
he asked Greeley to show that first letter to the commissioners in order that there might be no mistake about

it, and you remember how we were all dumbfounded when a portion of that correspondence was published, how we saw no escape for the President, and how it seemed to us and to the whole country that Lincoln had been trifling with these commissioners, had abandoned the position, and had misled and betrayed them; and when, in order to set himself right before the world, Abraham Lincoln asked Horace Greeley for the privilege of publishing the whole correspondence, merely omitting the phrase, 'our bleeding, bankrupt and flying country,' because he said it might discourage and dishearten the people at the North,— when he asked that his good name might be vindicated before thirty-seven millions of people, Horace Greeley refused. Horace Greeley joined in the cry against him, and by that refusal placed Lincoln in a false position before this country for two years; and not until the danger had passed, not until the storms of war had rolled away, was the correspondence published, and the name and good fame of our martyred President vindicated.

"They tell us the war is finished; perhaps it is. I ask every sincere Republican in this house to-night what he believes would be the result, provided we had at the next assembling of Congress a Democratic majority in either or both branches of our national Congress. They need not undertake to repeal the fifteenth amendment or the fourteenth, but you and I know that there is such a thing as unfriendly legislation. You know as well as I —there is not a man in this house that does not know it—that, with a Democratic majority in either branch of our national Congress, you might pile up facts mountains high, showing that the new freeman had been outraged, insulted and abused, and they would not see the facts. The time has not come when it is safe to withdraw from the hands of this great party the power with which, for years, you have entrusted it. It

is a question which we must regulate and decide as we do
all other questions; we must determine what men will do
in the future by what they have done in the past.

"If there should come to the cashier of the bank in this
city two applicants for the office of teller, both of them
with their platforms precisely alike, embodying the ten
commandments, Christ's sermon on the mount, and everything that is good in morals and business, still the cashier,
I take it, would not decide upon these applications merely
on the platforms which these men made; he would inquire
into their history; and if he found that one fellow had
robbed his employer's till, that his credit was bad and his
morals weak, and the other had never been suspected of
any offense, he would select the man whose record had been
good in the past, notwithstanding the old thief might say
he had taken a ' new departure,' and promised never to do
so any more. 'I am glad to hear you have taken a new
departure; I hope your platform is all right; I think your
platform is, but my dear sir, I must let you depart first
with somebody else's money than my own. Everybody
who asks us for political position, for power, for trust, can
see that reputation is not a dead issue. The reputation of
any party which solicits power is always in issue, and it
will always be in issue.

"Now, what issues do they present to us? Simply two.
In this liberal platform which they all seem so anxious to
put up, they clamor for the one-term principle. I am
opposed to it, and so are you. One term is too long for a
bad president and two-terms are not more than enough
for a good one. We needed no amendment of the
constitution to get rid of James Buchanan and to get rid
of Andrew Johnson. We did not need any amendment of
the constitution to shut off Martin Van Buren, James K.
Polk, and the rest of them; and the fact that we elected

Abraham Lincoln because the interests of the nation demanded it is an eternally convincing proof of the futility of such a plea as that the whole of the people shall be tied hand and foot by a clause of that kind in our organic law. I believe thirty-seven millions of people are quite competent to determine whether they want a man for president the second time or not. They have always been able to do it, and all the precedents of our history have justified their conduct whenever they have, as they have done in many instances, quietly thrown him overboard.

"But they tell us they are also in favor of local self-government. Now, what does local self-government mean? Why, it is the old exploded theory of state sovereignty, and nothing else under heaven. Read the Democratic speeches that are made at their meetings, indorsing Greeley and favoring his nomination by the convention, and election. It is the same talk we heard exactly, all through the war, of tyranny and oppression, and the iron heel of the tyrant. My fellow-citizens, go home to-night and ask yourselves, in the presence of your own conscience, and in the presence of God, whether you feel you have been tyranized over. Ask yourselves whether this magnificent spectacle which is now presented is the result of tyranny—that of a great people, led as they have been by the steady hand of this great captain, encountering a mighty volume of debt, and reducing that debt hundreds of millions of dollars, and at the same time reducing the burden of their taxation in equal proportions. Think, too, how our greenbacks are appreciating; think how our bonds are appreciating in the markets of the world; think how our credit has advanced; think how prosperity prevails throughout all our borders; and then, look at the President of the United States, and thank God that he is no genius, that he is simply a plain, honest, capable, faithful man, true to the interests of the great people by whom he was placed in his position.

"He declared to you at the outset, 'I shall have no policy opposed to the will of the people.' How did he illustrate it? He thought, early in his administration, that the interests of this country demanded the acquisition of the island of San Domingo. I thought it did not; the most of you thought it did not; I have seen occasion to change my opinion upon that subject; but finding that the will of the people was against it, General Grant sends his manly and noble message to Congress, and says, 'I thought that the interests of our trade, our commerce, and our nation demanded the acquisition of that island; I thought not only for commercial purposes, and in view of future complications with foreign powers, we ought to have it, but in and of itself we ought to have it. I thought so then, and I think so still. I sent my commissioners, among the best men in the country there, and they have reported as I thought. You, my fellow citizens, do not want it; I only want it for you; if you do not want it, do not have it; I have no policy opposed to the will of the people.'

"I tell you, in the years that are to come, standing up against all the glittering rhetoric of mere senatorial orators, that simple state paper, magnificent in its self-denying patriotism, will stand out like a great gigantic pyramid, challenging the admiration and gratitude of mankind.

"Yet, after having done what he has done, and accomplished what he has accomplished, it is insisted that he must be thrown overboard, and Horace Greeley substituted in his place. It is claimed that he has violated his faith with the people in the injudicious appointments he has made. I am here making no apologies; I am not here as a partisan, either; but I believe that there is, deep down in the popular heart of the people, a sense of fair play and of com-

mon decent treatment, that will vindicate, and protect and
defend him; that same great nation that has rallied around
our martyred President as with cords of steel, will rally
around their living captain as with flames and circlets of
fire, and protect, and justify, and care for, and defend
him. I ask you now to remember, whenever there has
been, in the history of the politics of this country, charges
so malignant and so base, and epithets so vituperative as
have been employed against Ulysses S. Grant, you would
stop and ask yourselves, ' What has this man done?' Has he
broken open a bank? Has he stricken down his neighbor in
the dead hour of the night? Has he robbed anybody? Of
what offense is he guilty? What crime has he committed?'
Run through the whole catalogue of crimes, and still the
denunciations that have been poured upon him have been
all too severe; and we answer and say : ' He has done
nothing except to save this nation.' We will save it again,
and save it, my fellow citizens, through him. The contest upon which we are just entering will be one of the
most animated which has ever occurred in the political
history of this country; the same old party stands up as
strong, powerful and bold as it ever did; its banner is
lifted just as high; it keeps step to-day, as it always has
kept step, to the glorious music of the nation; it knows no
faltering, it knows no shrinking of the spirit, no trembling
of the nerve ; and as we come into line, now at the opening of this campaign, here together in this great and magnificent county of La Salle, let the old fires burn, all up
and down the land, and let the word go all up and down
the line, let the old spirit rise up in every heart, and let
the old order be given from the beginning to the end of
the continent, ' Forward !' and victory is assuredly ours."

Mr. Storrs spoke the following week at Freeport,
going over the same ground as at Ottawa, and in pretty

much the same form. He commenced by referring to
a Republican meeting he had addressed there in 1861,
and another in 1864, when Abraham Lincoln was a
candidate for a second term. He then gave a running
history of the Republican party from its organization,
showing that the party had religiously performed every
promise which it had ever made, and kept its faith with
the people. He went on to say :

"The platform of the so-called 'Liberals' calls for
nothing which the people demand and which the Republican party is not abundantly able to carry out. The
Liberals demand the payment of the national debt; but
the Republican party is paying it at the rate of one hundred millions of dollars per year. They demand the reduction of taxation, but the Republican party has already
reduced taxation over one hundred millions of dollars.
They demand the resumption of specie payments, but the
policy of the Republican party has so far strengthened the
national credit, that we are hastening toward specie resumption as rapidly as the business interests of the nation
will justify. They demand the equality of all our citizens before the law, but to the Republican party alone is the nation and the world indebted for the fact that political in-
equalities have ceased to exist in this country. They demand a reform of the civil service, but fail to tell us what
reform they wish, or how it shall be effected. Mr. Trumbull proposed that postmasters be elected by the people;
but they have already scouted the idea as utterly impracticable. The present administration is the first and only
one which has ever undertaken, in good faith, to effect
practical reforms in our civil service. At the outset the
Liberals were loud in their demand for a reform in the
revenues; that they have skulkingly abandoned, and have
surrendered their free-trade theories to the most absurd

protectionists on the continent. They demand a restoration of order at the South; but the encouragement of the Ku-Klux is a poor way to restore order. The Republican party has restored order by compelling the Ku-Klux to behave themselves; and so long as they can be kept quiet order will prevail in the South, her industries be developed, and her prosperity be assured. But the Liberals also demand the one-term principle, and clamor for the right of what they call 'local self-government.' Do they establish the one-term principle by electing Greeley, or do they purpose to remit that to the people of each congressional district? Will they secure the one-term principle by an amendment to the constitution or by an act of Congress or by Horace Greeley's promise that he won't run again? The people are quite competent to determine whether they want a President for more than four years. When they don't want him for a second time they have a very plain way of giving him notice of the fact. We didn't have to amend the constitution to beat Andrew Johnson; nor did we have to amend the constitution to dispose of James Buchanan. They wanted Abraham Lincoln a second time. Greeley and Trumbull and Chase and several other very high-toned gentlemen thought that one term was enough; but as is usual in such cases the people were quite competent to determine that question for themselves, and had their own way. We propose to let them have their own way about these matters in the future. We think that one term would be too much for Horace Greeley, and two terms is all we ask for Grant.

"As to this point of local self-government, it is a mere sugar-coated method of administering the old 'State Rights' dose. Great clamor is made over what is called 'centralization,' and one would think that there was a great deal in it. The Liberals don't tell us what they mean by

it. We are familiar with the talk, however. We became
familiar with it during the war. That eminent 'Liberal,'
Beriah Magoffin, of Kentucky, denounced the first call
for troops as 'centralization.' Those distinguished 'Liberals,' Fernando Wood and Henry Clay Dean, denounced the
Emancipation Proclamation and the conscription laws as
'centralization.' The fact is, centralization was the death
of secession. As between the two, I am in favor of enough
centralization to crush out treason at home, to assert our
dignity and to punish our enemies abroad. The Republican party has, for the first time in the history of the
country, made American citizenship a fact. For the first
time in the history of this country, it is possible for a man
to start from the Penobscot and read the Declaration of
Independence in every town and county in every state to
the Rio Grande, and none to molest or make him afraid.
All this clamor about 'centralization' is meaningless, unless
it be shown that the general government has in some way
or other transcended its powers and invaded the reserved
rights of the states. Talk is cheap. But until the Liberals point us to some legislation, or to some act for which
the Republican party is responsible, of the character I have
indicated, we need bother ourselves very little about 'centralization.' The Republican party believes that this government is a union *of the people,* and not a compact of
states. It believes that these states are not like a lot of
marbles in a bag which touch but do not adhere, but though
'distinct like the billows, are one like the sea.' For half
a century or more we argued this question on the stump,
in Congress, and in the courts. We won in all of those
places. Not satisfied with the decision, the same men who
now howl about 'centralization,' submitted the question to
that tribunal of last resort, from which no appeal can be
taken, the arbitrament of war. They were again beaten.

It cost us three thousand millions of money, five hundred thousand lives, and over four years of war to win on that trial. I am opposed to a re-trial. Enough of money and enough of lives have already been wasted on the settlement of that question; and no such thin disguise as 'local self-government' will ever seduce us into the re-opening of that subject.

"A great deal of sentiment is expressed by these 'Liberal' gentlemen over what they call the distresses of the South, and much noisy vituperation visited upon the carpet-bagger. If under the new condition of things at the South bad men are elected to office, it is probably because the voters have made injudicious selections. The government can't help that, unless it gets up a new lot of voters, or prevents those from voting who now have that right. The negro votes because the fifteenth constitutional amendment tells him that he may; if he don't vote intelligently, it is because those 'Liberals' who denounce centralization at the South, have kept him for generations in ignorance. Intelligent voting, like intelligent workmanship, comes by practice, and unless the Liberals favor the repeal of the fifteenth amendment, they should quietly accept all the consequences that result from it. We think the temporary evils of unenlightened voting are much less serious than the permanent damage which would result from making the negro a citizen and then withholding from him the only weapon by which his rights of citizenship could be protected."

At Dixon, a few weeks later, Mr. Storrs went over the same ground in a stirring address. After comparing the Republican and "Liberal" platforms, he replied to the objection raised by the latter party to what they called the "centralization" of the National Government.

" Now, as to self-government, what do they mean by that? They generalize by calling it centralization. What do they mean by that? If it is something very bad, I am opposed to it. If it is something very good, I am in favor of it. If it is part way between the two, I do not care much about it. I wish they would tell me, when they use these words of fearful import and thundering sound, what they mean. If they mean that they are opposed to the general government transcending its powers and interfering with the vested rights of the state — so am I — so are all. But while I am in favor of the rights of the states, I am, at the same time, in favor of the rights of the nation. We have spent $3,000,000,000 of money, sacrificed hundreds of thousands of lives, and had four years of war, in order to save this nation from destruction. I am, therefore, in favor of a centralized government, so strong that there shall be some meaning in the words, ' American citizen.' I am in favor of its being so strong that in the remotest corners of the globe, whenever the meanest American citizens are molested, trampled upon, or oppressed, that this great government will put out its strong arm to defend the citizen and punish the oppressor. And not only that, but that it will do the same with all its citizens at home. I am in favor of a government which, when the organic law has declared that negroes shall be voters—that they shall be clothed with that right, and that Congress shall, by appropriate legislation, protect and defend them— I am in favor of a central power strong enough to see to it that the rights so conferred shall be protected and the negro justified in its exercise; and whenever that right is assailed, as it was by the Ku-Klux, I hold that it is the duty of Congress to see that it is defended. But they say that we must have peace, order, good-will, amnesty, and the shaking of hands across the bloody chasm. I am in favor of quiet. I am in favor of peace. I desire to see order reign through all the borders of this country, and over the whole earth; but if you would restore order, you must suppress disorder; if you would have peace, you must punish the men who are violating the peace.

"Who made the disorder at the South? Did the negro make it? No. Did the carpet-bagger make it? No. History has written it. Men masked, with blackened faces, by murder, robbery, pillage and outrage of every kind, inflicted upon these new-made citizens, made a very bedlam of that country. Would you restore it by putting the Ku-Klux in power? No!—put him down and make him behave himself. When that legislation was passed and the government clothed with these powers, order came. Why? Although their dispositions had not been changed, although the Ku-Klux were the same in heart as they had been before, yet because they knew there was a silent soldier in the presidential chair, and that the time had come when there must be no nonsense, therefore they behaved themselves. It is because this administration has done that that it is vilified, abused, and traduced in the way it is. I have desired to see the time come when you and I and all of us could travel wherever we pleased, could say what we desired to say, or think what we desired to think, and that there should be no one to molest us or make us afraid. That time is coming, but, gentlemen, that time will not come until, in the prosecution of his business, every man can do it without reference to the place of his nativity."

He reiterated his former argument as to the difference between platforms and practice, and illustrated the political situation with an apologue which his audience appreciated and heartily enjoyed:

"This is also well illustrated by the fable of the wolves

and the farmer. A farmer had been for years engaged in
the sheep-raising business. When he started, be bought a
magnificent shepherd dog to watch his flock, and he put
it in office. There was a party of wolves in his immediate
neighborhood, and as the time rolled on there never was
any cordiality of feeling between the wolves and that dog.
The wolf party gradually got smaller and smaller, because
the dog would make raids on it, and by and by they
dwindled down to a very small number. There were, however, a good many curs in the neighborhood, and they determined they would join this wolf party, and call A GREAT
LIBERAL MOVEMENT. They held a convention and resolved
that peace and amnesty should be restored between themselves, and they concluded that there was nothing whatever in their way but that dog, and if they could get him
out of the way, they would shake hands across this bloody
chasm. They passed a series of resolutions in which they
declared that the losses that had been caused by the
former depredations were atrocious, but that they were
dead issues. They said they had renounced all the habits
of their previous lives, and that they would, for the future,
be the safest defenders of these flocks. The boss wolf went
to the farmer, 'Now,' he says, 'all the trouble is attributable to this dog. To begin with, he is a dog you don't
want around your premises at all. He is unfit for this
purpose. Another thing, he cannot bark; there is not a
stub-tailed cur in the country but what can out-bark him.
Another thing,' he says, 'five of that dog's pups are in
position here—holding office. He is guilty of nepotism in
its very worse shape.' Gentlemen, that was a pretty rough
case on the dog.

"The farmer says, 'These things may be so; I know
that dog cannot bark much; but,' says he, 'he bites like
the very devil, as you know. I did not want him for a

house-dog, so that, as to his merits or demerits on that point, I have nothing to say. As to these pups, the clear truth about that is that they take after their father, and I have never lost a sheep out of my flocks; my flocks have prospered. I do not know about your logic; you may confuse me as to that, but the good straight way for me is to judge the future by the past, and I do not think that I shall be guilty of the atrocious nonsense and fearful ingratitude of removing that glorious old shepherd dog that has grown up with these flocks and with me, and has never been anything except entirely and forever faithful.'"

Contrasting the records of Grant and Greeley in the days of the nation's perils, he concluded as follows:

"Let us be generous; let us be just; let us give the credit where the credit is due. Let it never be said of us, in the years that are to come, that the great nation that has been saved by the quiet and silent soldier, turned their backs upon him because he was slandered by the very men whom he had defeated in the field of battle.

"I believe that the great people of this country love Grant as much as they ever did — trust him as implicitly as they ever did. During the years this faithful man has held the helm of state in his hand, how magnificently the old ship of state has passed through the storms we know, because we have been passengers aboard of her. Let us not leave the ship. Let us not desert Grant — the old captain; one more trip, and the thing will be done; order will be restored, our finances prosperous, and we will come up to those grand sunny slopes that spread themselves out in the great distance on the other side; and on this great continent, if we are true to ourselves, we will erect the most magnificent structure the world has ever known — sacred to the cause of human liberty — its dome as broad as the arching skies, its base as extended as the continent on which it is

built.   Here, in its mansions, there will always be space,
for all time, for the true and loyal and good men from all
corners of the earth to meet and celebrate the triumph of
free government among men."

In the meantime, the Democrats had met at Baltimore, and, in the hope of returning to power by the coalition method, had not only adopted the platform of the
Cincinnati convention, but had swallowed their candidates as well.   The tactics of the Baltimore convention
were doomed to failure, and the accession of strength
they hoped to gain from the renegade Republicans was
more than offset by the opposition of stiff-necked Democrats who refused to accept Greeley and Brown as their
leaders.   The irreconcilable Bourbons called a convention of their own, which met at Louisville, Ky., in September, and nominated Charles O'Conor, of New York,
and George W. Julian, of Indiana.   Both these gentlemen declined, and their supporters nevertheless kept on
voting for them, and thus nullified the "Liberal" Republican vote.   The nominees of the Philadelphia convention, Grant and Wilson, were elected.

The action of the Baltimore convention gave Mr.
Storrs a splendid opportunity for the exercise of his
powers of invective and sarcasm, of which he was
prompt to avail himself.   His next campaign speech was
delivered at Jacksonville, Ill., on the 12th of August.
To a large mass meeting there he delivered a powerful
address, reviewing the political situation.   The points
to which he directed attention were always the same,
but he had now a fresh argument to bring to bear in
regard to the position of the Cincinnati party.   They
were now embraced in the ranks of those who had
fought to destroy the Union ; and Mr. Storrs brought

the fact prominently forward, and prefigured the fate of the renegades when the enemy had no further use for them. He said:

"The campaign upon which we are just entering is, in many respects, the most important, and in all respects the most extraordinary, when we consider the manner in which it has thus far been conducted, that the country has ever seen.

"A great political organization, which, in the short period of eighteen years' existence, has accomplished more for the interest of freedom and good government than any party the world has heretofore known, having after successive triumphs over its old and persistent enemy so far demoralized it that it is rendered powerless for mischief in the future, is now, and for that reason, urged to voluntarily surrender to the enemy which it has, since 1860, never met but to defeat.

"It has finally been demonstrated that our old, long-time adversary cannot defeat us. It is equally clear that there exists in this country no power sufficiently strong to overcome the Republican party itself, and we are now met with the curious proposition that, because the Democratic party is not able to beat us, we should, for the purposes of reconciliation, turn in and defeat ourselves.

"The man who commits suicide for the accommodation of his business rival possesses a much more conciliatory spirit than the majority of mankind can truthfully lay claim to.

"Had Grant, after thoroughly penning Lee up at Appomattox, received an invitation from Lee to surrender, for the purpose of bringing about an harmonious state of feeling between the two armies, no serious fault probably would have been found with Grant had he declined the invitation and insisted, as he did insist, that the vanquished army should do the surrendering, and if harmony was what they were after they must be content to secure it in that way.

"No man would be more delighted to see the most brotherly and loving state of feeling established between the Republican and Democratic parties than myself, but, they having been thoroughly defeated, it is, I think, no more than fair for us to insist that, if there is any surrendering to be done, they should do it. Had they been left to pursue their own course that is precisely what they would have done; but it so happened that, just on the eve of stacking their arms and settling upon the terms of capitulation, a squad of disappointed captains and brigadiers from our own ranks joined them, and, thus encouraged, the brigadiers insist that the rank and file whom they have deserted shall follow them into the camp of the enemy, and trail their colors before the foe whose surrender they could easily have compelled. It is not strange that the enemy thus recruited should immediately resume their arms, tear up their articles of capitulation, and be loud in their demands for shaking hands across the bloody chasm. The wonder is not that the army that is whipped should rejoice at the avenue of escape that is thus opened to them, but that the rank and file who, after weary marches and bloody battles, stand just upon the threshold of final and decisive victory, should suddenly lose all spirit and surrender to an adversary no longer disposed nor able to encounter them. . . .

"There is no distinctive Liberal party. It was swallowed at Baltimore. Jonah did not swallow the whale, but the whale swallowed Jonah; and the whale did not consult Jonah as to the time, or place, or manner of swallowing him, nor of vomiting him forth. Do you suppose that this Democratic whale will consult the convenience of John M. Palmer and Lyman Trumbull as to the proper time of casting them out of its stomach, where they are now quietly housed?"

Reminding his hearers that in 1871 Mr. Trumbull and General Palmer supported a resolution in the Republican State Convention of Illinois endorsing "the eminently wise, patriotic, honest, and economical administration of General Grant," he asked:

"How are we privates, who are compelled to browse around in the valleys of political thought, to know what to do, when our great instructors, who have been upon the mountain tops and occasionally sent a solid boulder of wisdom crashing and tearing down the mountain sides for us to hammer away at, cut such extraordinary capers? Hardly knowing what to do last September, we reverently listened for instructions, and on the 20th day thereof, from the loftiest peaks, we heard Trumbull and Palmer shouting to us—'We refer with pride and admiration to the wise, patriotic, honest and economical administration of General Grant, and we confidently recommend it to the attention of the whole country.' In our feeble way we caught up the law as it was thus delivered to us, and supposed that we were singing the right song, and in the right key as we responded. 'We refer with pride and admiration to the eminently wise, patriotic, honest, and economical administration of General Grant.' Judge of our surprise, when, on the 1st day of May, suddenly from those lofty summits, and with hardly a word of warning, we heard Trumbull and Palmer in full chorus shout forth, 'The administration now in power has rendered itself guilty of wanton disregard of the laws of the land, and of usurping powers not granted by the Constitution.' We are all expected to join in the responses. The music is different, the words are different. They must be sung to a different key. Something is the matter with the leaders of our choir. Our voices are not trained to this new style of music. It is pitched too low for us. We cannot suddenly leave the 'Star-spangled Banner' for 'Dixie.' The words don't suit us. The result is that the congregation feel that this duet won't do for them, and they sing their good old pieces, in the good old words, to the good, familiar old music, and in the good old way.

"The result is the congregation is just as large and musical as ever. But our choir must seek employment from some other denomination."

After discussing the civil service reform question as he had done at Springfield, he next addressed himself to Greeley's famous plan for the resumption of specie payments:

"The Liberal Republicans are quite as vague and uncertain with reference to the resumption of specie payment as they are in regard to reforming the civil service. They say: 'A speedy return to specie payment is demanded alike by the highest considerations of commercial morality and honest government.' Precisely. But what do they mean by *speedy?* Do they mean within a month, or within a year, or within five years?

"Do they mean that we ought to resume specie payments as soon as, under the natural growth of the country, we can conveniently do so, or that resumption should be forced by legislation? Are they in favor of the national banks, or are they opposed to them? We are all agreed that specie payment ought to be resumed, but *how*, is the question. The sage of Chappaqua, who is never at a loss for a plan, has solved the whole question and relieved us from all difficulty. With $400,000,000 of greenbacks in circulation and less than $100,000,000 of coin in the treasury, he says that '*the way to resume is to resume.*' Certainly nothing is easier. Resume at once. Commence paying out coin one hundred cents on the dollar until it is all gone and then—having about $300,000,000 left that we have not coin to meet—we will find that the way to stop is to stop. But where is the money to come from to resume with? Judge Trumbull says our reserve is already too large, but it falls very far short of being large enough to justify us in resuming. How shall we get the balance? By taxation? There is no other way to get it, and we think our taxes are already quite large enough.

. "We must either have more coin or less currency. Shall we contract? Let the business interests of the country answer that question. The fact is, we will never resume specie payments through the immediate action of any legislation whatever. No more serious injury could be inflicted upon trade and business interests than an attempt to regulate and direct them by legislation. Experiments of that kind always result disastriously. But what might we expect should Horace Greeley be elected President? Filled with the conceit that the way to resume is to resume, he would in furtherance of his ideas recommend to Congress legislation to hurry and force resumption. I am assured, however, that Congress would pay no heed to his advice. They probably would not, but the effect of such a message upon business would be instantaneously felt at home and abroad. Every national bank would at once contract its loans, and a sudden contraction of loans means general pecuniary distress, panics and widespread disaster."

On the amnesty question, he cited the generous and noble words of the President's last message to Congress, and then said:

"If the gentlemen who are not embraced within the terms of the present amnesty bill desire pardon, why do they not then ask for it? It can be had for the asking. I do not think that it would be subjecting Jefferson Davis

or Raphael Semmes to any very cruel humiliation to insist
that they should show the genuineness of their repentance
by being compelled to *ask* for pardon. I submit that question to you.

"We are entreated to forgive and forget. We are
willing to forgive; but there are many things which they
ought never to forget. The father will never forget the
son who died in the great cause. The widow will never
forget the husband who perished that the nation might
live. The orphans will never forget the father who willingly met death that they might enjoy the priceless treasures of free government. We cannot forget the heroic
dead of this great rebellion, nor can we forget the cause
for which they fought and died. We may forget, but the
world will never forget, those glorious events in our and
the world's history, when a great nation, through four years
of war periled blood and treasure for a principle and that
idea—the capacity of man for self-government.

"Loud demands are made for the restoration of order
and for the return of peace at the South. We are all in favor
of that, but we differ widely from the Liberals as to the
manner in which order shall be restored and peace secured.
We would restore order by suppressing *disorder*. We
would secure peace by punishing those who disturb it.

"When a *mob* is raging in the streets it is possible that
order might be restored by surrendering to the mob; but a
better way by far is to disperse the mob and punish its
ringleaders.   For the disorders which have prevailed at the
South the negro is not responsible, nor is the carpet-bagger. The Ku-Klux alone are guilty of all the disorders
which have occurred there. What shall we do to restore
order? Surrender to the Ku-Klux, or force them to behave themselves? The administration has adopted the
latter course. It has interfered, and by legislation pro-

vided for the protection of the negro in the enjoyment of
his newly-acquired right, provided for the employment of
sufficient force to put down and punish all those who
would by force interfere with it, provided for the trial of
those guilty of violating that article in the courts when a
fair trial could be had.   And this is the Ku-Klux Bill.

"Of course, we must expect, in the event of Mr.
Greeley's election, that all this legislation will be at once
repealed. Where, then, will the freedmen be left? Oh, we
are told by the Democracy, we are in favor of the amendment.   But the amendment is self-enforcing.   The Constitution provides for a Judicial Department, consisting of
one Supreme Court and such inferior courts as the Congress may from time to time ordain and establish.   The
inferior courts are created by an act of Congress.   Suppose
that you repeal the legislation, what becomes of your courts?

"You have not touched the Constitution—you are earnestly in favor of that, but still opposed to all legislative
action which gives it effect.   So was the fifteenth amendment.   The right to vote is conferred, and Congress is
authorized to enforce it by appropriate legislation.   The
Democracy is in favor of the amendment, but opposed to
all laws which may be necessary to make it operative.
Repeal this legislation, and what becomes of the negro?
He is at once handed over to the tender mercies of the
Ku-Klux, driven from the polls, and no power can be
found to prevent it."

The earnestness and impressiveness of this argument
were never surpassed in any subsequent speech made
by Mr. Storrs during this campaign.   It duly impressed,
not only all his hearers at Jacksonville, but all who
afterwards read the report in the Chicago papers; and
no doubt had a good effect in keeping in the ranks
many waverers.

At Indianapolis, on the 28th of August, Mr. Storrs delivered an address which the *Journal* of that city characterized as "one of the best efforts of the campaign." The night was stormy, and the driving rain on the roof of the wigwam created an uproar that interfered considerably with the pleasure of those who desired to catch every word, but the opposition of the elements only served to pack the auditors more closely in the vicinity of the stage. Mr. Storrs began by paying his respects to Mr. Hendricks, as follows:

"'The most extraordinary feature of the present campaign is the industrious effort made by our adversaries to rule out all history and all past experience as guides for the future.

"Mr. Hendricks insists that we must keep our eyes fixed steadily on the future, and that under no circumstances must we seek to gather any instruction from the past. We must forget all that we ever knew, and unlearn all that we ever learned. If we were situated precisely as Mr. Hendricks is, we might think with him. If, upon looking back upon the past history of our party, we found what he finds when he reviews the record of the Democracy—a record stained all over with political crimes and offences of the most serious and damning character, we would undoubtedly feel as he feels—great anxiety to bury it out of sight and to detach himself from it.

"That man never lived who, after spending at least half of his lifetime in the violation of the law and in the commission of crime, did not, when he desired the confidence of his fellows, resent with great zeal any allusion to his past career, and seek to bury them out of sight as dead issues. But, dead as such issues are, it is wonderful how they stick to a man, and how they will continually rise up in judgment against him. The course usually pursued by such unfortunates is a new departure in its largest sense. They cut their hair, change their clothes, leave their country, adopt another name, and travel under an assortment of aliases. All these things the Democratic party is now doing. The trouble is that the disguise which they have assumed is too thin. We all see through it. We see under this gauzy covering of reform the old State-sovereignty, repudiation, negro-hating Democrat. They claim that they are really and in fact converted.

"We suspect the genuineness of the conversion. It is too sudden. The conversion of Saul of Tarsus is hardly in point, for although Saul, like modern Democracy, went forth breathing threatenings and slaughter, on his trip to Damascus he saw a light — I am convinced entirely different from the one which the Democracy beheld at Baltimore. The light which Saul saw was from heaven. That which the Democracy beheld was from Cincinnati. By it they were enabled to see the treasury department and all the other departments of the government, a spectacle which had not gladdened their eyes for years. Saul didn't ask the disciples to join him, but he joined them. Saul did not propose that the famous liberal Christian, Judas, should join him and the high priest for a great reform movement. Saul not only changed his views, but he changed his name, and henceforth was no longer known as Saul of Tarsus, but as Paul the Apostle.

"Our party has always been a great political missionary organization. We have to-day within our ranks thousands and hundreds of thousands of converted Democrats. We expect to have hundreds of thousands more. With us they feel that glorious freedom which the truth alone can give, that 'joy which passeth all understanding.'"

Mr. Storrs was quite in a biblical vein, and his

speech throughout was pointed with scriptural illustrations.

"The overthrow of the rebellion liberated four millions of negroes, but it liberated even a larger number of Democrats. The colored man had sense enough to seize his liberty. But many Democrats seem to be afraid to take out their manumission papers. Don't be alarmed, my Democratic friends. Freedom won't hurt you. Avail yourself of it, and the longer you enjoy it the better you will like it.

"We think it most ungenerous that, after having liberated the Democrat from the thralldom which bound him for years, after having saved for him the country which his party sought to destroy, after having freely forgiven the manifold sins of omission and commission of which he has been guilty, he should seek to deprive the negro of even the slightest benefits of his newly-acquired freedom, and should exact from him the full measure of the little debt he owes even unto the uttermost farthing.

"It is an old story, but in point here — that of the king who took an account of his servants, one of whom owed him ten thousand talents; having nothing with which to discharge this heavy debt, the servant begged for patience and promised to pay all. Moved with compassion, the king pardoned him and forgave the debt.

"How much like a modern Democrat that old servant behaved. Going into the streets, rejoicing in his freedom, he meets a fellow-servant who owed him an hundred pence, and he laid hands on him and took him by the throat saying, 'Pay me that thou owest!' This fellow-servant begged for mercy, promised to pay all, but the big debtor cast his fellow-servant into prison until he should pay the debt; and then, we are told, his lord was wroth, and delivered this unjust servant over to the tormentors until he should pay all that was due.

"Let these Democrats take heed from this story. Nothing torments the average Democrat like an exclusion from office. He must deal fairly with his fellow-servants, or the torments of disappointed hopes which he has suffered the last twelve years he will be compelled to endure forever.

"I am constrained to believe that the Democratic party is not yet converted. But if it really is, why should it not be quite willing to give a proof similar to those furnished by Saul of Tarsus? First, let it cease breathing threatenings and slaughter against Republicans and the Republican party, and show that they were in fact good Republicans by joining our party, preaching our doctrine and voting our ticket. Second, like Saul of Tarsus, let them mark the period of their conversion by changing their name. Their willingness to 'shake hands across the bloody chasm' with some of our Judases won't answer the purpose."

He repudiated the idea that the renegades who had gone over to the Democracy ever were, in any sense, "leaders" of the Republican party. Then he showed the incongruity of the Democratic platform and candidates, and contrasted both with the plain, honest, consistent declarations and performances of the Republican party and President Grant:

"Horace Greeley is the most intensely high-tariff man in the country, and always has been. Brown is a free-trader from principle, and never has been anything else. Greeley is in favor of Ku-Klux legislation. Brown is thoroughly and bitterly opposed to it. Greeley is a temperance man, to the extreme of total abstinence; he eschews all meats, and is a Graham-bread man on principle. Brown is a man who, according to his own confession, occasionally relapses into total abstinence, who favors soft-

shell crab and butters his water-melon. Now, my Democratic friend, which of these two worthies are you going
for? You cannot go for them both, for they are as diverse
and opposite as the poles. Then, the candidates do not
agree with their platform, either taken together or sepa-
rately. They do not agree with their platform any better
than they agree with each other. Sumner says he will go
for Greeley because the Democracy has been converted.
Semmes says he will go for Greeley because Greeley has
been converted. Sumner says he is going for Greeley
because Greeley favors the negro race, while Semmes says
he is going for him because he advocates the right of secession. Trumbull goes for Greeley because Brown is in
favor of free trade, and the protectionist goes for Greeley
because Greeley is in favor of protection. Now this party
designs to swindle somebody, and if God should see fit to
visit Horace Greeley upon us, somebody is as certain to be
swindled as that two and two make four. It is either the
Republican who votes for Greeley on the strength of his
Republicanism, or it is the Democrat who votes for him on
the strength of his Democracy; whichever way you take
it, one way or the other, you must have it; there can be no
middle ground."

He showed that the new doctrine of local self-government was nothing else than the old doctrine of
state-sovereignty and the right of secession in disguise:

" We fought through five years of war to put down
that accursed political heresy, and, now that we have succeeded, we mean that it shall stay down, and we intend to
trample out the last vestige of its existence. That is
Republican doctrine.

" But you tell us we have been cruel in not extending
amnesty to our Southern brethren. Well, they all have
the right to vote, and the disabilities existing against them

are simply such as are created by the fourteenth constitutional amendment. Now, my Liberal Republican friend, if you are opposed to the existence of those disabilities, you are opposed to the fourteenth amendment, by which they were created, and if you are opposed to that amendment, let me ask you to stand out like a man and say so. If you want to reargue that question, if you want to open up either the fourteenth or fifteenth amendments, we are prepared to reargue both of them. But what is the truth about these disabilities? What do they amount to? Just this: about one hundred and forty Southern gentlemen are deprived of the glorious privilege of holding office. Now, there are thousands of Democrats at the North who have been ever since 1860 laboring under political disabilities of exactly that character. Since that time how many a Democrat has been prevented from holding office? The disability was created in a different way, to be sure; it was imposed upon them by the voice of the people in that case, and in this it was imposed by the constitution.

" But would it not be fair and decent, to say the least, that these Southern gentlemen, Davis and Toombs and Wigfall and Semmes, should ask for pardon before they get it? The great God of infinite wisdom, while his capacity for pardoning is infinite, never pardons the sinner until he prays for pardon. You know it is said, ' Knock, and it shall be opened unto you,' 'Ask, and ye shall receive.' And whenever, on bended knee, with a broken spirit and a contrite heart, with his hand upon his mouth and his mouth in the dust, the sinner humbly confesses his sin and begs for pardon, then, and not until then, does he get it. Are we asking too much when we ask that Davis and Semmes and Toombs shall ask to have these disabilities removed? If you think it is unkind to make that requirement, take a pardon with you and go down South, and, on bended knee, supplicate Jeff. Davis graciously to be pleased to accept a pardon from your hand. You may do it if you wish — the Republican party never will."

In September Mr. Storrs was stumping the state of Pennsylvania, and on the 17th delivered a stirring address at Reading, in the Library Hall. At the outset he urged the Republicans to do their utmost to elect the Pennsylvania state ticket. He said:

"The interest felt by Republicans throughout the entire country in the result of the October election in this state arises not so much from any knowledge of the individual character of the candidates as from the controlling effect which this election will or may have upon the general result throughout the whole country. We feel that the Republicans of Pennsylvania have no right to defeat the Republican party in the nation, nor even to imperil its success upon any merely personal considerations. We do not believe that they will do so. In the times past the Republicans of the old Keystone have, with a patriotism and unselfishness which has secured for them the gratitude of the whole country, cheerfully set aside all personal considerations, and regarded, not their individual wishes and feelings merely, but the best interests of the nation. This much — no more, and no less — will be expected from them in the pending state election. It is not for me to say what, in this state, would be the effect upon the presidential ticket of the defeat of General Hartranft. But this I do know: that in every other state in the Union such a result would be most dispiriting and disheartening; it might be disastrous. Pennsylvania holds the key to the position, and the Republican party will hold you to the strictest accountability. Your state election can in no proper sense be said to be local. Where the key of the position falls, the position itself falls with it. A man may have a disease of the heart. In one sense it would be local. But when the heart stops beating the man stops breathing, and the whole man dies. We would hardly think of attempting to comfort his mourning family by assuring them that the disease was merely a local one.

"To the Republicans of Pennsylvania may the defence of your nominees be safely entrusted. It is quite clear that they are entirely competent to perform that work. I invite your attention, therefore, to the broader questions involved in our national politics. The most extraordinary feature of the present canvass is the attempt made by our adversaries to rule out as an element of human calculation for the future all past history and experience. Men certainly never do that in their dealings with each other. In judging whether a man's future course will be straightforward and upright, we are apt to give him the benefit of the fact, if it exists, that his past course has always been such, and however valiantly a party whose history is a record of crimes might disclaim against any allusion to the fact as a discussion of dead issues, we would certainly, in deciding its future course, be greatly influenced by those dead issues. Our opponents ask us to believe, and to act upon that belief, that a political party whose course has always been honest, faithful and patriotic will for the next particular four years reverse its history, and pursue a dishonest, unfaithful and unpatriotic policy, and that a party which for the last twenty years has never been on the right side of any question will for the next four years be on the right side of all questions."

Mr. Storrs then rapidly sketched the history of the Republican party, claiming that for what it had actually achieved it was entitled to the gratitude of good men everywhere; that it had done nothing and omitted to do nothing which would justify the people in withdrawing from it their confidence, and that the mission of such a party would never be ended so long as there remained one forward step to be taken in the pathway of human progress.

He reviewed the record of the Democratic party, its opposition to the constitutional amendments, and its proposal to repudiate the national debt, and pointed out the inconsistencies of the coalition on the questions of revenue reform and civil service reform. The veto power was vested in the President by the express letter of the constitution; yet Horace Greeley had agreed to abdicate this function in respect to the tariff at the bidding of the Cincinnati reformers.

"Thus we are to secure a purer administration and a more faithful execution of the laws, by a deliberate agreement to neglect the performance of a constitutional duty, by the surrender of a constitutional right, by basely deserting all convictions of public interests, by a clear violation of an official oath. A political convention which will be permitted to demand of its candidate the surrender of a portion of his official powers as the price of his nomination and election may, with equal propriety, demand the surrender of them all, and thus practically abolish the office of President altogether.

"The price which Horace Greeley has agreed to pay for his nomination and election, is one which no convention at any previous period in our history has had the impudence to demand from its candidate. The price which Esau received for his birthright was a liberal one in comparison, for Esau received the mess of pottage Jacob had to give. To no such depths has a Presidential candidate ever sunk before, and it is to be hoped that on this 'bad eminence' Horace will stand alone—the solitary instance of a public man bartering the convictions of a lifetime, for the empty honor of a Presidential nomination — selling his birthright for the mere promise of a mess of pottage.

"Moreover, this new party returns clearly to the old and exploded heresy of state sovereignty Its platform declares that 'local self-government, with impartial suffrage, will guard the rights of all citizens more securely than any centralized power.' The consequence of the doctrine of state sovereignty was the right of secession and the denial of any right of coercion in the Federal government. It is clear that if local self-government attempts to secede, nothing but the 'centralized power' of the Union can prevent it. But this centralized power is repudiated, and under any and all circumstances local self-government must have its way. This is 'reforming' us back to the dismal years immediately preceding the war. The question which we supposed we had settled, at the expense of 500,000 lives and $3,000,000,000 of money and four years of war, is again presented to us. Our views upon it are the same that they have ever been, and we hope by this blow to crush it out forever."

Mr. Storrs then proceeded to the discussion of Mr. Greeley's record, showing that he was not to-day, and had never been, on the great fundamental question in our politics — the right of secession — a Republican, that he denied the right to coerce, that as commander-in-chief, if true to his principles, an attempt to secede must inevitably succeed; that his course throughout the war was factional, variable and damaging to the Union cause, and finally demonstrated that in the Peace Conference at Niagara Falls, he willfully and deliberately placed Abraham Lincoln in a false position before the country and refused to relieve him from it, thus placing himself beyond the pale of Republicanism, Republican sympathy and Republican support.

VI.

THE CAMPAIGN OF 1876.

"Liberal" Republicanism — Civil Service Reform — Revision of the Tariff — Resumption of Specie Payment — General Grant's Record Contrasted with that of Horace Greeley — Scriptural Illustrations.

IN taking the field in 1876 on behalf of the nominees of the Republican convention, which met at Cincinnati, and with such names as Conkling, Morton and Blaine before them, chose R. B. Hayes as the standard-bearer of the party, Mr. Storrs was eloquent as usual in eulogy of the party record, and vigorous in his denunciation of the Democracy, but, for the first and last time in his career as a Republican advocate, there was a noticeable falling off in his enthusiasm for the candidate. He would, in common with a majority of the party, have preferred a known leader at the head of the ticket; a man who was stalwart in his convictions, and who could give effect to the demand of the party as expressed in the platform of 1876, for the vigorous and continuous exercise of the powers of the Federal government until all classes were secure in their civil and political rights. How Mr. Hayes would carry out this programme was entirely a matter of conjecture, as he was almost without a record when he unexpectedly rose into the most prominent place before the nation.

A ratification meeting was held in Chicago shortly after the adjournment of the convention, and Mr. Storrs addressed the Republicans there assembled. He said:

"As I look about on this platform and in the body of this hall, I see many of the most conclusive evidences of the wisdom of the Republican convention which has recently been held at Cincinnati in the nomination of Hayes and Wheeler. I see many of my good old Liberal friends returned to the Republican fold. I welcome them back. I am sorry that they ever left — I am glad that they have returned. My friends were foolish, but, after having learned that the adventure of the prodigal son always results in a husk dividend, it is to be hoped that in future we will stand together as we do to-night, and as we will in the canvass, upon the threshold of which we are just standing. We will come to the conclusion that the Republican party is strong and virtuous enough to effect its own reforms, and that one of the poorest methods on earth to reform the Republican party is by voting the Democratic ticket.

"I ratify the nomination of Hayes and Wheeler, of course, because they are both good men, because they are both fit men, because they are both men unassailed and unassailable, and for another reason — because they are the Republican nominees. I would not vote for Hayes or Wheeler, or any other man running on a Democratic ticket. I have that confidence — that sublime and perfect confidence — that, in a tight place and in a delicate position, the Democratic party will do the wrong thing as a party — that no nomination that they could possibly make could combine in itself virtue enough in the candidates to overcome the inherent cussedness of that great aggregation of men. I am for the Republican nominees because the Republican party is as good as the nominees; because, taken as a great mass, it represents the loyal sentiment and the patriotism and the honest desire for reform in this country. I believe that the Republican party, as a party organization, with

all its mistakes, with all its errors, and with all its shortcomings, has within itself to clean the Augean stable, to
elevate our civil service, and to march all the time, if not
a little ahead, fully abreast of a wise and honest public
sentiment.   When the Republican party ceases to be a
party of movement, and forward movement, it will cease to
be the Republican party.   It was a party organized, not for
a day, but for all time.   It takes things as it finds them,
but it never leaves them as it finds them.   It found 4,000,-
000 of chattels — it has made 4,000,000 of voters in their
place.   It found a great nation, the hope of civil liberty
all over the globe, struggling in the arms of a gigantic
rebellion, and it carried it safely through its flaming perils,
and has guaranteed to our republic the eternity of success
and glory.   It found a depreciated and almost exploded
currency and a crippled national credit.   Steadily and
persistently it began eight years ago to denounce the fraudulent conception that our national debt should be paid in
greenbacks; it has never swerved a moment from the course
it then took; it has pursued it unceasingly ever since, and
it will never abandon the question until the word of the
United States finds its redemption in coin, in the currency
of the world.

" It is impossible that all the reforms which the people
demand shall be wrought out by the election of Hayes and
Wheeler, or by that of anybody else.   Their election is
simply the expression of the public will that there shall be
a reform.   An honest man, standing at the head of the government, and backed up by a constituency which has a lack
of moral sympathy with him, is as helpless as a baby.   I
approve and ratify these nominations, because they repre-
sent the average sense and the best matured judgment of
the whole people of the whole country.

" It has been my habit, in looking at political questions,

when I was in doubt as to the best course to pursue, to see what the Democratic party desired, and then select the opposite. I am perfectly certain that we have followed the wisest course, because the nomination of Hayes and Wheeler has unlimbered their every gun, and demoralized the crowd. They must seek for a great unknown, but there is one thing that is known, and that is the rebel record of the party which the great unknown must head. The past of their career weighs down upon them like a mountain load, and no man, snatched from any obscurity however great, can carry that record forward safely, and triumph in the face of the united Republicanism of the nation which we see to-day.

"I observe that they say that our candidates are color-less. Good. It is probably because their garments are absolutely white. There is no genius for plunder, no audacity for rings. We belong to that party which to-day has an infinitely profounder belief in the goodness of God than it ever had in the dexterity of the devil. Our party platform is so clear that everybody understands it. Reform in administration; not work to be accomplished by a spurt; one election does not achieve it. The army capture an outpost, but the citadel of corruption for which our party is not responsible—of that corruption which began and gathered strength a quarter of a century ago—will never surrender without the most unwearied, patient, and per-sistent exertion. Every man—every private in the ranks— can contribute his mite in that direction. A reform of our civil service ; how, and exactly by what method, we will tell by one experiment after another, if experiment be necessary, until the result be achieved. An honest cur-rency, the redemption of our promises to pay in coin by the fulfilment of the national engagements,—these are the principles upon which the Republican party stands to-day, absolutely unchallengeable, and they commend themselves to the good judgment and the loftier patriotism of the whole people."

On the 14th of July, he addressed a large and enthusiastic meeting at Aurora, Ill., and criticised very keenly and minutely the sophistical platform which the Democrats had adopted at the St. Louis Convention, and which Mr. Storrs characterized as "the cheekiest platform ever witnessed in political history or literature." The concluding part of his speech was devoted to a telling review of Mr. Tilden's record:

"It has been my pleasure, for every political canvass of any national importance since 1861, to address the Republicans of this growing and very beautiful city, and I, by no means, feel that I am among strangers, for as I look about I see those whom I saw on the first occasion I ever visited Aurora, who have stood with me during those long and terrible years of the war. I see those who never faltered when dangers of the most serious character threatened us. I see those to-night who, after the war had closed, were as resolute that the fruits of our victory should be gathered and garnered as they were that those effects should be, in the first instance, achieved. I see those who have always been Republicans ever since there has been a Republican party, and who always will be Republicans as long as there is a Democratic party. When I am asked, as I sometimes am, how long the Republican party will live, I say it will live at least one election after the final and eternal death of the Democracy, for so long as the Democratic party keeps above ground and exhibits any signs of vitality so long is the existence of the Republican party a military necessity. It will not—this Democratic party—always endure, for we are a great evangelizing and missionary agency. We began the good work of converting that party in 1860, and we have been pursuing that purpose steadily and persistently and unwaveringly ever since. Thousands and hundreds of thousands of those original Democrats have been converted to Republicanism and are now safely within the ample folds of the Republican party.

"They complain of us that we are waving the 'bloody shirt,' that we will not let by-gones be by-gones, and that we are continually singing the same old song, and making the same old speeches. It is unfortunate that it is so, but the misfortune arises from the fact that it is necessary it should be so. When one of my dear, deluded Democratic friends says, 'For God's sake, why don't you stop talking these same old things?' I say, 'For God's sake, why don't you stop being that same old party?' We must talk about the antecedents and the history of the Democratic party, because the party of to-day is the same party, identical in material, identical in its membership, identical in its spirit, identical in its traditions, identical in all its purposes — the same old party that declared that the great chart of American liberties was a glittering generality, that scoffed at patriotic feeling as a delusion and a sham, that asserted the right of secession, that involved this nation in rebellion the most stupendous in its purposes that the world ever witnessed, that obstructed the fair and patriotic reconstruction of these states, that attempted the repudiation of the national debt and the destruction of the national credit. It is the same old party that has been guilty of all these crimes and offenses, and the men who now make up that organization, and give it tone, and character, and life, are the individual men who have been guilty of all those political offenses which ought to have consigned them to eternal political oblivion. In the nature of things the Democratic party must expect to face its terrific record.

It comes once every four years before the people of this
country and demands their recognition and confidence.
The Democratic party comes before the people of this
country to-day and asks that it shall have the management
of our national debt, the control of the national finances,
and be intrusted with what it calls the reform of both. It
makes loud and lofty promises of its performances in the
future. But as wise men, as absolutely unimpassioned
men, if such a thing were possible in the presence of questions so great in their magnitude — as wise men, I say, we
must take you, not by the assurance you make to day, but
by your performances in the long past which stretches
behind you.

If we had such a record as theirs wouldn't we be anxious to bury it ? If they had such a record as ours wouldn't
they be anxious to exploit it ? If behind us were blighted
faith, violated honor, ruined homes, ruined credit, wars,
rebellions, treasons — if that was the record that this
Republican party had made, we would deafen our ears and
call upon the mountains to fall upon and bury us rather
than hear it denounced or commented upon. But the
Republican party glories to talk of its record — it is a glorious record to talk about — and the Democratic party
hides its head when it is mentioned, because it is a record
in the presence of which every patriotic head ought to be
bowed. The party has not changed ; its character has not
changed ; its membership has not changed. It is a question beyond and infinitely above the mere personal charac-
teristics of the men placed in nomination.

" You are here to-night to ratify the nomination of
Hayes and Wheeler. ' Their nomination was wise. It is a
nomination which combined all the elements of the Republican party. It brought the Liberals back home. It
brought the Independents back home. If there are any

Liberals or Independents here to-night who wandered off with Greeley in 1872, I say to them, 'We open wide the door; we bid you welcome, only don't do so any more.' You are all back, safely housed in that glorious old Republican temple, the walls of which are decked with the most heroic achievements of the past century, with a record that is as enduring as time, and history will never willingly let die — that splendid temple whose dome is lifted even among the very stars, and whose foundations are as secure as the eternal rocks; you are back again within it, and see that no inscription ever goes upon those walls, that nothing is emblazoned thereon, except such as can shine along with the deeds that already adorn it.

"We are to-day a united, a powerful, and — I feel it in the air — a victorious party. It is the same old organization, with the same old patriotic fire and nerve that carried this great nationality through the Rebellion and saved it. It is the same party that faced the results of its own logic as courageously as the young David of old faced the great Goliath. It knew in its early days — and it knows to-day — neither 'variableness nor shadow of turning.' It found the negro a slave; it made him free. Making him a free man, it made him a citizen. Making him a citizen, it clothed him with all the rights and privileges of citizenship, even unto the power of voting. True still to its trust, what it said in 1868 it said again in 1872. No talk about negro equality or competition could frighten it; and to-day we have, through the agency of the Republican party, a nationality — not a mere aggregation of states, but a nationality, the United States of America, powerful enough and always willing to protect the poorest and meanest of its subjects even in the remotest quarter of the globe when his liberty is assailed. The old party said, 'The men whom we have made free men, citizens, voters, we will protect, if the states in which they live will not protect them. If the states in which they live will not protect them this General Government, which we call the United States of America, will protect them.' And that promise the Republican party of the United States, with the help of God, proposes to keep. Down to to-day we have come. The great debt, which hung like an incubus upon us, is gradually melting away — taxation reduced, coming back by slow degrees, but sure, nevertheless, to the good old times when the basis of our currency was specie. We may look with the most perfect and absolute confidence that, at no very distant period of time, with the debt placed beyond all doubt, the integrity of the nation thoroughly vindicated, its faith absolutely approved, our currency recognized all over the globe, good times come again, spindles turning as they were before, mills in full blast, business prospering, no bondman on the soil of the Republic — at no very distant day, all these splendid results we may look upon as the natural outcome of the policy of the Republican party."

The Democrats, in their St. Louis platform, had denounced the financial policy of the administration. Mr. Storrs' answer was complete and crushing:

"In 1866, again in 1868, going into a national canvass, they demanded the payment of the government bonds in greenbacks, which would not only have utterly destroyed the national credit, but would have of necessity so inflated the national currency that the resumption of specie would have been eternally and everlastingly postponed. And yet this party, with the smell of repudiation on its garments, with the recent history of the Indiana and Ohio campaigns fresh in the minds of the people, with their miserable record behind them of a steady, persistent, willful opposition to and interference with every scheme which looked to the reëstablishment of the national credit and the payment of the national debt — they denounce the Republican party for imbecility or immorality, because it has taken no step in that direction ! Let us see what the facts are. What was gold in 1865? What is gold to-day? Have we made no advance toward resumption during the last eleven years? This truthful platform says we have not. Gold was in the neighborhood of 150 in 1865; it is 112 or thereabouts to-day. Is not that a long step forward? Is it not an immense stride in advance that this growing nation has taken? How is the debt? In the eleven years of which this lying platform speaks this Republican party, which is denounced for its imbecility and immorality, has paid the enormous sum of $456,000,000 of the national debt. Has it taken no step in the way of decrease of the expenditures? Our appropriations have been reduced from 1874 to 1875 over $27,000,000. Our expenditures in 1866 were $520,000,-000, and in 1873 they were $290,000,000. Gold reduced from 200 to 112; $456,000,000 of the national debt paid; hundreds of millions of taxation removed from the shoulders of the people; our bonds largely appreciated in every money-mart in the world; and yet ' we, the Democratic delegates,' in national convention assembled, solemnly denounce and arraign the Republican party for taking no steps towards making the promise of the legal-tender notes good !

" Figures sometimes become very eloquent, and in this connection they are eloquent. Let me read a little more of figures. Our tariffs have been so that the people hardly feel the burden; every expense of the government has been so removed that the burden is but lightly felt to-day. Our internal taxes that would have been paid in the several years, had the laws remained unchanged, under Grant's administration, calculated on the basis of the taxes collected

in 1868, would have been in 1869, $63,919,416; in 1870,
$58,295,182; in 1871, $92,726,132; in 1872, $110,810,083;
in 1873, $123,533,307, etc. In 1877 there would have been
collected on that basis $129,700,000. This shows a saving,
an absolute decrease of the taxation, on an average of $104,-
696,190 per year during the last eight years. And yet the
Republican party, which has accomplished those magnificent results, is denounced by the ' Democratic delegates,' as
guilty of imbecility and immorality ! But that is not all.
' We, the Democratic delegates,' also say that ' reform is
necessary in the scale of public expense. Our Federal
taxation has swollen from $60,000,000 gold, in 1860, to
$450,000,000 currency, in 1870.' I ask you whose fault is
it that the expenses of this government have ' swollen from
$60,000,000 gold, in 1860, to $450,000,000 currency, in 1870?
It is the war that has imposed those terrible burdens upon
us, and while you are sweating and groaning over them
Ben Hill comes up from Georgia, and Henry Clay Dean
from Iowa, and denounce the mild men of Kane county
because, in putting down their rebellion, they were compelled to incur additional millions of expense. I say it is
the cheekiest platform ever witnessed in political history
or literature. Why, I would suppose that whenever the
occasion occurred you could not drive a Democrat into the
mention of the tremendous burdens under which the people are laboring, for right back of us looms up the memory
of this great rebellion ! Right back, fresh in our minds,
is the memory of the war which compelled us to raise the
expenditures of the country. It is none of their business
how much that war cost. Treated as they deserved to have
been treated, as any other nationality would have treated
them, this $157,000,000, which the people of this country
have been compelled to pay since that time as a yearly
burden for putting down and crushing the rebellion,

would have been shouldered by the Democratic party and paid by them, even to the confiscation of everything they possessed.

"I suppose that in the interests of conciliation we must submit to it without murmuring; but it does seem hard that the recently reconstructed Confederates assembled at St. Louis, and doing business under the name, style, and firm of 'We, the Delegates of the Democratic Party,' should denounce us because, as they say, we expended more money in putting down their rebellion and whipping them back into the Union than was absolutely necessary.

"We next come to the question of defalcations. The history upon this point is very short. One would think, from the clamor that is made, that corruption was in every branch of the public service,—that there was not an official anywhere who was not guilty either of stealing public funds or of taking corrupt money. This is a great deal bigger nation than it was fifty years ago. We collect and expend to-day millions of money where we handled and expended only thousands half a century ago. I am one of those sanguine men who believe that this world is all the time getting better. I believe that even the Democratic party is slowly improving. It is a great deal better world, officially considered, than it was in the days of Old Hickory ; it has improved since the days of Martin Van Buren ; it is an immense improvement over Polk ; it is a great way ahead of James Buchanan's time. The fact of the matter is just this : There is not a first-class merchant in the city of Aurora who does not lose by little petty defalcations on the actual amount of his business a much larger sum of money than does the United States on the enormous expenditures it has been compelled to make under Grant's administration. Now I will read from an authentic report the history of all those proceedings : 'The losses on every

$1,000 of disbursements were, in the administration of Jackson, $10.55; Van Buren, $21.15; Harrison, $10.37; Polk, $8.34; Taylor and Fillmore, $7.64; Pierce, $5.86; Buchanan, nearly $6.98; Lincoln, $1.41; Johnson, 48 cents; Grant, the first four years, 40 cents, the second four years, 26 cents.' That is the veritable record, and it is an immensely satisfactory one. It is a record, however, that you would not dream of amid the clamor and clatter made about thievery in every branch of the public service.

"We are asked if we approve of Grant, and if we indorse him. I do not suddenly change my opinion of men. I have yet this to say: that when the memory of 'We, the Democratic delegates,' shall have perished in oblivion and forgetfulness, when the generations to come will have forgotten that such men ever lived, the real, solid, patriotic achievements of U. S. Grant will, growing brighter and brighter as the years wear away, make a record for him that shall be absolutely imperishable. In all this terrible storm of obloquy—and no man has ever suffered more in the frightful flood of calumny which has been poured upon us—silent and patient and steady, has he sat, conscious that the hearts of the people beat with and for him, and conscious in his own heart that he never breathed a breath that was not a patriotic one, and never entertained a purpose, so far as this great nation was concerned, that was not patriotic as well.

"'They speak of some 'false issues': 'The false issue by which they seek to light anew the dying embers of sectional hate. . . . All these abuses, wrongs, and crimes, the product of sixteen years' ascendancy of the Republican party.' My Republican friends, will you stop to think of that? 'All these abuses, wrongs, and crimes, the product of sixteen years' ascendancy of the Republican party!' That carries us away back to 1860; carries us back to when many of us were boys; carries us back when the great party was new and fresh and young; carries us back to the time when, with the watchword ' Liberty' on our banners, we won our first great victory; carries us back to the time of Lincoln; carries us back to those years of trouble through which we passed; and the Democratic party speak of that ascendancy — the ascendancy of Lincoln, his first and second term, the first term of Grant, the whole history of reconstruction — speak of that as a history of 'abuses, wrongs, and crimes,' which 'we, the Democratic delegates,' purpose and intend to reform! And yet they say, ' Let the dead past bury its dead — forget these old issues.' At the same time there comes trooping up from the South, from every Confederate cross-roads, the bearer of a Confederate heart, filled full of Confederate hopes, believing that the Lost Cause is finally won, flaunting in the face of this great nation, just out of its terrible perils, the denunciation of sixteen years of wrong, outrage and crime of this Republican party! If this Democratic party, insulting the grandest history of the nation in that charge, insulting the memory of the heroic dead and the heroic living as it does, could take some visible shape, would not the strong Republican army of Kane County, with the old nerve and vigor and its old heart back of it, feel like grinding it into powder? We can bear taxation; our treasures may be sunk into the seas, but this glorious record, which challenges the admiration of all the world, and which is the work of a great loyal people, shall not be spit upon and defiled. You cannot smite it directly, but, carrying this infamous charge in your hearts, keeping it warm on your lips, when the day of November comes, go up to the polls and say to them, ' You, the Democratic delegates, that sought the destruction of this great nation, we repel your slander and now bury you for eternity.'

" Now what are the ' false issues ' ? Let us see.   A word
or two about sectional hate : What is the danger from sectional hate—from what source does that danger spring? You
have seen some exhibitions of it in the past and during the
present session of Congress, when the old fires of rebellion
have been rekindled, when the old illustrators of plantation manners again appear on the floor of the House, and
when unrepentant rebellion flaunts its horrid front in the
face of the people and denounces the nation and the party
that crushed that rebellion to atoms—Hill, Lamar, all the
prominent leaders of secession, back again into the councils
of the nation they sought to destroy?   And in the presence
of such magnanimity as that we have this sympathetic
blubber about 'bloody shirt,' etc. Do you suppose that there
would have been one prominent improvement, national in
its character, made had this Democratic party, which
to-day prates of reform, succeeded since 1860 ?   Contemplate such a result as their success, if you can without shud-
dering.   Think of the success of the Democratic party in
1864 ! Down from its high pedestal our nation would
have come.   Home would have come our conquering
legions, with their banners trailing in the dust and in the
mire of defeat! The dishonor and disruption of the
nationality—that would have been the sure result had the
promises of Democratic reform been listened to by the
people and had their solicitation for public confidence met
with any response in 1864. Then, again, 1868.   Contemplate, if you can, their success then.   Every measure
for the reconstruction of the nation which they sought to
destroy would have been rendered utterly fruitless, our
gigantic debt would have been rendered still more gigantic,
our credit would have been gone, and we would have been
to-day a disgraced and discredited nationality in the eyes
of the whole world.   In 1872, think of the calamities that

would have followed a Democratic triumph, when one of
their own candidates pronounced the reconstructive measures 'revolutionary, unconstitutional and void.' What
has occurred to make the evil of a Democratic success less
to-day? What has occurred to make the necessity of a
Republican triumph less imperative now, than it has been
every hour since 1860? The time has not come when this
ideal sentiment of hand-shaking shall take the place of
that recognition of principles which the great emergencies
of the occasion demand. And what has the Republican
platform said that calls from the Democrats these reproaches? This is all : 'We sincerely deprecate all sectional feeling and tendencies. We, therefore, note with
deep solicitude that the Democratic party counts, as its
chief hope of its success, upon the electoral vote of a united
South.' It is its only hope. The success of the Democratic party means a united South, secured at the expense
of the colored vote. It makes an appeal for that southern
vote directly, as in the days of old, to sectional prejudices
and sectional hate. It means that every newly-made citizen shall be deprived of the privileges which he is entitled
to under the constitution. I shall not appeal to any sectional feeling, but to the broad, catholic spirit of nationality. The Republican party demands the suffrage of every
citizen, North and South, East and West, black and white,
—every citizen, of whatsoever race he may originally have
been, who desires the largest, truest, broadest measure of
national prosperity for the land we love so justly and so well.

"Now, about this platform : They have lost none of
their old differences. They are the same old issues. It is
the bitter, intense spirit of state rights working against
a distinct and united nationality that has been waging war
for the long years that are passed. We stand upon the
threshold of a new century. We will inaugurate it well,

I am sure, and say that this nation, one and indivisible, shall be perpetual.

"Upon this platform they have placed in nomination Mr. Samuel J. Tilden, of the city of New York, as their exemplar and illustrator of reform. What has he done? Who is Samuel J. Tilden? One of the most expert railroad lawyers on the continent. That is not a first-class recommendation. A man thoroughly imbued with the corporation spirit, so completely that, like the client he represents, he has no soul. It has ordinarily been the case that physicians are prosperous in proportion as they have cured their patients. He is a great railroad doctor—the great corporation physician; but all precedent in his case is abolished,—the patients have died and the physician has prospered. Wherever and whenever Samuel J. Tilden has been called to stand by the bedside of a sick railroad there was a funeral in the near future. He is the father of watered stock. He is the great absorber and absorbent. He is the author of farm mortgage bonds, and I don't need to explain to you what those instruments mean. There never yet came into the door of his office a healthy corporation which did not hobble out from the other door on crutches and in bandages. All along, up and down this great West, are the wrecks of disappointed hopes and blasted expectations that stockholders and corporations have had, when they have passed through the gentle but death-dealing treatment of Tilden.

"I might bring myself to such a frame of mind as to vote for a Confederate. I can understand how a man living in the South might have voted for the South; but not until my heart has ceased to beat, not until my whole being is changed, will I ever, on any ticket, nor under any circumstances, cast my suffrage for a man living in the North, who in 1864, denounced the war as an experiment,

as a failure, and abjectly and meanly sued for peace! I
follow him still further, back to the state of New York —
worse than that, back to the city of New York — back to
the embrace of Hoffman and Tweed — back to the associations he seemed to love so well. Chairman of the central
committee, he approved and aided in the most stupendous
frauds upon the rights of franchise ever committed by any
party,— a great fraud, which wrested the state of New
York from the Republicans to whom it belonged, and
polled in four wards over 20,000 fraudulent votes. This
was done under the direction of the modern reformer, the
friend of peace in 1864, Samuel J. Tilden! I go still
further. The gigantic robberies of that great ring had
finally excited the alarm of the whole nation. During the
time when millions and millions were being shamelessly
plundered from the people of New York, the chairman of
the state central committee, the recipient of Tweed's bounty,
was curiously and marvelously silent. But the Republican
press, Republican speakers, the Republican party, denounced
and denounced again and again those gigantic frauds.
A great newspaper brought them to light; exposure came;
the lightnings of public wrath visited the head of Tweed
and his gang. When escape from detection was no longer
possible, then, from behind the loopholes of his safe retreat,
from behind his barricade of law books and railroad bonds,
Tilden comes forth as a patriotic reformer, and demands
the punishment of Boss Tweed! The Republican carriage
was all ready, and he jumped in and rode! Is he entitled
to the credit? As I said the other night, the whole history is in a nutshell. Tweed was tried by a Republican
judge, before a Republican jury, prosecuted by a Republican attorney-general, convicted in Republican style, sent
to a Democratic jail, in charge of a Democratic jailer, and
ran away in true Democratic fashion.

" Mr. Tilden claims in the little Pecksniffian speech he made at Albany, that he has had great experience in administrative reform, and there must be a reform in the civil service. Well, how, Mr. Tilden, how? We want a reform, not in salaries, we want a reform in the men ; and, having a reform in the men, we want reform in the methods of their selection and appointment. I put this question squarely and fairly to you: ' Do you think that, with that embodied corporation at the head of our nation, and with the woods full of the Confederates and Democrats flying to the capital for an office, there would be any improvement? What, in the name of God, would be the *personnel* of the civil service that would be picked out of that measley crowd? And it is out of that crowd that Tilden would have to select. They have tried the operation in their Confederate congress; and see what an exhibition they made of themselves! Why, Washington was absolutely alive with men who were looking for offices, because they supposed, there being a Confederate House of Representatives, the Lost Cause was won. Think of a Democratic triumph all along the line, and what the results must be ! We have seen this Democratic crowd in 1864. The Saturday before the great national convention which nominated McClellan met, this city was full of them. I made a speech over there in the park, on the same stand with Dick Oglesby and John Farnsworth. I started to go home to Chicago Sunday morning, and what a sight there was! Every fellow dressed in gray; breezes, in comparison with which the odors from Bridgeport were sweet as those from a bank of flowers, came from every car. Train after train, the engines all doubled up, and not a seat to be had on the cars. They were the Democratic delegates on their way to the convention. After I arrived in Chicago, a good old Democrat said to me: ' I was very much surprised a little while ago. I saw a great mass of men going down Wabash Avenue, and I thought it was a procession of rebel prisoners on there for exchange, but I'll be damned if it wasn't the Democratic delegation from Missouri.'

" In the presence of that same savory crowd Samuel J. Tilden appeared in 1864. Some fellows had an ear bitten off in a joint debate; men with their noses broken in an election contest; fellows with short hair. Those men came on with banners with doves upon them, engaged in the olive branch business, and all swearing for peace. At the head of this crowd in 1864, was Samuel J. Tilden. The crowd has not changed, and the leader of the Democracy has not changed one single bit since that time. I think there can be nothing more suicidal than to intrust into the hands of these men, who sought the destruction of our national life, the direction of our national interests. I believe in this nation. I know what it is,— it is the sacred custodian of the priceless treasure of free government for all peoples and all nationalties. I hope to see it endure forever. I cherish in my very heart of hearts the memory of the great heroes who have lived and died, the great leaders of our great party. I hope to carry in my heart as the most sacred thing which it bears an intense, indulging, never-ending love of this great nation, embalmed, sanctified, and glorified as it has been by the blood of so many hundreds and thousands of noble men; and I believe in my very soul that this nation can be saved, and that, with all its faults and shortcomings, this Republican party, whose cause I to-night advocate, is the real custodian of our national honor and integrity. All hail, then, the great cause! We stand upon the threshold of this great contest. Let the old fires be everywhere relighted; let the old spirit be again rekindled, and let the word come up from the old leaders, as in the olden time, 'Attention! forward!'"

At Detroit, the Republicans opened the campaign
by the dedication of a large central wigwam on the
24th of August. In compliance with an invitation from
the State Central Committee, Mr. Storrs was present,
and addressed one of the largest and liveliest indoor
meetings ever witnessed in the State of Michigan. Referring to the platform adopted by the Democrats at
St. Louis, he said:

" Here are the Democratic delegates from all parts of
the country representing the Lost Cause, denouncing a
period of crimes and abuses which the Democratic party
propose to right. These sixteen years embraced four years
of war, four years of the administration of Lincoln and
eight years of the administration of General Grant. Sanctified by the blood of a quarter of a million of brave men,
these years are denounced by such men as Ben Hill, Lamar
and others. If there is a particle of the old spirit in Detroit I know that you will consider this an insult. Tilden's
letter of acceptance and the St. Louis platform are full of
accusations of the Republican party and are much alike in
this respect; they are shocked at its thefts and immorality,
and promise peace and good times. If the government
was turned over to the Democratic party it would be indeed the time when the lion and the lamb shall lie down
together, with the very small difference that the lamb
would be on the inside. I do not propose to defend the
Republican party. Wherever stealing has been done, it has
been done by individuals, irrespective of the principles of
the Republican party, and those individuals are the ones
to blame. The Democratic party is a robber as an organization, and I say to you that the stealing and corruption in the Republican party are too small to be noticed
when compared with a party that would steal arms, steal
states, and that finally attempted to steal the whole nation.

Precisely how the Democratic party propose to carry out the reforms about which they talk so much they do not tell us.

"'The Democrats propose to reform the civil service, but how ? Tilden says by selecting a higher grade of men ; but from where ? Where will you find them ? The offices must be filled by either Democrats or Republicans. If you want loyal men, men of refinement, men of culture, the Republican party is full of them. At Washington this winter we have seen the kind of men that the Democrats propose to reform the civil service with, the emissaries of the Lost Cause. Culture ! Men who can't tell whether the Saviour of mankind was crucified at Calvary or shot at Bunker Hill. Why the roads through the country are full of tramps, Democratic office-seekers, hoofing it from Washington. Another instance : What a great moral city is the City of New York! How piously the Democrats there can stuff a ballot box, and count this man or that man out. How very quietly they go about doing good — so quietly that no one ever hears of it.

"Who is the Democratic candidate ? Samuel J. Tilden. Some people say that they shall vote for him because they are tired of machine politics. Why, gentlemen, Samuel J. Tilden is the perfection of a machine. He is a reaper and mower combined, a self-sharpener, and has never been anything else. They tell us that Mr. Tilden is a patriotic man, but how very quietly he went about saving the Union, his left hand on the Chicago convention, and his right hand didn't know anything about it. Here was a war where millions of men met on the field of battle, where hundreds of thousands of lives were lost, where an immense amount of treasure was expended; and I ask you, was there a man about whose position there could be a particle of doubt ? Why, every schoolboy in the land was able to define his position in regard to the war, but, skulking behind his law books and railroad bonds, Samuel J. Tilden was not heard from. We all have the right to say to him, you were no obscure country lawyer, why could you not at once say, ' God speed to the good cause. God speed to the noble soldiers.'

" They say he is a reformer, and that he unearthed the frauds of Tweed. Tilden and Tweed were personal friends for many years, and long after all Tweed's villainies had been exposed by the Republican press, Tilden met him in convention and took him up as a political equal and friend. After the Republican party and the Republican press had exposed Tweed, Tilden came to the front and rolled into office as Governor of New York on the tide that swamped Tweed. Now, Tweed was tried before a Republican judge, by a Republican prosecuting attorney, and convicted by a Republican jury, but he escaped from a Democratic sheriff. It is truly wonderful to mark the progress of reform. Confined in a small room not much larger than this, poorly furnished with marble-top table and tapestried throughout, eating but five or six meals per day, and seeing only fifty or sixty visitors each day, Tweed pined for a sight of his wife ; he never loved her so much in his life before. The jailor took him in a carriage to his humble dwelling, in that pauper street, Fifth Avenue, and he went in at the front door. From that moment to the present time the places that knew him know him no more forever.

"Tilden is reform governor of New York ; he has broken the canal ring. Eighty thousand dollars has been expended, three men indicted, one of whom was convicted and is now imprisoned out of doors on bail. This is the great ring-smasher. Now I suppose you all know that if there is anything that will make a man love his fellow-men all through and through, it is to consolidate railroads.

That is where Samuel J. Tilden has proved himself a success. He is the great railroad physician, and whenever he has stood at the bedside of a railroad there has been a railroad funeral in that immediate neighborhood very soon thereafter. Generally, you know, a physician's success depends upon his ability to save his patients, and it seems strange that when railroads have died on his hands Tilden has achieved great success. He is the author of watered stock and the finisher of blighted railroad stock. There is hardly a farmer in this broad land but that has a little piece of paper stowed away somewhere that he occasionally takes out, and, as he looks at it and mourns its worthlessness, he can trace it to the great reform candidate, Samuel J. Tilden."

On his return home, Mr. Storrs accepted an invitation to address the Republicans of Freeport, and fulfilled his engagement on the 15th of September. The announcement that he was to speak, and the meeting of the Congressional Convention in the afternoon, had filled the town with people, and the large hall which had been secured for the meeting could not hold the crowds, Republican and Democrat. who thronged to hear him. He said :

" I by no means feel in addressing the magnificent audience here to-night assembled that I am among strangers, or that I am speaking to strangers. I have known Freeport, its people, its surroundings, it patriotic spirits, its loyal impulses, for the last sixteen years. I am somewhat renewing to-night an acquaintance commenced sixteen years ago, and I am renewing that acquaintance on an occasion very much like that under which we met when the acquaintance began. It is curious to me, and, perhaps, may be so to you, to see how long a time it takes to wipe

out old political issues, and to substitute in their place entirely new ones. We have all waited, watched, and hoped
for the day to come when bygones should be really bygones,—when the past with all its dreadful memories
could be erased,—when all the troubles which we had
overcome would be behind us as a bad dream; when, with
new issues, new parties, new organizations, this great
nation, starting afresh upon its career, might say to itself
that, whatever else may happen, the past is safe, and to
the future alone are we called to look. That time, every
heart that beats before me to-night tells me, has not yet
arrived. Bygones are not bygones. The past is not altogether past. The past is not quite secure. We do not
stand to-day a nation with that past absolutely safe, with
the broad future before us absolutely untrammeled by any
history which lies behind us. We confront to-day — and
it is one of the wonders of this century — the same great
political organization, consisting of the same membership,
inspired by the same feelings, devoted to the same purposes, holding precisely the same ideas, that that party
held sixteen years ago, when it organized treason and sought
the destruction of the national existence — that we met and
defeated in 1860. We had hoped — and you all had hoped —
that, long before the centennial year had arrived, this
Democratic party, from which the cause of human freedom and of good government everywhere had suffered so
much, would have utterly passed out of existence and
would have vexed us no more. You had hoped that all
those old political ideas on which that party was based,
and to maintain and enforce which it organized a gigantic
rebellion, would have been buried in oblivion and absolutely be regarded among the things of the past. But, you
are doomed to disappointment. In the year of grace 1876
this same organization, whose record is a record of broken

promises and violated pledges,—this same political organization, which has carried within itself all the most dangerous political heresies that have threatened the destruction of our national life,— is proud, asserting, dominant, demanding that the custody of the affairs of the nation whose destruction it sought shall be by a loyal people turned over to its keeping. And the solemn question which you are to answer to-night, is this: Shall those who would have murdered this nation, the grandest on the face of the earth, within eleven short years after their attempt had failed, shall they be called back into power, and intrusted with the life and integrity of that nation whose destruction they sought? This is the question which is constantly recurring. I am told that these are bygones, and that we are making the same old speeches that we made in the years that are past. This question of loyalty, of devotion to the national existence, is as old as virtue, and the vices of the Democratic party are as old as sin. As well might you ask a preacher to hush his voice and let the pulpit go untenanted because preachers before him have denounced sin, as to ask Republicans to hush their voices and close their meetings as long as a Democrat lives above ground.

"I am in favor of conciliation — thoroughly and altogether in favor of conciliation. The simple question in my mind is who shall be conciliated ? I turn to the old Republicans on this platform ; I turn to the old Republicans in the body of the hall ; I ask them if they remember the days when we started out in our procession, twenty-two years ago ; I ask them if they remember how small a procession it was ; that we went afoot ; that the going was bad ; that our feet were sore ; that the winds blew through every hole in our garments ; that the skies were inclement, and that there were conservative gentlemen standing on the side-walks heaving mud at the procession as it passed ?

I ask them if they remember the days when the old procession grew, when it came up a great party, when it crystallized about itself all the holiest objects, the loftiest impulses, the best purposes of the country, and called itself the Republican party? I ask them if they remember when that great procession swelled in volume so that it embraced the whole continent, when it met a rebellion in arms, when it throttled the life out of it, when it saved the great nation? I ask them if they remember when these loyal people buried their loyal sons in every valley and on every hill-side in the land? I ask them if they remember the thousands and millions of dollars and the countless thousands of lives sacrificed that this nation might live? I ask them, finally, if they remember, when peace came, and when, to protect the national credit, another war, quite as great in its proportions as the first, to vindicate and maintain the national credit has been fought and won against the same adversaries; and I ask them to-day if, when the victory is finally achieved, we may not be permitted to sit down by the hearth-stones which we have saved, and ask that the robbers and plunderers of the national honor shall conciliate us?

"I speak of the Democratic party. It comes to you to-day asking that the confidence which you withdrew from it twenty years ago nearly shall be again restored to it. What has it done? Twenty years ago this same Democratic party made human sympathy a curse, and made charity an indictable offense. Twenty years ago this same Democratic party, which to-day demands the suffrages of the people, organized itself into a party which said the sunshine of freedom shall be local, and the black shadow of slavery shall be national. This same party organized secession in the war, and, having failed in meeting reason by the bullet and argument by the bludgeon, took its political principles to the last field to which those questions are ever referred. It carried them into battle ; its banners went down in defeat ; its hopes were crushed ; its arms were defeated. If, when Lee's armies surrendered at Appomattox, they did not surrender the damnable heresies out of which the war grew, the war was a failure as base and shameless as Tilden declared it in 1864.

I supposed, we all supposed, that when their armies were annihilated their political ideas were annihilated as well. Has there been any conversion ? Point me to a single Democrat south of Mason and Dixon's line, big or little, who to-day will tell you that he entertains on the question of state sovereignty an opinion in the slightest degree different from that which he held when the war began. Point me to a single leading Democrat North, prominent in politics, who was a Democrat when the war began, who to-day will tell you that he believes on the question of state sovereignty one iota differently from what he did sixteen years ago. Is it possible, then, that a party made up of the same members, each individual member holding the same belief that he held twenty years ago,— that the party has changed when there has been no change in the opinions of its individual members ?

"In 1861, Samuel J. Tilden, with James Buchanan, declared as his opinion that, although a state had no right to secede, the general government had no right to coërce it into the Union. Has Tilden changed ? Is there a Democrat in the whole length and breadth of the land that has changed ? Not one. If no individual member has changed, how, then, has the party changed ? If they have changed, if they have revolutionized that belief, if they are now honestly of the opinion that this nation is one and indivisible ; that the right of secession does not exist ; that there is inherent in the general government the power

to crush out the attempt whenever it is made ; if, to follow
this out, there is a single Democrat who has to-day reached
those conclusions, there is but one way in which the genuineness of his change of conviction can be demonstrated,
and that is by leaving the Democratic party and joining
the ranks of Republicanism.   When the heathen ceases to
worship his idol of block or stone as the real God — when
he believes in the divinity of the Saviour and in the truths
of the Old and New Testament — he doesn't stay among the
heathen, but joins the Christian church.   And if these
Democrats are converted, I have this advice to give them :
Get out from among your heathen associations, stop wor-
shiping your images of brick and of stone, change your
soiled and battered clothing of Democracy, wash yourselves
clean, put on a new shirt, come into the ranks of Republicanism, don its garments, and thus prove the genuineness
of the change of heart which you claim to have experienced.

"This Republican party of ours comes to you to-day
with substantially the same membership.   It is the same
party, with its unbroken record of glory that made four
millions of chattels freemen and citizens.   It found the
old structure of state filled with the rotten and decayed
timbers of African servitude.   It removed them all amid
the thunders of war, and replaced them with the everlasting granite of freedom.   This same Republican party
that crowded into four short years of war the most
colossal and resplendent results ever recorded in history,
confronted at its close a vast debt, and honestly, manfully,
faithfully, it has pledged the credit of the whole nation
that it shall be paid, and reduced it more than $400,000,-
000 of money.

"It has lifted millions of dollars of tax from the
shoulders of the people.   It has decreased by millions of
dollars the national expenditures.   It has increased by mil-

lions of money the national revenues; and this brings its history down to to-day.

"But while I am discussing questions of this character, some Democrats tell me, 'Why, those are old issues.' 'The freedom of the slave,' they say, 'is secure beyond all questions. His citizenship, as you have said, is imbedded in the constitution.' His right to vote, they tell us, is secure. And when they make that line of argument they seem to think that the whole discussion is closed. Right here, let us pause and think. Let me suggest to you that there is hardly a clause in our Federal constitution which is self-enforcing. We have a provision that there shall be Federal courts, and I think I see a conservative Democrat — one of the old-time Democrats who respects the constitution beyond all measure — stand with his toes turned out and his back to the fire, and with his hand under his coat-tail, saying. 'I am in favor of the constitution — I am in favor of that clause which provides for Federal courts, but I am not in favor of this congressional legislation by which the court is created.'

"We have these constitutional amendments by which citizenship and freedom are both conferred upon the negro, but they are not self-enforcing. Each one of these amendments provides that they shall be enforced by appropriate legislation. Now, what is that appropriate legislation, and what is its precise value? Let me tell you, if you will strike out all congressional legislation upon the subject and leave the amendments standing alone, they are as idle for all useful purposes 'as a painted ship upon a painted ocean.' The Republican party is a practical party. It imbedded those great rights in the constitution. It took them down to the solid rock upon which the nation lives, and it said. 'We will make these no idle gifts. These shall be no treacherous benefactions. We mean precisely what we say.' We gave freedom to the slave. It were base not to protect him in its enjoyment. We gave citizenship to the negro. It were base not to protect him in the enjoyment of all its privileges. We gave him the right to vote. It were outrageous if it were an idle gift. We protect him in the full and complete enjoyment of the right, and therefore congress has by legislation provided that, whenever any privileges thus conferred shall be interfered with, this great central power which we call the general government may intervene, and may protect the negro in the enjoyment of every privilege which the constitutional amendment confers upon him. It says this: ' We give you by the constitution the right to citizenship and to vote, and more by legislation. This is no ideal gift. If, when you go to deposit your ballot, that right is interfered with, if the state in which you live cannot or will not protect you, this great government will protect you. If you are interfered with by force, we will protect you by force. If armed men threaten you in the enjoyment of any of those privileges, armed men shall march to your support, and assert your full and complete enjoyment of them.' This is what the Democratic party calls centralization.

"It is a centralization of which I am enthusiastically in favor. I would give nothing for that government so utterly powerless and helpless that it could not, even at the cost of war, at the extremes of the globe, protect the meanest and poorest of its citizens when insulted and outraged. I would spit upon that government which would not at home protect, even at the cost of war, the meanest and poorest of its citizens in the enjoyment of every privilege which the constitution conferred upon him. And the man to-day who is in favor of the constitutional amendments, and is opposed to that legislation by which they shall be enforced, is a coward and a sneak, and fittingly belongs to the Democratic party.

"I will pursue this subject still further. Let me illustrate a little. I think I am familar with this Democratic party. I have read its history. It has been burned into me and into you. During the war all through the North, you found magnificent Democrats who were in favor of a vigorous prosecution of the war. Certainly they were. They were in favor of a vigorous prosecution of the war, but were opposed to drafting a single man. They were in favor of the suppression of the rebellion, but were opposed to buying a gun. They were in favor of the suppression of treason, but opposed to invading what they call a sovereign state; opposed to secession, and opposed to putting it down; opposed to a dissolution of the Union, and opposed to preventing anybody dissolving it.

"One more question on this point. You have seen one-half of a Confederate congress. They cannot disturb the amendments. But place the whole of the affairs of this nation in the hands of the Democratic party, and where do you suppose, within thirty days after attaining power—where do you suppose every single syllable of legislation will be left that was intended to enforce the provisions of those amendments? Away back in 1863, in the Democratic, patriotic, honestly-governed City of New York, there was inaugurated a little one-horse Democratic rebellion. The draft law had been enforced. Seymour, Tilden, all good Democrats, had assured the rank and file that all that legislation was revolutionary, unconstitutional, and void. If there ever was a man that loved the constitution and talked about it all the time, that carried it about with him, and slept with it under his pillow, it is one of the meek and lowly followers of John Morrissey and Isaiah Rynders. If there ever was a class of men up in science

who denied privileges to the negroes on the ground that
they were not men, and that their astragali differed from
that of a white man, it was the learned *savans* whose noses
have been broken and whose ears have been bitten off in
those discussions in the City of New York. At that time
these good, zealous Democrats really believed in the bottom
of their patriotic souls that the constitution had been violated by the draft law, and organized a mob and brought on
a great riot, in the midst of which Horatio Seymour wrote
a letter to President Abraham Lincoln. He said to him
practically: 'We are all in favor of the prosecution of the
war. We all devoutly pray that the Union may be saved.
We pray every night when we retire to our couches that
the Union may be restored. But this draft law opposes
and violates, as we think, some of the fundamental provisions of the constitution. The temper of the loyal people
of this state,' he said, ' is greatly aroused,' and therefore he
proposed to Abraham Lincoln that the draft be suspended,
and that a lawsuit be commenced in some court in the city
of New York and carried through to the supreme court of
the United States, which, in the course of two or three
years, might be terminated, and by which it might be ascertained whether the draft was all right or not. Mr. Lincoln wrote back to him: ' My Dear Sir: I cannot see how
your proposition will work. The difficulty is our Confederate friends south of Mason and Dixon's line won't
wait for your lawsuit. They go right along and fill up
their armies.' And he says, ' My dear Seymour, go on
with your lawsuit one or two, or as many of them as you
please. I will go along with my draft, and we will run
them in parallel lines,' and, as it turned out, the other
Democratic rebellion south of Mason and Dixon's line was
crushed into powder long before Horatio Seymour's suits
would have been reached upon the docket. It is the same

party precisely that acted thus when such dangers as those were threatening us which now asks that the affairs of this nation shall be turned over to its keeping. It is the same party, reeking all through with its political crimes, that insists upon it that from the hands of this great loyal organization that saved the nation, it shall be taken, and passed over into the keeping of that disloyal mob who sought its destruction. I do not believe that the time has yet arrived when this loyal people has so far forgotten the history of the past twenty years that they are prepared to accede to this request.

"It occurs to me that here is a proper place to be scriptural. I have watched, as I have told you, this Democratic party curiously — watched its promises. It is a party absolutely without performance, and depends altogether upon promise. If there is a banker in this town, or a citizen who is not a banker, that has loaned some fellow $100 which the fellow has never paid, he may forgive the debt — let that be a bygone; but I don't believe he will make another loan. How may I know that this Democratic party is to keep its promises? By judging from what it has done? Oh, no. They say, 'We will save the nation.' We saved it. We have saved you that trouble. They say, 'We will protect it.' Why, you sought to destroy it. They say, 'We will maintain the national credit.' Why, you sought to ruin it. They say, 'We will make greenbacks equal to gold.' We say, 'You sought to destroy them altogether.' They say, 'We will lift up the national credit to where it belongs, and pay the national debt.' We say, 'It was eight years ago that you sought to repudiate it.'

"These are the promises it is making to-day. These are the performances of the past. How are you going to judge from promises? Suppose there comes into your place of business a young man magnificently adorned with a platform. He shines and glistens all over with it. He has brought, perhaps, the Ten Commandments, the Sermon on the Mount, the Saints' Rest, and Taylor's Holy Living, all rolled into one, and he says, ' I would like to be treasurer of your insurance company,' and you produce to him a record from the police court simply showing that he has been indicted and convicted twice of larceny — what on earth becomes of his platform? And when this Democratic party comes to you with its platform, ' We, the delegates of the Democratic party in National convention assembled, in the city of St. Louis, insist upon it that the country demands immediate reform,' you say, ' All right; but in case anybody should doubt you, I propose to take a hand in. Try it on yourselves first.' I saw an announcement some days ago of a meeting of a ' Tilden Reform Club,' I asked them which they intended to reform, Tilden or the club.

Now, then, as to the Scripture. A noted ex-Senator is on the stump again, and he is always scriptural. A good man, but his heart is running over with this milky kind of goodness that would arrest a thief, capture the spoons from him, and then give him your hat and overcoat, that there should be no misunderstanding nor unkind feeling in the future. He says that we should treat our brethren of the South with the same Christian spirit that the father in the parable treated the prodigal son. I have read the parable of the prodigal son. I am willing to accept that test ; and I, for one, will be willing to treat the Southern prodigal precisely as the old man in the story treated his prodigal. The prodigal of the parable was a pretty good sort of boy, as the world went. He came to man's estate. He left home when he had a perfect right to leave. Nobody questioned it. No soul doubted it. His portion was paid over to him. He didn't take a single dollar that did not belong to him. If I have read history aright, that was not precisely the

course which the Southern prodigal pursued. The old
Scripture prodigal was a boy standing just upon the threshold of life, foolish as hundreds and thousands of boys
have been since, with his pocket full of rocks. He went
out to see the world, fell among the Democrats, and naturally enough was cleaned out. He did not seek the
destruction of the old homestead when he left it. He
went away with no ill-will. He did not attempt to plunder
either the old man or the brother he left behind him. But
he found that playing prodigal didn't pay. When his
money was gone, and his credit was gone, and his Democratic friends had no further use for him, he went to feeding swine, and then went to feeding with swine. He got
about as low down as he could, and, sore, sick, disheartened, covered with blisters and scars, the poor, foolish boy,
loaded down with his unhappy experience, but with his
heart still in the right place, got up from among the hogs
where he was groveling and says, 'I will go back to my
father,' and back he went. And, as he was tottering on
the way, the old man was looking out the gate watching
down the long and dusty highway for the poor boy to
return, as he knew he would; and he saw him coming hob-
bling along, ragged, and wretched, and miserable; but he
was his boy still, and he went out and threw his arms
around him and bade him welcome and gave him a suit of
clothes and a ring and a veal dinner, and that was all.
Now that is all that boy got. I want you to observe he
didn't come back headed by a band-wagon and a banner
with 'Tilden and Reform' on it. What did he ask for?
He did not come back after the fashion of these large-
headed gentlemen from the South, saying, 'I will run
this farm.' No sir. He came back saying, 'Father I
haven't a cent; take me as a hired servant'; and, so far
as I have been able to discover,—if there are any preachers

here they will correct me,— he did kitchen work forever
after.   And yet the loyal stay-at-home boy was not quite
satisfied with that arrangement.   He looked at that calf
when about immolating him in congratulation for the
return of the boy, and he said to the old man: 'Father,
I never went off to be a prodigal.   I never spent my money
and substance in riotous living, and you never killed any
fatted calf for me.'   And, the loyal, patriotic father turned
around to him and said :   'Son, thou art always with me.
All that I have is thine.   Not a dollar in money, not a
foot of land, not an office, not a smell of an office, goes to
this returning prodigal.'   But this loyal, patriotic Northern ex-Senator says that we should let the Southern prodigals take this government — this farm — and run it for
all time in the future.   Now suppose we do offer the Southern prodigals this nation.   Suppose they do come back
kindly.   They say they accept the situation.   It is remarkable ; is it not a little extraordinary, after the surrender at
Appomattox, that they accept the situation ?   Isn't it a
little extraordinary that the rebel army accepted the situation at Vicksburg ?   Isn't it quite strange and startling,
and doesn't it make the world come out in violent gushing
kindness, to think that Bragg's army accepted the situation at Chattanooga ?   Isn't it curious that the Confederate army accepted the situation at Five Forks?   Isn't it
strange that Floyd and the rest or them accepted the situation at Donelson ?   Ah, of course they did.   There was
nothing else under God's heavens that they could do.   They
did accept the situation, and that is all there is about it,—
not only when their armies were beaten in the field, when
the last ditch was reached, when their banners were trailing
in the mud and mire of everlasting and eternal defeat, with
their arms stricken from their hands, with their cause
hopelessly lost.   This was done after the nation had been

filled with mourning, and the Northern people burdened with a debt of three thousand millions of dollars ; after the little hero to-day at the head of the government had Rebellion by the throat and choked the life out of it. Then the courteous rebels accepted the situation.

"It is this same party which to-day demands the custody of the national finances, and at the head of their ticket they have a great financial reformer, and stumping in various sections of the country are Democratic orators, eager and earnest, introducing their arguments to the people in order to convince them that a sound currency, a restored credit, must be the necessary result of a Democratic administration. Somewhere in the State of Indiana is a distinguished senator denouncing the Republican party in that it fixed a day for the resumption of specie payments. He says if that policy is carried out there will be such a contraction of the greenback that it will be quadrupled in its value, and that, therefore, every debt which every citizen owes will be practically quadrupled in amount. Isn't it a terrible calamity to think of ? Let us stop and consider it. Has it ever occurred to you whether it is very probable that any time within our prospects of living a greenback will be worth very much more than gold ? Suppose some enterprising citizen of Jo Daviess County concludes he will start a dairy. He gets his cows and his machinery for running the business. He issues his milk tickets, and he finds by and by, so many tickets has he issued, that he has a great many more tickets than milk. What is he going to do ? Can he contract his tickets so as to resume ? Suppose he began contracting—that he calls in his tickets—the time will never come when the milk ticket will be worth more than the milk. What is the policy of the Republican party ? If you cannot contract your tickets,—if you cannot call them in—inflate your

dairy; get more cows ; get no more tickets, but for God's
sake get more cows.   What is the policy of the Democratic
party ?   It is to inflate your tickets, and to inflate your
milk at the same time.   Instead of having a tendency
toward honest resumption of your tickets, instead of
enlarging your dairy, they have immediate recourse to the
pump.   When it is inflated by that process, have they got
any more milk ?   I am asked by Democratic orators, 'Do
you pretend to claim that Congress cannot make money ;
that the inscription which it puts upon a piece of paper
doesn't confer upon it actual value ?   Do you,' they say,
' deny the power of Congress to do that ?'   Yes.   I have
the utmost reverence for the power of Congress, but there
are many things that Congress cannot do.   Congress cannot make a horse.   Congress cannot make two hundred
acres out of one.   Congress cannot make actual value by
saying that it is actual value.   Take a $20 gold piece, fresh
from the mint, with the inscription clear and bright upon
it.   Obliterate every letter and every figure; leave it an
absolutely smooth surface; twist it into any shape you please;
make a round ball of it, and it is then worth $20.   Take
a $20 greenback.   Obliterate the inscription from it; make
it a blank piece of paper; roll it up in a wad, and it isn't
worth a—Democratic curse.   It is absolutely good for
nothing.   There is no inherent value in it; and the only
worth it possesses is the belief of the holder of the paper in
two things: first, in the ability of the nation to make the
promise good; and, second, in the willingness of the nation
to make the promise good.   You cannot enforce a liability
against a nation by an attachment proceeding.   It is to a
certain extent idle to say that every blade of grass and grain
of wheat is pledged to the payment of the greenback and
of the bonds.   So long as the Republican party is in
power that is true; but with the Democratic party in

power it is false. The credit of either the greenback or the bond depends upon the integrity of the party in power, and the just management of the national affairs. Place to-day—if the Almighty in His wrath should see fit to do it—this Democratic party at the head and in custody of our national interests, with its long black record of repudiation behind it, and where, so far as the national credit is concerned, would the national credit be? Let there come up from the South, from every Confederate crossroads, a bearer of a Confederate heart full of the belief that the Lost Cause is won; let the Government be made up in that way, and where would our national credit be? Do you gather grapes from thorns, and figs from thistles? Is this Democratic party, characterized to-day by being a solid South, is that party, which for years and years has waged relentless war against the national life, to be trusted with its old doctrine still fresh upon its lips, and its old bitterness still lingering in its heart? It is to be intrusted with the care and protection of the national credit? Let the wires carry the intelligence abroad that the old Rebel Democratic party has triumphed, that it has charge of the national debt, that it has charge of the national credit, knowing that that party has always sought and desired the ruin of both, where would our national credit be? Where would be the pledge of your blades of grass, your gold and your silver in your mines, your coal in your coal-field, your grain on your prairies—where would the pledge of them be with the Democratic party in power?

"There is nothing in this world more sensitive than national credit to the slightest outside interference. Place in charge of it a party punctured all through with the name of repudiation, and this national credit which we all hold so dearly to our heart would perish in a night. I am told that we cannot interfere with the national debt.

I may overstate it. I am assured, however, that in the
last session of this Confederate Congress more than 1,000
bills for private claims from the South were presented, and
smuggled in by that most astute Northern Democratic
gentleman having charge of those affairs in committee.
Imagine the condition of those claims if they should
triumph! Cords and cords, scores and scores, of claims of
that character would come into Congress, and millions,
countless millions, of additional indebtedness be saddled
upon the people, which would render the time of resumption of specie-payments not only an indefinite postpone-
ment, but an everlasting impossibility.

"But they assure us they desire to reform the civil
service. How? Have you ever heard a Democrat say how?
Have you ever read a Democratic speech that told you how?
Has there ever stood up in Washington, in the Senate or
in the House, a single Democratic legislator, and made one
single recommendation of a practical character looking to
the reform of the civil service? Wade through their long-
winded platform, if you please. Balance each dreary plati-
tude with the utmost care; search it all with the keenest
analysis and criticism, and then tell me if you can. Can
you see a practical remedy suggested by the Democratic
party for the reform of the civil service? My good friends,
without reference to platforms, without reference to letters
of acceptance, let us take this business as it is. We all
know that, as long as this form of government continues,
the nation must be managed by parties. I believe in political organization. I believe that men are so constituted
that upon great political questions they do not think alike;
and I think two pretty evenly-balanced parties, eager and
zealous, are the most healthy indications that you can find
in any free government. I believe, moreover, and you believe it, that the party in power will fill the government

offices to a great extent with men holding the same political belief that the party entertains. This is a necessity. You will never reach that beatific condition of government when it will be otherwise. Suppose that the only issue were hard or soft money; a large majority of the people vote that they will have hard-money, and they elect a President upon that basis, what would you say to him if, continuing upon that basis, representing that idea, he placed at the head of the treasury, as its secretary, a man who believed in inflation? I have this to say: If I were a hard-money secretary of the treasury, and believed in it as thoroughly as I believe in it to-day, I would see to it that my first assistant, my second assistant, my third assistant, my chief clerk, and my subordinates, if I could command it, should be hard-money men too. I should see to it that they talked, when they talked anything, hard-money; that they talked hard-money out of the office; that they would be hard money all the way through. When I desired to advance hard-money ideas I wouldn't go to the soft-money men to help me. Suppose you undertake to reform the civil service. Let me say to you here that out of one or two of these great aggregations which we call the Democratic and the Republican parties must these offices be filled — either by Republicans or by Democrats. From which aggregation will you fill them? If you desire men who can write, where will you find the most men who can read and who can write? In the Republican party or in the ranks of the Democracy? If you want to find the great mass of the intelligent, honest, patriotic thought of the country, where will you go? The question is answered by your own hearts the instant it is asked. You know that within the boundaries of this Republican party of the nation, within its great temple, on the walls of which are inscribed the grandest records either of ancient or modern history,—

that in that temple are to-day assembled, and have been
gathered for a quarter of a century past, the wisest, and
purest, and best, and the most patriotic men on the continent.

"I ask you one other question.   From either one of
these two aggregations must your choice be made.   Imagine
such a thing as a Democratic success.   I do not care how
well-intentioned Mr. Tilden may be; I do not care how
resolute he may be; that man doesn't live sufficiently
strong to encounter a solid party against him.   There
would come floating down upon him like the resistless
waves of old ocean a tide that would sweep that little
bachelor clean up into the clouds if he didn't obey; that
would demand for these Confederate Democrats, who have
for sixteen years been dieting on east wind, a reward
for their services.   Think of the city of Washington.
Think of the congregations that would be there assembled.
Think of the thousands, and tens of thousands of the helpless, hopeless, hatless, shirtless, and lost Confederates there
appealing for an office and in search of a reform of civil
service.   Is that your remedy?   Straws show which way
the wind blows.   We vainly thought that the old Union
cause had triumphed.   We saw the old flag floating above
our heads, and supposed that the cause which it represented had triumphed.   We thought we had triumphed,
but in an idle hour, in an evil hour, our outposts were un-
guarded and the rebel host rushed in, and when they came
in they threw their pickets out.   The old skirmishers of
the Union army, the old Boys in Blue, who had watched the
doors and attended to the messages of Congress, have surrendered — surrendered to the foe who but eleven years
ago surrendered to them.   In went again the old conquered
Confederate soldier.   Out went the victorious soldier of
the Union.   Soldier after soldier who had fought that the

Union might live was driven from his place. Soldier after soldier, with the old plantation threat on his lips, who had fought that the Union might be destroyed, was put back in his place of triumph. Doesn't it seem as if Samuel J. Tilden, in 1864, spoke the words of prophesy when he said the war was a failure?

" Point me to a city under Democratic rule where the treasury has not been robbed. Point me to a city under Democratic government where the revenues have not been plundered. Point me to a little patch of land, I do not care how small it is, that has been under Democratic management for years, and I will show you withered fields and blasted political crops. Point me to any place where their policy has had its full swing, and I will show you poor schools, bootless men, shoeless children and ruined wives.

"They tell us that we have forced upon the nation an ignorant vote, that the black man is ignorant. But the black man knows he is ignorant. He has learned that much. We erect school-houses; the rebels tear them down. We send teachers; they slaughter them. And yet, with the blood of the innocent citizen upon their hands, and with the smoke of burning asylums and school-houses on their garments, they turn around to this great loyal North, and spit upon their history for the last twenty years, and ask that *they* may be permitted to take charge of our national affairs. More than all that. Not only have they embodied assassination in their creed, but they have, by a reign of terror which is a disgrace to modern civilization and would be a discredit to a Turk, driven every white man from their midst. Farmers of Stephenson county, business men of this thriving city, send your son with his youthful hopes and bounding ambition to the South. Let him take that free tongue with him, the free thought and free speech which he has enjoyed here, and go there. He

goes there in pursuit of an honest living in an honest way.
How is he met? Broad-hatted Democratic lawyers demand
of him, not what he can do, but what does he think. And,
if his views on some political question do not agree with
those of the worthless men who were born there, he is denounced as a carpetbagger and shot in the night. I spit
upon this cry of carpetbagger. I believe in the carpetbag principle. I believe that there is no state in the Union,
no foot of soil in all its broad domain, upon which I am
not to be permitted to tread, a free man; and where I am
not to be permitted to utter what I think. And the man
who would deny me that privilege is a sneak, and if it
comes into the politics of the nation, the war is not yet
ended. I say, throw down every barrier, remove every
obstruction, open every avenue of enterprise. Let us have
it, for God's sake, if we have to fight for it; let us have the
largest, broadest freedom of thought and opinion of which
any government is capable. Who are you, what are you,
who talk about carpetbaggers? Were you born here?
Hundreds of thousands of you are from old fatherland,
where patriotic feeling is an instinct with the people —
thousands from the old Empire State. From all the hills
and valleys of New England and New York you have come
here, young men, poor men, filled, however, with that un-
conquerable spirit which is characteristic of a carpetbagger;
and you have reared here the most magnificent empire that
the world has ever seen. I say, go on with the carpetbag
spirit. Send it all over the South. Make its fields blossom.
Make every swift-running stream active with the wheels of
swift-running machinery; develop its mines; increase its
resources; develop everything of a material character;
educate its people; and then we will have what we will
never have otherwise,— a united, homogeneous nationality.

"The Democracy have nominated Samuel J. Tilden on a platform which reads well enough, but who is he? I desire to say no unkind thing of Mr. Tilden, but the unkindest things that I could say of him would be truthful things. Suppose that I should say that he was born with a Democratic platform in one hand and a railroad charter in the other; that, at the early age of twelve years, he was incorporated; that he has had no soul since; that he was consolidated with the Democratic party and run in connection with Bill Tweed as a great railroad wrecker and great railroad physician, under whose ministrations there have been more corporation funerals and at whose door have been seen larger processions of corporation hearses than all the corporations that have ever flourished in all the times before. I ask this simple question of him: Mr. Tilden, where were you during the war? What were you doing during the war? It is an important question for us to ask. I ask the loyal men to-day, whose hearts and all whose sympathies and feelings were with and are with the great cause, where was he? Now and then we have a stray affidavit from some inconspicuous individual that Samuel J. Tilden quietly, modestly, unobtrusively, was, away down at the bottom of his little corporation heart, a genuine, all-wool, yard-wide, patriotic man. I have never found it out. I do not believe in patriotism that is so stealthy; I do not believe in loyalty that is so shy; I do not believe in an emergency as great as that was that made so good a man hide the whole of patriotism under so small a bushel."

Returning to Chicago, Mr. Storrs again addressed an enthusiastic mass-meeting in that city. Being one of many speakers on this occasion, his remarks were brief. He said: ·

"The Republican party had a great mission during the war. It has had a great mission since the war. Its mis-

sion since the war has been to convert the Democratic
party. And how splendidly it has succeeded is evidenced
in the fact that in their last platform of principles they
unhesitatingly declare that they are opposed to stealing.
Within twenty-five years we expect to get them to ratify
the whole Decalogue. Think of it! The Democratic
party opposed to larceny! And in favor of reform! A
party not satisfied with stealing trivial things, but that
runs off with a whole state. A party that undertook to
force the nation to steal the government opposed to larceny! God save the mark! I desire to enlarge the proposition of the next governor of this state. He insists that
the only question before us is, ' Who are the best men for
president and vice-president of the United States? It is a
broader question, a more serious question. The question
is, Which of the two parties is the safest to be intrusted with
the management of our national affairs? If you took the
Blessed Saviour and put him at the head of the Democratic
party, elected him its president, with its feeling, its history, its traditions, its spirit, he would be absolutely helpless for the accomplishment of reform. I am opposed to
the Democratic party because it has a consistent, unvary-
ing record, injurious to the best interests of the people,
and destructive, if carried out, of our national existence.
I am opposed to the Democratic party because it sought
the destruction of our cause, and I don't believe it wise to
intrust the affairs of a great empire to the members of a
political organization within ten years after they sought to
annihilate it. The logic is short, it is clear, it is plain, it
is unmisunderstandable. I am prepared to accept with
certain qualifications their protestations of repentance, but
the repentance has not been long enough.

"I want them to be engaged in good works as long as
they have been engaged in bad works, and if we wait for

the expiration of that period of probation, we will be dead, and our children afterwards, before the Democratic party succeeds to power. The Democratic party is in favor of purifying the civil service of the government. How do they propose to do it? Have they told you? They are in favor of an honest currency. What currency do they propose to give you? Have they told you? They say they are in favor of the resumption of specie payments. How are they to resume? Have they told you? Their platform is full of denunciations from the beginning to the end, and the curious feature of the platform of 1876 is that it denounces every Democratic measure since 1860. They insist upon it that the Republican party which they arraign has impeded that desired result. What financial policy has the Democratic party had since 1860? None whatever, except in 1868 they did invent a platform and put forth a principle insisting upon it that the national debt should be paid in greenbacks, a policy that would have resulted in the repudiation of the national debt and the destruction and swamping of every national interest.

"No single living Democrat occupying a prominent political position since 1860 has proposed a scheme for the reform of the Civil Service. They have had the power this winter in one branch of the National Government. How have they reformed the service? No measure has been introduced for that purpose. They have had control over the appointments, and such a raft of Confederates, believing that the Lost Cause was finally won, was never before seen as gathered in that City of Washington to catch the crumbs that might fall from the Speaker's table. Tray, Blanche, and Sweetheart, sutlers, commissaries, privates, and officers in the Confederate service from the beginning to the end, knowing that their victory had finally been achieved, rushed to Washington by countless hundreds and made night hideous by their howls for place, demanding the reward of their services.

"They ask us, ' Will you shake the bloody shirt ?' Who is responsible for the blood on the shirt ?   Whose blood is it ?   I would not as a Republican, and, as I think, as a patriotic citizen, needlessly engender the bitterness which the war brought about, but if I am to choose, and my thousands of fellow-citizens who surround me to-night, if you are to choose — if the choice is to be laid between the boy who shed his blood that your nationality might be preserved, and the man who shed his that it might be destroyed, no gushing talk about shaking hands over the gaping chasm will make you hesitate long about the decision. You can call it the bloody shirt or not, as you please. First, last, and all the while, as long as I have the capacity to distinguish the difference of men when public benefactions are to be bestowed, I am, thank God, in favor of giving them to him who fought that the nation might live, rather than to him who fought that the nation might be destroyed."

VII.

THE CAMPAIGN OF 1880.

"LEAVING that wonderful city of mine, enthroned on the edges of the great inland sea, coming away across 2,000 miles of plain and mountain to this gem on the Pacific coast, this jewel which rests upon the edge of that wonderful ocean, I find they are both patriotic cities, both born of patriotism. Will you allow me to carry back to my fellow-citizens when I return home the message from San Francisco to Chicago that this wonderful city is true to her birth which made her a free state, and is true to that great party which made us a nation. I come from the Atlantic to the Pacific and one flag covers us; wherever I am I am a citizen of the United States; and when I think of all these splendid achievements and of our party, we did it, we did it, and the poorest of us, however little we may have of other worldly possessions, these splendid achievements are our patrimony, and with these we are rich indeed. This great party, the pride of humanity everywhere, confronts to-day the Democratic party, a party that asks that the past be buried, and I do not wonder at it; a party that insists that no previous record shall be examined — I am not surprised at it; a party that wishes to look to the future only — I am not astonished at it, for if the record of the party to which I belong and you belong

199

were leprous with guilt as theirs is, and were stained all
over with crime as theirs is; if the political history of our
party were as theirs is, not merely criminal but crime
itself, I would ask, as they ask, that the past be forgotten.
Are these dead issues ? They claim so ; I think not.   The
great effort of the Democratic party of to-day is to unload
its history, to run away from its reputation and its character.   It is a hard thing to do.   They discover that character is always in issue.   No man asks for employment
without he puts his character in issue.   You don't employ
men on their platforms or on their promises.   The banker
would not employ the pilfering clerk of last month, even if
his platform of next month embodied the Ten Commandments and Christ's Sermon on the Mount.

"You perhaps by this time have discovered that I am
not in favor of a change, except in the better and qualified
sense.   I am in favor of all changes that look to improvement.   I would be in favor of a change from hell to purgatory, but not from earth to purgatory."

These words were the beginning of a speech, delivered by Mr. Storrs in the Grand Opera House, San
Francisco, on the 15th of September, 1880, which called
from the *Chronicle* the following day the statement
that—

"It is risking nothing to say that the great audience
which crammed the Grand Opera House last night from
pit to gallery, to hear the famous orator from Illinois,
Hon. Emery A. Storrs, has not been surpassed in San
Francisco in point of numbers, intelligence and enthusiasm.
Long before half-past 7 o'clock, half an hour before
the time announced for the opening of the meeting, hundreds reluctantly turned from the doors, unable to squeeze
their way into the immense-edifice.   There were ladies
willing to brave the discomforts of standing if they could

but get within the theater, men so anxious to hear Mr.
Storrs that they stood in the aisles and passage ways packed
liked sardines in boxes, able to hear the fine voice of the
speaker but unable to catch a glimpse of him, The enthusiasm, as might be expected, was unparalleled.   Every
telling point made by the speaker — and his speech fairly
bristled with them — was applauded to the echo."

But this political harangue — one of a short series
on the Pacific slope — was not the first of the labors of
Mr. Storrs during the great campaign of 1880. He
had inaugurated the fight in a splendid address at a
mass meeting, at Chicago, of those favoring the nomination of Gen. Grant for a third term, held immediately
prior to the nominating convention. The address, setting forth the attitude of a great commander, the colossal
egotism of "the independent scratcher," and the
"third term" issue, was a field for common quotation
by the after-campaign speeches of that fall.   Mr. Storrs
said :

"I can say without the slightest degree of extravagance that it has never been the fortune of any man to
face, on a political occasion, an audience more splendid in
enthusiasm, grander in its tone and quality, than the vast
assemblage gathered here to-night.   It is an audience
called together on no common occasion and assembled for
no ordinary purpose.   It is an audience of the leading men
and women of the chiefest city of the great Northwest.   It
is an audience gathered together here in an emergency to
protect the fair escutcheon of the great state of Illinois
from an impending stab of dishonor, and, God knows, it
will protect it.   It is an audience gathered to celebrate the
praises of no common man, an audience met from all over
this State, merely to testify what all the world has testified,

that we have in our midst the chiefest citizen of the world.
And the broad-browed men of Chicago that have, within
the period of nine years, lifted it from ashes and made it
the proudest city of the world, seated like a queen enthroned
by the shore of her great lake, have no apologies to offer
because they are here to night demanding the nomination
of U. S. Grant. The city of Chicago, Mr. Chairman, never
begged a favor ; it never won a fight that it didn't win in
front, and it never yet trembled in the presence of an
adversary.   The city of Chicago is a great Republican city;
it is the imperial city of the carpetbagger who has carved
out in this Western world, within the period of twenty-five
years, an empire the most splendid that the sun in all his
course shines upon, an empire of the light of which the
'independent scratcher' never dreamed.

"Who is this man that has called this vast audience
together, utterly untitled, who holds no office, who wields
no patronage, who manages no bureau ? He is a great
majestic prince, enthroned in the hearts of 48,000,000 of
people.   He reigns there by their suffrages ; and this side
the Plutonian region of Democracy, this side the purgatorial region of the half-way house of independentism,
there is no man to molest or make him afraid.   I speak
to-night not alone of this hero.   I cannot speak for this
great citizen without speaking of the Republican party.
From boyhood up to manhood I have been and am a member
of that party, stalwart at the outset and stalwart now, per-
pendicular as a ramrod, believing in its faith in the inner-
most recesses of my soul, never doubting that from its birth
down to this hour its supremacy has been absolutely essential to the well-being of this country.   I talk, then, of that
grand old party ; I talk of its grand leader, as grand as the
party and as great.   I can say, that when I look back on
our history I can discern a great party which has for a

quarter of a century preserved its identity ; a party often depressed, never extinguished ; a party which, though often tainted with the faults of the age, has always been in advance of the age ; a party which, though guilty of some errors, has the glory of having established our liberties on a firm foundation ; and of that party I am proud to be a member. It was that party which, at the very threshold of its career, confronted the shameful doctrine that freedom was sectional and slavery was national, rescued the Territories from the grasp of slavery, and dedicated them forever after to freedom — to free men, free thought, and free speech. It is that party which, in vindication of its ideas of freedom, elected Lincoln president of the United States ; which found treason in every department of the Government ; which found its fleet scattered over every sea ; its arsenals plundered, its forts in the hands of traitors, its little army shivered to fragments ; which found every branch of the public service paralyzed, the national flag dishonored even when flying over its own forts ; which found hostile armies arrayed against it ; which, compelled to appeal to the patriotism of the people for national salvation, made the appeal ; which met an armed rebellion vast in extent and malignant in spirit ; which saved this nation to be the custodian of free government among men. It is that party which, true to the great cause which it represented, made the promise of freedom to the slave and kept that promise good. It is that party which, when the war for national preservation closed in victory, declared that forever after slavery should be extirpated from the soil of the republic ; which declared that all persons born beneath the flag, or naturalized here, should be citizens ; which guaranteed to all citizens equality of civil and political privileges ; which placed beyond the possibility of repudiation our national debt, and made firm and secure

the national credit. It is that party which has restored
our currency, and made every paper dollar in the pockets
of the laboring man worth one hundred cents. It is that
party which compelled the British Government to pay to
our own people millions of money, for damages inflicted
upon our commerce by rebel cruisers fitted out in their
ports. It is that party which by wise legislation has sought
the execution of all our constitutional guarantees to the
citizen, the purity of the ballot-box, and the protection of
the polls against violence, terrorism, and fraud. It is that
party which has ranked among its leaders the purest
patriotism, the staunchest courage, the wisest thought, the
best culture, and the loftiest statesmanship of the nation,
and among its rank and file that solid citizenship which
demands just and honest government, and will be satisfied
with nothing less. I look with pride on all that the
Republican party has done for the cause of human freedom. I see it now hard pressed, struggling with difficulties,
but still fighting the good fight. At its head I see men who
have inherited the spirit and the virtues, as well as the blood,
of the old champions and martyrs of freedom. I see pre-
siding here to-night the only living son and descendant of
Abraham Lincoln, whose name and whose memory are
enshrined in every patriotic heart. I see here to-night the
son of that great patriotic statesman, Stephen A. Douglas,
who, when treason raised its hands, cast party to the winds,
stood like a rock for the Union, and died with patriotic words
upon his lips. I look at the call in obedience to which this
magnificent audience is assembled, and see at its head a
name which we all delight to honor; one steadfast and
ever reliable as a legislator, wise in counsel, prompt in
action, earnest in opinion, dauntless in courage, incorrupt-
ible in integrity; who for nearly twenty years maintained
the honor of our state in the councils of the nation, always

speaking for freedom ; who for eight years dignified and honored the American name and character abroad, and who, as Minister to France, during the terrible siege of Paris, when every other foreign representative had fled, remained faithful at his post, gathering in safety under his country's flag the citizens of every land who sought the protection of its sheltering folds — Elihu B. Washburne. To the same call I see the name of the peerless soldier, the ever-faithful Republican, the true man, the firm friend, the stalwart senator, the smiter of treason — John A. Logan. The last words of the great Michigan senator, Chandler, patriotic and eloquent words, uttered the language of this call, and declared, with Lincoln and Douglas and Logan and Washburne, that he, too, believed that the success of the Republican party would be best promoted by the nomination and election of Ulysses S. Grant as President of the United States. The millions of oppressed, bullied and terrorized Republicans of the South, white and black, speak the same sentiment. To this party — to these men — I propose to attach myself ; and, while one shred of the old banner is left flying, by that banner will I at least be found.

"I confess that I am not independent of these considerations. I have not scaled, and shall not attempt to scale, those dizzy heights from which I could look down upon them. I am content to remain in the valleys, where I find such company as I have named, rather than to seek those drearier and colder, if loftier, mountain peaks to which that select few aspire who profess to see in the nomination and election of General Grant as President of the United States dangers which the wisdom of the country is not able to perceive. Who am I, to threaten that wisdom, patriotism, experience, and intelligence, that unless it surrenders its opinion for mine I will refuse obedience to orders, and bolt the ticket ? This colossal egotism is called 'independence.' This man who parades it is known as the 'independent scratcher,' independent of the party to which he belongs, save when the minority to which he is attached can rule ; whose ticket he votes, whose principles he condescendingly espouses, and whose candidates he patronizingly supports at spasmodic intervals, the recurrence of which it is given to no one to foretell. I do not include among the 'independent scratchers' those true Republicans who honestly prefer the nomination by the forthcoming National Republican Convention of some other candidate than General Grant. Those true and earnest Republicans who prefer either Mr. Washburne, or Mr. Sherman, or Mr. Blaine, or Mr. Edmunds will surely find the claims of their favorites fairly considered by that convention, and will as surely support its nominee as I am sure to support him, not haltingly, and unwillingly, but with whole soul and in dead earnest. The friends of General Grant do not bolt, and they neither boast nor threaten ; but they do better — they succeed. The 'independent scratcher' is either that ambitious young man very proud of knowing what older and wiser men have found it convenient to forget, or that ambitious man of any age who, itching for notoriety, must find some one more distinguished and greater than himself to scratch.

"In 1864 the 'independent scratcher' in the state of Illinois engaged in a scheme to force the withdrawal of Abraham Lincoln, and attempted to carry through our state convention at Springfield a resolution condemning Lincoln and his administration. The outraged patriotism and good sense of the people, the dangers of insurrection in our very midst, frightened the 'independent scratcher' back into the ranks which he attempted to desert.

"In 1872 the 'independent scratchers,' wretchedly in

the minority, organized a free-trade and revenue reform party at Cincinnati, but at its head the most rabid and ultra protectionist and the bitterest hater of the Democratic party on earth, and in a body melted into the Democratic fold. The combination was terribly beaten. Many of them returned to us in 1876, and we were well nigh defeated; and but for the fact that there was then at the head of the government a man with whom no one could either trifle or trade, surrounded by a cabinet inspired by his own courage and patriotism, the nation would have been involved in another rebellion. From this coalition thousands of honest, earnest but deceived Republicans have withdrawn themselves. They have by years of faithful service expiated their offense. They are with us now. They are here to-night, and after having once tasted the bitter fruits of bolting experience, they are comfortably back in the old mansion, feeling ' themselves again,' and determined to never wander more.

"General Grant is to-day, and has been for the past three years, a private citizen, out of office, with no patronage at his disposal, resting his claims purely upon his strength with the people as a man. It is idle to talk of the precedents of our history, for our history furnishes no precedent. There is no instance in our history where a president, after holding the office for two successive terms, retires to the ranks of private citizenship, and is afterward called upon to again fill the position. Washington retired after serving two terms. Jefferson did also, and declined a successive nomination for a third term after it became clear that it was impossible for him to secure it. Madison held the office two terms, and no renomination was tendered him. Jackson held the office two terms, and no renomination was tendered him. Grant held the office two terms, retired at the close of his second term. After an interval of four years, a nomination is again tendered him, for which our history furnishes no precedent whatever. Why should the people of this country, after having had four years' opportunity to calmly and justly judge the man, be deprived by a sentimental objection of this character of his services through another trying period in our history? Who has made such a law? With a wider experience and a riper judgment than he ever before possessed, with an emergency upon us through which we know he could safely carry us, who is there to say the majority of this people shall not again elevate the private citizen of their choice into the highest place? The people of this country have never found any difficulty in ridding themselves of a president whom they did not like at the end of his first term. They found no difficulty in retiring both the Adamses, Van Buren, Polk, Pierce, Buchanan and Johnson, after they had served one term. The people have never yet made a mistake in electing an incumbent to the second term. They have made several mistakes in electing a man to the first term. Quick to discover such a mistake, however, they never repeat it. The people of this country are better judges of the fitness of their public servants than any little band of philosophers who have vexed us with their theories. Conceding that there is no constitutional objection to the election of General Grant, it is still urged that it is unduly honoring one man at the expense of all the others. I am in favor of General Grant's nomination, not to honor him, but to benefit the country. This great office is to be filled, not for the accommodation of the individual, but to promote the public interests. It is not, as some people seem to conceive, an office to be passed around among certain invited guests like refreshments at a picnic, but a great office, to be filled for the public good.

"While the friends of General Grant sincerely believe

that there is before us such an emergency as can best be filled by him — while they sincerely believe that his election will do more to insure quiet and a finally just solution of our political troubles than that of any other Republican — while they believe that he possesses the confidence of the people North and South in a larger measure than any other man in the nation — they do not believe, and they are very far from saying, that he is the only man whom the Republican party can elect. But it nevertheless is true that the most serious problem in our politics to-day and for the future grows out of the constant menace of a solid South. Who can divide that solid South, and thus solve the problem? I do say that General Grant is the only man in all this country who can solve the problem of the solid South by dividing the South, so that it shall not be solid. I do say that he is the only man in all this country whom the Republican party can nominate for whom the negro will risk his life and property to vote. I do say that he can carry three and probably five Southern states, and can divide the vote in all the others, and that no other Republican can carry one. If Grant is nominated, the negro will vote, and will vote for him. If he is not nominated, the negro will not vote at all. If Grant is nominated, the terrorized and outraged Southern white Republican will vote, and vote for him. If he is not nominated, he will not vote at all.

"The country demands for its leader a man whose very name stands for peace, whose very presence is a restraint upon the law-breaker. Grant means peace. He smote secession hip and thigh in open warfare; it fears him now as it feared him then; it respects him now as it respected him then. I am doing no injustice to any living man when I say that for all such emergencies General Grant fills the requirements of the occasion in a larger measure than any other living man. It is idle to claim that all our dangers are past, because during the present session of congress the Democratic party has suspended for the time being the prosecution of its revolutionary schemes. The very fact that Grant is the probable candidate of the Republican party, and that the complete development of their schemes would render his nomination a certainty, has awed them into silence, and they stand, even in his prospective presence, tongue-tied and dumb before the world.

"This great character stands forth to-day, bright and shining, the admiration of the world. Palsied be the hand which would strike it, and blistered the tongue which would defame it! It is not merely because he is so well worthy of this great honor, but because we sincerely believe that, more than any other man, can he serve his country and promote its best interests in that position. From first to last he has never known defeat. His record from Belmont to Appomattox is one unbroken chain of victories which honored his country and secured for himself the admiration of his foes. He never left a duty unperformed. He never made a promise which he did not keep. He never turned his back upon a friend. There is more wisdom in his silence than in the speech of most men. There is not a boast in all his long and splendid career. Bitterly and malignantly as he has been assailed, no word of slander ever escaped his lips. Prudent and cautious in counsel, he never fails to act when a conclusion has been reached, and is as prompt in action as he is prudent in preparation. In his first inaugural he met the clamor for an inflated currency by a demand for the payment of our national debt in coin, and by his veto struck a blow at all schemes for a depreciated currency from which they never recovered. He inaugurated and carried through a plan of peaceful arbitration by which grave international disputes were settled and made our flag and our country respected throughout the world. As modest as he was great, he never set his individual judgment against the clearly expressed public will, but, renouncing his desire, he declared that he had no policy opposed to the will of the people. Leaving his high office, he has made the circuit of the globe, and has been received under every flag with such honors as no man ever received before. Unaffected by them, he never for one moment lost that wonderful pose which has carried him through so many great events. Returning home, thus honored and thus laureled, the brave, the honest, the patriotic, the modest soldier, statesman, and citizen, places all these honors in the hands of his countrymen.

"'There is no elevation so high that he is dizzied by it. There is no place so low and humble which he may fill that he does not uncomplainingly and faithfully perform all its duties.

> ' Draw him strictly so
> That all who view the place may know
> He needs no trappings of fictitious fame.'

" This is our true knight, 'without fear, without reproach,' and without a plume. Here, in his own state — here in the chief city of that state, have the thousands who are assembled here to night met, not to place fresh laurels upon his brow, not to add an additional honor to his long roll of honors, by uttering the voice of his own state in his behalf in National convention, but to save the state from such a dishonor as any halting upon our part would surely reflect upon it.

" He has enemies here, as had Lincoln and Douglas before him. They can and they will be silenced. Joining hands with the other states, Illinois shall stand in the line and shall utter her voice for her honored citizen. Assailing no competitor, the rank and file, the Old Guard, declare that they are for Grant, because again and again they have marched under his banners, but never to defeat,—and every battlefield over which his flag ever floated was a field of victory. The work of our great leader is not finished, and will not be until he has led the hosts of freemen to that future, when there shall be within all the boundaries of the Republic not one foot of ground over which the flag floats and upon which a citizen stands who may not speak, and think, and vote as he pleases. Prostrate to-day are millions of our fellow-citizens, our equals before the law, but shorn of that equality. Under the banners of of our chosen leader shall they be lifted up?

" When justice reigns throughout all our borders, and every citizen, white and black, stands equal before the law, when North and South, and East and West, there shall be found no privileged class, then, 'let us have peace;' that Peace which shall come to us with her silken banners floating in every breeze, with Justice and Mercy bearing her train. Justice to all, friend and foe. Such a peace leaves no traces of bitterness behind it, and smiling fields and the roar of thriving cities, and the hum of busy machinery, and happy homes, and a prosperous and prospering people mark its pathway, and, better than all and grander than all else, there shall be in all its march neither shackled wrists nor fettered tongues."

The entire campaign, succeeding the exciting nomination of James A. Garfield, in the face of "the 306" Grant adherents, was a succession of orations to the orator Storrs. The simple reading of his political addresses — and political addresses are usually reckoned most interesting from the occasion — create enthusiasm ; but the influence they wielded when delivered can only be imagined from their reception at the time. There was a bitter fight over seats in the Illinois State convention, on the 19th of May, preceding the national assemblage, and Mr. Storrs was the champion of one delegation. The *Illinois State Register*, a Democratic paper, said of the debate:

"The speech of Emery A. Storrs was an extraordinary effort. It was surpassingly brilliant, burnished, as it was, by the genius of the orator and of the poet. Mr. Storrs exhibited his gifts to the best advantage. He bore down upon the rioters, the bribe-givers and bribe-takers of Chicago with all the blazonry of his unequaled powers of denunciation, of ridicule, of sarcasm, of humor, leaping the difficult places in his pathway by a glowing appeal for Grant, an apotheosis of Republican stalwartism, a shining tribute to the flag, and crowned his cause with a trumpet-tongued cry for harmony, for conciliation, for peace, that won his audience, and supplied an ample apology for the claim which he so fervently espoused. He wanted only thirty-six of the ninety-two delegates — wanted them in the name of justice, in the name of popular rights, and above all, in the name of the great leader who had done more for his country than any other living man, and whose splendid form towered into the very sunshine of eternal fame. The orator closed his speech with a peroration, the classic finish of which, though capping a faulty argument, was worthy of Sheridan in the British Parliament, or of Sergeant S. Prentiss, when, pleading for his contested seat as a representative, he electrified the American Congress forty years ago. The victory was complete. The orator had swept triumphantly the chords of human passion, and the vote then promptly taken gave Grant all that had been claimed for him in Cook county. This episode in Illinois politics sets a notable precedent in party organization, and illustrates the highest ingenuity of party leadership."

John A. Logan called it " the magnificent speech ". The argument was carried from the State to the National convention, and, as Mr. Storrs battled for the seating of the Grant delegates in that memorable assemblage of June, 1880, the scene became one of intense excitement. A hurricane of applause from the stalwarts in the gallaries interrupted Mr. Storrs as he drew his masterly argument to a conclusion. The Blaine men answered with cries and yells. The Grant men cheered again and even louder, and then occurred a chaos of uproar such as has never before or since been known in a National convention. Flags were stripped from in front of the gallaries and waved madly. Delegates rushed excitedly through the hall, interchanging jubilations, some loudly singing patriotic songs. For nearly an hour Babel prevailed, and the chairman's gavel was powerless to restore order, while Mr. Storrs, standing upon the platform, looked quietly around him and smiled, until, in a sudden lull, he concluded his speech with the words:

" Gentlemen, give the grand old State that never knew a draft, and never filled up a regiment with paper soldiers — give the grand old State, the home of Lincoln and Douglas and Grant, a fair chance. Put no indignity on the honor of her sons. Then, if you can nominate the worthy son of Ohio, John Sherman, do it fairly ; and when the hysterical gentlemen who are afraid that he is not popular enough to carry Illinois are inquiring their way to the polls, the grand old guard, whose representative I am, will have planted the banner of victory on the citadels of the enemy. By all means, let us be free and absolutely untrammeled ; put no just cause for complaint on us ; have no hesitancy in a candidate who exhibits scars, provided they are hon-

orable scars, won in honorable welfare. Select no man
without a record; pull no skulker from under the ammuni-
tion wagon, because he shows not upon him the signs of
battle; take the old tried hero,—let us take him if we can
get him; and then I believe, with the old guard behind
him, who have never kept step in this world to any music
but the music of the Union, and with the friends of Blaine,
and the friends of Sherman, and the friends of all good
men, a victory will be achieved, the like of which has
never been recorded in the annals of our national politics.
Citizens of one country, members of one party, let us
remember that, while we accept no indignities from our
enemies, we hope and trust and pray our friends will put
none upon us. Here in the midnight, with the storm without, and these assembled Republicans within, we are first
to be just, first to be fair, and victory is ours as sure as the
morning comes."

Such was the scene evoked in "a convention of
statesmen" by Mr. Storrs' oratory, and it is probably
unexampled in our nation's history. His argument at
Burlington, Iowa, July 16, 1880, was a type of his clos-
est reasoning; and was regarded by the Republican
Central Committee as so convincing that it was made a
campaign document. Its style is shown by an excerpt
from his discussion of the various planks of the Democratic platform, entered into after a telling review and
comparison of the records of the two rival parties:

"Their fourth plank announces this doctrine : 'Home-
rule, honest money consisting of gold and silver and paper
convertible into coin on demand, and the strict maintenance of the public faith, state and national, and a tariff
for revenue only.'

"What does the democratic party mean by 'home-

rule'?   The evidences which they have furnished us of
home rule in these states from which the one hundred and
thirty-eight electoral votes are to be derived are not
encouraging.   From the practical evidences they have
given us, home-rule means with them the right to fetter
opinions, to stifle speech, to terrorize the voter and bully
the courts at home.   It means the White-Liner and the
Ku-Klux at home ; it means the argument of the shot-gun;
it means the persuasion of Chisholm and Dixon and hundreds of others by the gentle methods of assassination ; it
means the enlightment of the negro and the white Republican voter, by midnight raids, by burning homes and
indiscriminate slaughters.   This is the practice of the
home-rulers in the south, and this is the practice which
this platform ratifies and endorses and the right which it
demands.   Nothing, however, more impudent in politics
can be found than the declaration of this plank in the
platform for honest money.   Let us compare the practice of
the Democratic party in the past with its present professions.

"The Democratic platform in 1868 called for the payment of the public debt in greenbacks, which, had it been
adopted, would have resulted in such an inflation of our
currency as to have rendered the resumption of specie payments an absolute impossibility, which would have been
the dishonor of not only the public debt, but of the greenback itself.   They aimed a fatal blow at the national credit,
for they demanded 'equal taxation of every species of
property according to its real value, including government
bonds and other public securities.'   Had this policy been
adopted, my fellow citizens, do you suppose that it would
have been within the range of possibility for us to have
reduced the interest upon our public debt?   Would not
the national honor have been so shaken that resumption

would have been an impossibility, and honest money something in a distance so far removed that we could never expect to live to reach it ? In 1869 the public credit bill, which pledged the nation to the payment of its debt in coin, was opposed in Congress by the almost solid vote of the Democratic party. Clamoring to-day for honest money, they opposed the resumption bill which makes the greenback and national banknote honest money. Their platform in 1876, written by a shrewd capitalist who had an eye to the vote of the state of New York, and supposed that he would have the South at all events, for the purpose of catching the capitalist vote, declared for honest money and denounced the Republican party for hindering resumption, the entire Democracy having previously opposed the scheme of resumption, but in January, 18.6, but a few months after this convention met, the bill to repeal the resumption act received 112 votes in the House of Representatives, all Democratic but one. In June, 1876, as a rider to the civil appropriation bill, an amendment repealing the resumption act received solid Democratic support. Does this look like honest money ? The party was not converted by its platform, for the party understood the purpose of the platform. A bill to repeal the fixing of the time for resumption August 5th, 1876, received in the House 176 votes, all Democratic except three, more than a year after the declaration of the platform of 1876. In October, 1877, Mr. Ewing reported from the committee on banking and currency a bill to repeal the resumption act. This is the practice of the party as against its profession. It was the practice of the party not only in our national Congress, but throughout the states. In this honest state of Iowa the platform of the Democratic party for 1877 declared: 'We demand the immediate repeal of the specie resumption act.' In 1878, still unconverted, the Democracy of the state of Iowa in its platform declares: 'We favor the immediate repeal of the resumption act.' This is the sentiment of the party. Its constitutional doctrines and traditions, and its votes, wherever its votes would tell, have been from the beginning down even to to-day against honest money, for which in its platform to-day it lying and hypocritically declares.

"Their fifth plank declares: 'The subordination of the military to the civil power, and a thorough and genuine reform of the civil service.'

"This simply means that the military power shall not be used to protect the citizen, nor to put down armed and organized resistance to the enforcement of the laws. It means that the moonshiner shall go unpunished; it means that wherever an independent Democrat determines that he will not pay the revenues which the government imposes upon the business which he is pursuing, that no military power shall be employed to compel such payment; it means that acts of Congress may be resisted in their execution by organized bodies of armed men; that no military power may intervene to enforce these acts of Congress, nor to put down such armed and organized resistance to their enforcement. It means that an act of Congress providing for an honest ballot, and for a peaceable poll, shall be rendered nugatory by the surrounding of polls by armed and organized bands of ruffians, and that the military powers of the nation shall not be invoked to protect the citizens in the enjoyment of their privileges, the enjoyment of which the constitutional amendment solemnly guarantees them.

"It is well that the Democratic party was exceedingly brief in its demand for a thorough and genuine reform of the civil service. It states no plan — it states no evil that it seeks to remedy. If it is patriotic men — men thoroughly devoted to the nation and to its preservation, thoroughly devoted to the support of the great guarantees furnished by the constitutional amendments that we desire — shall we find them in the Democratic party? Does it possess more of the intelligence of this country than the Republican party?

"This party has organized in itself the bulk of the ignorance, the violence, and the crime of the country. If culture and superior education are desired in our office-holders is there even a Democrat who will claim that better facilities are furnished for procuring these requisites from the Democratic than from the Republican party? Will you, with the experience of the organization of the House of Representatives before you, contemplate what kind of a reform that will be which will result from the election of Hancock? Not only would the triumph of the Democratic party fail to promote any genuine reform of the civil service, but it would render such reform utterly impossible. No one expects the civil service to be reformed through any such curious and extraordinary channels.

"By their sixth plank the Democracy declare 'the right of a free ballot is a right preservative of all rights, and must and shall be maintained in every part of the United States.'

"From reading this platform one would almost come to the conclusion that the Democratic party had decided in its platform to state great truths which it had always opposed, and to assert great rights which it had always denied. The election laws of Congress, so called, were passed to secure a free and honest ballot, and to prevent fraud and violence at the polls. At the time they were passed the Democratic party solidly opposed them, and denounced them as unconstitutional, and has since that time, even by revolutionary schemes, steadily sought their repeal. The courts have sustained their constitutionality of those laws, and yet their repeal is as steadily sought.

"The whole current of Democratic History gives the lie to this protestation in favor of a free and honest ballot.

"They have never advocated a registry law, the purpose and fair operation of which where they have been in power would be to secure a free or honest ballot   No law for the registration of the voter and for the protection of the purity of the polls has ever been passed that has not encountered the opposition of the Democratic party, and when it has been in power such laws have uniformly fallen under their administration.

"The fraudulent vote of the city of New York for years and years is a steady commentary upon the falsity of this protestation. In 1868, as was subsequently demonstrated upon the trial of Tweed and the examination of his affairs, over twenty thousand votes were cast, or at least a fraudulent vote of twenty thousand in but very few wards of that city. In several precincts there were more votes counted—double the number of votes counted—than the entire population. This was under a Democratic administration. They opposed every registry scheme by which these gross and outrageous frauds might be prevented.

"But is there a free ballot in the South? Does any man of ordinary honesty and ordinary intelligence claim such a thing? Let us take a few examples. In 1872 the Republican vote of Alabama was 90,272, the vote of 1878 was nothing; and yet the Democratic vote was not increased to a larger extent than the increase in population would justify. Is that a free ballot?

"In 1872 the Republican vote in Arkansas was 41,373; in 1878 it was 115. The Democratic vote in the meantime had not increased, but this Republican vote had been terrorized, bulldozed and driven from the polls, and by threats, fraud and violence the expression of public opinion by the ballot was absolutely and utterly stifled; and yet the party guilty of this most stupendous crime sneakingly and hypocritically, in its platform, protests that the right of free ballot is a right preservative of all rights, and must, they say, be maintained in all parts of the United States.

"In 1872 the Republican vote of Mississippi was 82,175; in 1878 it had dwindled down to 1,168. This tremendous change cannot be accounted for by conversions. It is simply a dropping off of the vote, not an accession of Democratic strength, but a denial of the right of suffrage. Is this a free ballot?

"In their tenth plank the Democracy say: 'We congratulate the country upon the honesty and thrift of a Democratic Congress, which has reduced the public expenditures forty millions a year, and upon the continuation of prosperity at home and national honor abroad.'

"The first commentary upon that is that it is false; but this glaringly false pretense of economy will bear examination. How has this economy been exhibited? Is it economy? In the reduction of the army and in cutting down the pay of our officers. The spectacle of a crowd of rebel brigadiers in Congress, sitting in judgment on the pay of Sheridan and Sherman and Union soldiers and officers, is one which the loyal men of this country do not contemplate with any great degree of pleasure or satisfaction; but we have been compelled to witness it. Our army cut down and so crippled that it is absolutely inefficient to protect our frontiers, or indeed to protect us against mobs in our large cities throughout the entire country—is that economy? I regard it as the most wasteful extravagance.

"It refuses to make appropriations for the payments of

judgments procured in the court of claims against the
United States, and proclaims this as economy.   It refuses
to make appropriations for the payment of the expense of
our courts, and has left the federal courts throughout the
whole country so crippled that there has been no money to
pay jury service, and in numberless instances the marshals
have been compelled from their private funds to pay the
expenses of the administration of justice in the federal
courts.   This is not economy: this is a shameful neglect or
duty; a shameful denial of justice to the citizen; a shameful and a wasteful extravagance.

"It refuses to make appropriations to finish uncompleted public buildings, thereby vastly increasing the
expense when completion must ultimately be made.   It
has cut down the service in the department of the interior
and other departments to such an extent that the patent
office and pension bureau have been almost practically
closed.   It has refused to make sufficient appropriations
for the revenue cutter service, to the prejudice of the customs revenue, and has lost tens of thousands of dollars
from revenue where it has derived one from its niggardly
appropriation for that service.   It has refused to make
adequate appropriations for the signal service; it has practically refused appropriations for the repair and protection
of the navy yards, stations, armories and arsenals, suffering
these great properties to go to wasteful and ruinous decay.
It has refused to make adequate appropriations for the
increased expenses devolved upon the mint and assay offices,
rendered necessary by recent legislation, thus tending
to defeat the object of legislation.   It has refused
to make adequate appropriations for the survey of the
public lands; it has made grossly inadequate appropriations for lighthouses, beacons and fog stations, thus imper-
iling the safety of our merchant marine.   And, finally

by one great effort, to cut off the supply of lemonade to the members of the house of representatives; but, as history tells us, the supply was sought for by individual members from the senate department.

"At the close of this remarkable plank which I have just read to you, the country is congratulated by the Democratic party upon the continuation of prosperity at home and national honor abroad. But how in the light of history has this prosperity at home been secured, and this honor abroad been maintained? But for the large reduction of public expenditures, resulting from resumption of specie payments and strengthening of the public credit, and reduction of the rate of interest on the public debt, the thoroughness, efficiency and honesty with which all our custom duties and internal revenues have been collected and paid over, the country is indebted to a Republican administration."

Of his 4th of October speech at Toledo, Petroleum V. Nasby telegraphed:

"Storrs' meeting the largest ever held here. Speech a most brilliant one. Intense enthusiasm."

Said the Toledo *Blade*, in an editorial comment upon the occasion:

"The orator of the evening was worthy of his magnificent audience. Mr. Emery A. Storrs has no superior in the art of reaching the popular heart, of presenting great truths in a way that will at once charm and convince his hearers. He is a magician in the use of the English language to convey grand thoughts and pregnant facts. No wavering man in that vast assemblage left the hall unconvinced that the salvation of the country lay in Republican success."

General Garfield telegraphed from Mentor:

"Our people are crazy over you."

The Cleveland *Herald* in a report said :

"Nothing but a full report can do justice to Mr. Storrs' speech. His speech was the best of the campaign."

Regarding him as "golden-mouthed," the Cleveland *Leader* referred to him as "the Chrysostom of Chicago."

The Boston *Herald* said of a speech Mr. Storrs made at Newburyport, Mass., Oct. 7 :

"It was the ablest, cleanest cut and most impressive campaign speech that has been heard in Newburyport for years, many old residents saying they have heard nothing like it here since the days when Robert Rantoul was in his glory."

The *Gazette* of Boston said of a speech in that city :

"The speech of Mr. Emery A. Storrs, of Chicago, was the most brilliant piece of campaign oratory that has been heard for years in Boston — ardent, aggressive, and slashing into the Democratic lines with a vigor that reminds one of a dashing cavalry charge on the field of battle. In compliance with General Arthur's invitation, he addressed a mass meeting at the Cooper Union, in the city of New York, on the 20th of October. The New York *Times* said that his speech on that occasion 'gave the Republicans of New York a taste of a style of oratory to which they are not very much accustomed, and which has many other attractions than that of novelty. It was direct, pungent, witty, and forcible. Mr. Storrs kept the attention of his immense audience from the first to the last, and was frequently and heartily applauded. If any Democrat imagines that the laughter which he so frequently elicited was produced by tickling mere partisan prejudices, he will be undeceived if he undertakes to candidly explain away the points of Mr. Storrs' witticisms.'"

The very variety of styles in his great speeches prevented any evidence of existence of wearisomeness in any audience which ever listened to him. Take, for illustration of this quality of Mr. Storrs' oratory, another selection from that same Burlington speech, the argumentative portion of which has already been quoted from. Take an instance of his colloquial style, enlivened by his fun:

"We have seen nothing in the past performances or present professions of the Democratic party that leads us to conclude that it is any different in spirit than it ever was. It was the same party in 1860. It had a solid South then, and it has one now. It relies then on New York, Indiana, and New Jersey to help it out. It relied on them now, and for the same purpose. The conditions were precisely the same. In 1863 all the draft rioters were Democrats, and all of them who now survive are Democrats. Bob Toombs, Jeff Davis, Ben Hill and Chalmers were its leaders in 1860, as they are its leaders now. In 1860 it had Hendricks, Bayard, Seymour, English of Indiana, Thurman, Dan Voorhees, and Ben Butler and the same men are leading it to-day. There has been no change in the rank and file. Some of them have died from natural causes. Some have been overtaken with delirium tremens. The cavities have been filled up by immigration and by births in precisely the same quarters where large Democratic majorities are found. In 1860 the solid North was too strong for the solid South, and it will be in 1880. There has been no change in doctrine. It declared the negroes chattels in 1860, and bulldozes them in 1880, though in the North it cries out to them to vote its ticket."

And in the same speech read his sensible digression upon the colored question:

"It is but due to the colored people of the whole country to say that they have given the lie, by their subsequent conduct, to the gloomy foreboding and predictions of the Democratic party, and that they have agreeably disappointed the highest expectations which were formed on their behalf by their friends throughout the country and the world. It is but proper justice to say that South and North the negro has turned out to be, when he was free, an entirely self-sustaining institution. It has turned out to be entirely true that the best method in the world of teaching any class the benefits of liberty was freedom itself, and that no better method could possibly be employed to secure the acquisition of seeing to one confined in darkness than a free, speedy, and immediate translation into the light.

"While these general remarks are entirely true of the colored people throughout the country, and while these results are exceedingly gratifying, it would be strange if there had not been here and there mistakes among them which I believe they will correct, and to which their attention ought to be every now and then directed by themselves. In the first place I want you to understand that no man has any right to an office because he is a colored man. Not a bit of it. And it is absurd, and wild, and crazy to make a demand to the country, or of a party, or of a convention, that a man should be nominated and elected to a particular office because he happens to be black. There is no more propriety in insisting that a man shall be nominated to an office because he is black than there is in insisting that he shall not have the office because he is black. Not a bit. And I just hope you will remember this: you are entitled to office, if you are entitled to it at all, not because you have any claims upon your party, your country, your state, or your city—

you haven't; nobody has; not because you are black nor merely because you are a Republican, but because, being black, and a Republican, you are, in addition to all that, a first-rate citizen, an honest and upright man, and capable of intelligently performing the functions of the office for which you are nominated.

"I want to see the colored people compact in their Republicanism and know no other color. I want to see them Republicans, not merely because they are free, but because intelligently considering the merits of the two great parties which divide this country as men and as citizens, they shall reach the conclusion that the best interests of the country demand the continued supremacy of the Republican party. I have always hated all sorts of class legislation, all sorts of caste, and I want to see, politically, the most complete and perfect fusion of all colors, races and conditions into one great, loyal, splendid mass of American citizenship. And I don't want to distinguish one citizen from another because he is black or white, German, Irish, or native-born; but if any distinctions are to be drawn I prefer to draw them on the line which every citizen makes for himself and by his own achievement. You colored men must remember that you are watched very narrowly. You are frequently and unjustly criticized. You have exhibited a great deal of fidelity. Knowing that you are observed very closely, it behooves you to watch yourselves and each other very closely, and to see to it that whenever you find a colored man false to the history of his country and of the party which made him free, because of official or pecuniary considerations, while no personal malice as matter of course is to be inflicted upon him, yet at the same time you must remember that exhibitions of that character are exceedingly damaging to you all."

Or take again his sudden transition from the humorous to that beautiful, which almost touches sublimity of thought, as exhibited in his Cleveland speech during this 1880 campaign.   He had been referring to the Democratic predictions in 1868, when it was stated that the pillars of the government were rocking on their base.   Said he:

"Have you seen any trouble with the pillars of the government? The trouble was not with the pillars of the government: they did not rock; the trouble was with the gentlemen who were looking at the pillars of the government.   They were like the gentleman who had been attending a lecture on astronomy. Going home loaded with a great deal of Democratic logic, with a step weary and uncertain, with the earth revolving a great many times upon its axis, he affectionately clasped a lamp post and said, 'Old Galileo was right about it: the world does move.' And should it, the Republican party, succeed in November next and inaugurate the president, we will meet as a subdued and conquered people amid the ruins of liberty and the scattered fragments of the constitution.   I have been from the tempest-tossed waters of the Atlantic to the peaceful seas of the Pacific, over the mountains, along great rivers, across magnificent plain and prairie, through deserts, down into caves, and I have not seen a single ruin of liberty nor discovered a solitary fragment of the constitution.   We do not meet as a subdued and conquered people.   General Grant was our nominee for president, and he was elected.   He being the candidate, there was a strong probability that he would be inaugurated if elected.

" Forthwith we banded this great continent with ribs of iron and steel. Forthwith this Republican party carried the gold ore across those seas back to the lands of old

Egypt, and back to the shadow of the Pyramids, back to old Damascus, and bought all the history and tradition, spices and gums, incense and myrrh, and landed them in this fruitful West, where we received them with one hand and distributed them all over the habitable globe with the other. This great Republican party interfered with no pillars of the government. It found in that edifice the decaying timbers of human chattlehood. Bless God! it removed them, and replaced them with the everlasting granite of universal freedom. It broadened out that splendid edifice, its base covered the whole continent, each ocean washed its base. It reared that splendid dome, decked with stars, clean above the clouds, where, thank God! it shines and shines to-day, bathed in the glorious sunshine of everlasting fame. It has taken out the old, foul records of the olden time, the old pestilential heresies, states rights, secession, the thumb screw, the faggot, the chain, the whip, all these; the manacled slave, the padlock for the lips, the throttled thought, all these; the deep damning and almost ineffaceable shame of national dishonor, all these it has effaced from its walls, and written there, shining and resplendent, living forever, the grandest record of achievements that the history of the world has ever inscribed."

VIII.

THE CAMPAIGN OF 1884.

FRIDAY night, June 6, 1884, the great auditorium at Chicago, in which the Republican National Convention had been held, was overflowing with a restless crowd, assembled in the expectation of hearing some of the orators in attendance speak in ratification of the nominations of Blaine and Logan. The convention, however, quietly devoted itself to finishing the uncompleted routine business. Late in the evening certain speakers arose and attempted to make addresses, but the now disappointed audience hissed them severally to their seats. A motion to adjourn had been carried, and a movement was started for the doors, when a loud call was made for Robert G. Ingersoll. He was not present; and then there arose a cry for "Storrs! Storrs!" Said the *Tribune*, the following Sunday, " He was fairly carried to the platform, and, without any other inspiration than the excitement of the moment, made an address which will rival any of Ingersoll's brilliant efforts. It was full of sarcasm and humor, and as sparkling as a glass of champagne. His characterization of Blaine was admirably concise and to the point, and his arraignment of the Democracy was the most scathing and

severe — and all the more severe because it was studded
with humor and satire — that that party has ever been
called upon to face." An allusion he made to the
Democratic party has often since been quoted :

"I have seen," said he, " in one of their platforms
that they propose to enter on business with no capital
except the purity of their principles. Was there ever such
a bankrupt concern with such a capital? They say that
is all they have to offer for the suffrages of the people.
My God! my friends. A man that will work on these
terms will work for nothing and board himself. Won't
you think of that dear, delightful old daisy, if she could
take physical form, which we call the Democratic party,
entering into business upon the purity of her principles?
She has kept a house of political ill-fame for more than
twenty years. She has entertained every dishonest political notion and every disreputable political tramp on the
continent during that period of time. I think I see her
marching up to the ingenuous American citizen, with her
shawl twisted around her shoulders, with brass jewelry in
her ears, out at the toes, with a drunken leer of silly invitation in her eye, with a maiden coyness, professing to do
business on the purity of her principles. I would not
for the world say anything disrespectful of the Democratic
party. There are certain things about it that attract me;
but I regard it a little as I do a waterspout, which I like to
look at from a distance, but dislike to get too near to; and
when I see one of its processions — and we will see many
of them during this campaign — I feel about them as our
old friend Strode, in this state, did when he described an
experience of his own in the Black Hawk war. He said:
' By the dim light of the setting sun, on a distant eminence,
I saw a hostile band. They were gentlemen without hats;

I did not know who they were, but I knew d—d well they were no friends of mine.' "

Proceeding, he described the triumphant march of that party to which the years of his manhood had been devoted in a way which produced the wildest cheering, heated as were his hearers by convention scenes and moved by the magnetic power of the orator.

"The night is closing down upon us, the old diabolism of the Democratic party is not yet gone. Another convention will be held here next month. Tilden will probably be nominated. It is possible that he is already dead, but, with a slyness and secretiveness of the author of the cipher dispatches, he might be dead two years and never let anybody know it. We will run substances against shadows. We will run living, breathing men, with bone and flesh, and muscle and appetite, against ghostly reflections such as he. They tell us that he may carry New York. New York is a great, practical, splendid business state. It was my great good fortune to be born there. It is the old Empire state. It stands like the angel of the Apocalypse, with one foot resting upon the sea and the other upon the land, the mistress of both. It has the spirit of Blaine and Logan in its bosom. The old Republicanism of that state which challenged the diabolism of Democracy thirty years ago has still within its heart the old undying and imperishable faith. It will carry this banner, you may rest assured, forward through the storms and fires of the conflict upon which we are about to enter to triumph and to victory. There may be those who will hesitate and falter by the roadside. There may be those who will weary in this magnificent march. The campaign is now upon us. We have no time for liniments or poultices. We cannot stop to heal the infirm. The lame men must fall behind, the cripples be relegated to the rear. The great,

healthy, splendid marching of the Republican millions
taking up this banner will place it, you may be sure, upon
the topmost eminence of magnificent victory. Yes, music
is in all the air. I feel its old pulsings in my very veins
to-night. I know what this feels like, and I know what
the awakened excitement and enthusiasm of a great and
mighty party indicate. I hear the old songs of the old
days. I see the old flag with every star glistening like a
planet, filling all the skies. I see the old procession
formed. I care not where my place in that procession
may be — whether it be up in the front, under the light of
the blessed old banner, or down near the rear — I listen to
the order 'Forward,' and I march, as you will march, with
your faces toward the flag."

The scene which succeeded some of his bursts of
eloquence. said the *Times*, the following Sunday, "was
a demonstration of the powers of a bright and adroit
orator over a vast and turbulent multitude such as is
rarely witnessed."

The campaign of 1884, thus unexpectedly begun, Mr.
Storrs found impossible to push aside until the months
which intervened between that date and the day of
election were passed. James G. Blaine wrote:

"The boys in Maine are crazy after you. You must
come."

Jewell urged:

"There is no use dodging California, for they clamor
after you."

From every part of the country came letters and
telegrams begging for a speech. Devotion to party,
love of public speaking, did the rest. Throwing aside
his own interests, sacrificing, perhaps, more than any
other man in the country, he responded to every call

in his power. The week following the convention, he opened the campaign in Ohio by a speech in the Music Hall of Cincinnati, amid stirring scenes which followed his voice all over the land. The *Enquirer*, an organ bitterly opposed to Blaine, wrote of this meeting:

"The audience, hundreds of whom were ladies, seemed to have gone daft. People stood up all over the house waving arms and flags, until from the stage the scene presented the appearance of a vast field of grain violently swayed by cross currents of wind. It was useless to attempt to check the tumult." "Mr. Storrs," said the same paper, "dapper and wiry, arrayed in a faultlessly fitting dress suit, stepped to the front, where, with easy self-possession, he waited for a cessation of the applause before he spoke. A master of oratory, his voice, full, deep, and round, rolled out in perfect utterance, filling every corner of the hall. It was oratory without effort. Every word, clearly cut and distinct, was delivered with that rare quality—an agreeable sound."

In this speech at Cincinnati, speaking of our foreign policy, he said upon the subject of our navy what every true citizen must applaud:

"What kind of a foreign policy do the wants, the emergencies and necessities of the nation imperatively exact? We are not respected abroad. I say we should be. We are not respected at home. I say this should not be. I want no war; I want only the summer days of prosperous peace. I know of but one way to secure it, and that is promptly and at once to place ourselves in such a position that all assault can be so readily resented that none will ever be made. Without a navy—the sport of every foreign power, with an inadequate coast defense—the sport of every foreign power, we invite assault. We stand, a great, big, sturdy nation, with our hands helplessly by our sides, utterly unable, not only to protect our interests elsewhere in the world, but utterly unable to defend ourselves at home.

"The condition is one of shame, indignity and outrage upon ourselves that every spirited American will see is at once corrected. I want something more than this. Now I am speaking merely for myself : I am binding nobody. The time has come when the old notion of our insularity and freedom from attacks by foreign powers must cease. We are to-day six days from Europe; nearer, much nearer, than Cincinnati was to New York fifty years ago. We have trade with every port; we have our products in every civilized land beneath the sun. Our commercial interests are extant everywhere; our citizens are all over the globe. There is not a gun-boat over which the flag of the great nation floats adequate to protect an insulted American in the meanest seaport of the smallest nation of the earth. We are interested in what is going on all over the earth. Our trade must be protected and cared for wherever it extends. That nation is unfit to be called a nation which will not defend the imperiled rights of its citizens at home and abroad whenever they are assailed. I give to my country allegiance ; I recognize its laws; I obey loyally and willingly in all cases when obedience is required. I pay that for protection, and when my government fails to give it to me, it is my right to take their constitution in my hand and say : 'You blundering, bullying, bragging, non-performing fraud of a government, protect me as you have agreed to do or quit business."

Brackets and parentheses do not, ordinarily, dignify composition; but perhaps nothing — since his marvelous voice and action are stilled in death — can so adequately convey an idea of the effect of the rare powers of expression and mimicry which Mr. Storrs possessed, as to append exactly as reported in the *Herald* of Boston a "stump oration," which he delivered in Tremont Temple, that city, September 7, 1884. The speech could not be surpassed for campaign eloquence and wit. After telling of the great and sympathetic audience, the newspaper report ran :

" Mr. President, Fellow-Citizens, Ladies and Gentlemen:

" At this hour of the night it would be presumptuous for me to make anything like a full and elaborate discussion of the principles involved in the pending presidential campaign. It seems to me, since I have read the papers of this morning, that the necessity for very much discussion is past, and that political oratory has resolved itself, after all, pretty much into a howl of wild delight on one side, and wailing lamentations on the other, with an occasional bleak, dismal whistle coming from the brush or from some obscure place, intended, no doubt, to keep up the courage of the whistler. I am not unmindful, fellow-citizens, whom I am addressing. [Applause.] I know I am in Boston, in the state of Massachusetts, in the New England states. I am a resident of the state of Illinois. I am a citizen of the United States. [Applause.] I am, with you, joint proprietor of Bunker Hill [applause], made so by the fourteenth and fifteenth constitutional amendments. [Cheers and applause.] I have a common interest in Paul Revere [cheers], and in that remarkable cargo of tea, the unshipping of which led to such splendid results a good many years ago. I am from what in New York has been characterized the 'rowdy West' [renewed applause]—what one, at least, of New England's famous clergymen has denominated as the 'riff raff of the West.' [Cheers and laughter.] May I say to you, because I know it will be soothing [laughter], that this characterization, Mr. Chairman, has not greatly disturbed us in the West. [Applause.]

It has not broken our rest; not disturbed our slumbers [cheers], nor interfered with the quiet and usual transactions of our business. [Renewed applause.] Now, as Senator Hawley will tell you, we don't lack spirit on a proper occasion. We have an abundance of it. [Cheers.]

"Our state was the only state in the Union, Mr. Chairman, that filled its quota without a draft. [Renewed cheers and applause.] We sent over about 18,000 more to Missouri, a strong Democratic state, which will cast its electoral vote for Cleveland. We give 40,000 Republican majority. [Tremendous applause and cheers.] We have not been made angry by this characterization. May I tell you why? [A voice, 'Yes, tell us.'] We are the sons and daughters of New England. [Cheers and applause.] We have left these old fields and farms, and the blessed old firesides in New York and New England, many of us, with nothing save the lessons of splendid thrift and frugality which we have learned in these old New England homes. A thousand miles or more separate us from those old firesides. Our heartstrings may have been stretched; they have not been broken. [Cheers and applause.] And we have built in the valley of the Mississippi the most colossal, the most splendid empire of free men, free thought, free speech, as splendid a government as the sun, in all his course, has ever shone upon. [Renewed applause.] It does not make much difference what preacher calls us the riff raff. The sons and daughters of New England propose to turn over the settlement of the whole question to their fathers and mothers in New England. They will settle that question. [Cheers.] Well, fellow-citizens, there is no man living in the West that is not gratified to speak in Boston. [Applause.] And, if any man living in the West pretends to say he does not like to speak here in Boston, he is guilty of willful and deliberate hyperbole.

[Laughter.] We are citizens of a common country, united in our interests. We are becoming in the West great manufacturers. We are proud of this country, as you are proud of it. [Cheers.] We give Republican majorities, as you give Republican majorities, and for the same reason.

"We believe that the glory and the honor of the American name are bound up in the success of this Republican party. [Cheers.] I started with that great party when I was a boy. The first ballot I ever cast was for John C. Fremont, many, many years ago. [Cheers.] I look back upon that time and that standard-bearer, and it looks all bright and radiant, shining with the glory of the birth of a new party — a party which contains within its ranks the best thought and the loftiest sentiment and the most exalted conscience of our people. [Loud applause.] I have been with that party as an humble follower, a private in its ranks, never giving orders myself, but always, as near as I could be, under the folds of that starry, blessed, old banner [cheers] taking directions from our magnificent leaders, Lincoln [cheers], and Grant, and Hayes, and Garfield [cheers], and Arthur, and Blaine. [Loud applause.] And, fellow-citizens, it makes very little difference to me where in that splendid procession of the millions of the inhabitants of this country I may be placed, whether I am up near the standard-bearer under the stars, or down near the foot of the procession. I march to the old music, Mr. Chairman, and it is the music of the Union. My heart beats my own time. [Applause.] I am certain of one thing — that I shall always, so long as I live, march with my face toward the flag. [Tremendous applause and cheers.] I am not an independent in politics. [Cheers.] I recognize no purgatorial politics [cheers and laughter], no halting, half-way station between heaven and hell. [Laughter and cheers.] To me it is the heaven of good

Republican government, or it is the hell of that diabolical, old, infernal party [prolonged laughter and cheers] that has never in all its long, consistent, bad, criminal career, done a right thing except at the wrong time. [Laughter.]

" I wish to say of the Democratic party nothing unkind [cheers], nothing ungentlemanly. [Laughter and applause.] Of the independents it is my purpose to speak in terms of the utmost tenderness. [Laughter.] They have left us. Why should we mourn departed friends? [Laughter.] When I read the announcement a few days ago, Mr. Chairman, that they had gone [laughter], I heard the news with a great deal of solid comfort [laughter and cheers] — a great deal of resignation. But when I read along a little further, and found that their absence was to be only temporary, that they intended some day to return, I confess — who should not confess it? — that my mind was filled with the direst apprehension. [Cheers and laughter.] Our party has made some mistakes. If you will allow me to make a suggestion, it has grown too rapidly at the top. [Cheers and applause.] I for one am prepared to exchange the political æsthetes for the horny-handed, hard-fisted workingman. [Applause.] My feelings have been lacerated, my heart has been wrung many times by the departure of the æsthetes. [Laughter.] They have played too many farewell engagements. [Cheers.] I recognize the first rule of private hospitality in their treatment — I 'welcome the coming and speed the parting guest.' [Tremendous applause and laughter.] We have heard in the West something about the better element of our party. [Cheers.] In our plain way — because we have been building up states, cities and empires — we have not had time to think much about the matter.

"We have always thought, however, that the better element was the bigger [cheers], and that the wisdom of

th.s great party of ours was in the majority. Now don't
you think so? [A voice, ' Yes,' and applause.] Every
time I have read an announcement in the West (we take
the Atlantic Monthly there and have gospel privileges),
[laughter and cheers] I have read that these gentlemen
are exceedingly solicitous as concerning the question of
the purity of our youth. [Laughter]. May I be permitted
to suggest, Senator [turning to General Hawley], and I
wish you would tell them so in Connecticut, the farmers
of Illinois, of the great West, those strong, splendid broad-
browed, great, big-hearted men, those men who buried the
nasty doctrine of fiat money under a majority of 40,000,
those men are quite capable themselves of taking care of
the morals of their sons. [Cheers.] At least they don't
propose to turn the custody of those morals over to an as-
sorted lot of gentlemen, one-half of whom deny the existence of a God and the other half of whom believe that
mankind, themselves included, developed from an ape.
Now, just what does it mean to be an independent in
politics? If the word has a practical significance at all, it
means the refusal to acknowledge allegiance to either of
the great political parties of the country; is not that so?
[A voice, ' Yes,' and cheers.] These gentlemen are simply independent of the Republican party, to which they
formerly belonged — spasmodically, occasionally belonged.
[Laughter.] They have attached themselves to the Democratic party. They are not independent of that, are they,
when they acknowledge allegiance to it? How absurd it is!
[Applause.] If a refusal to vote the Republican ticket, to
indorse Republican doctrines, to support Republican candidates, is an evidence of independence, then the Democrat is
a great deal more independent, because he in that regard
has been at it a great deal longer. [Cheers and applause.]

    " Will some astute logician tell me the difference be-

tween a genuine old-fashioned Democrat and the new article, the independents? [Cheers and applause.]   They
support the same men, and for the same reasons. The old
Democrat and his ally support Grover Cleveland because of
his high moral character. [Applause and cheers.]   Mr.
Chairman [turning to the chairman], I cannot understand
what that last applause was for. They support him because he vetoed the five-cent fare bill, he vetoed the bill
shortening the hours of labor for street car conductors and
drivers, and because he vetoed the mechanics' lien law in the
state of New York.   Now the old Democrat and independent both support him for those reasons, among others.
Now, they refuse to support Mr. Blaine for the same reasons exactly. There is no difference whatever. Mr. Curtis
and Mr. Schurz both withhold their support from Mr.
Blaine for the same reasons that Hubert O. Thompson and
Mr. Davidson withhold theirs.   They use the same
methods, work through the same channels and seek to accomplish the same end in exactly the same way. Both
mourn when they are defeated, and rejoice when they succeed, and both will be buried in the same common grave.
[Applause and cheers.]   When they are dead and their
skeletons are bleached, you cannot tell the skeleton of an
independent from that of a Democrat. [Applause and
cheers.]   This is a very extraordinary party of ours, the
Republican party.   It never, in all its long, splendid and
illustrious career, has allowed a leader to take it one single
step in any direction it did not want to go. [A voice:
'That's so,' and applause.]   Never.   I want you to think
of that. [Renewed applause.]   Our leaders have sometimes left us by wholesale. So much the worse for the
leaders, and so much the better for the party.

"In 1872 governors, ex-governors, senators and ex-
senators, judges and ex-judges, left us, because the party,

as they said, was corrupt. And yet, how that splendid old
ship did righten itself up after they had gotten off!
[Laughter and applause.] How magnificently it made for
the harbor of a splendid success! How desolate and discomfited have been the leaders who jumped overboard ever
since? [Applause and laughter.] There is another very
remarkable feature about our party, which quite distinguishes it from the Democratic party. To write a platform for the Democratic party requires the very highest
degree of rhetorical and literary ability. I think I possess
some ability of that kind myself [laughter], and I would
not try it under any circumstances. [Applause and cheers.]
On the other hand, there is not a Republican in all the
55,000,000 of people upon this continent that cannot write
a Republican platform that is not good Republican doctrine
everywhere. Gentlemen, did you ever think what would
happen to a Democratic orator if he put his platform in
his pocket at night and got on a train which landed him in
a direction that he did not suppose he was going. Suppose, for instance, he started from Chicago and was going
to Boston, and by some curious freak was landed at Atlanta
or Savannah, and, thinking he was in Boston all the time,
began to clamor for a free ballot and a fair count. [Laugh-
ter and applause.] So you see that is a thing which is
liable to spoil with a change of weather. [Cheers.] Suppose that a patriotic Democrat, and there are many such,
construing the platform, after days and nights of anxious,
hair-pulling, headache, has made up his mind as to what
it means on the subject of the tariff, and he starts off on a
trip and lands at Lancaster, Pa., and there begins to talk
about a platform for free trade. What kind of a funeral
awaits that man? [Cheers and applause.] So you see that
it is full of difficulties. They say we are all the time talking about our record. They decline to talk about theirs,

and I don't blame them. [Cheers and laughter.] In the few words that I shall have occasion to say to you about the Democratic party, remember that I treat of it as a party. I make a distinction between the party and the member of the party, the same as I would between a corporation and a stockholder of a corporation.

" For instance, I know stockholders of the Standard Oil Company, and they are excellent gentlemen, but the company——. [Laughter.] I know Democrats who are a great deal better than their party, but I never knew any one worse. [Cheers and laughter.] And so it is about their party I would like to talk. And it is the party to which the conscientious independent citizens have attached themselves. Let me say here, it is a party that has shown how potent the silent vote is in Maine [laughter] and in Vermont. But we are told, when we speak about the record of the Republican party, that we are discussing old issues. To be sure, that is very bad, but it is no objection, gentlemen, to an issue that it is old, if that issue has not been settled. [Cheers.] The preachers of the gospel for a great many hundreds of years have been denouncing sin. That is a very old issue, and yet I suppose they will keep up their denunciations until sin quits. [Laughter.] The people of this country want to have confidence in any party to which they propose to intrust the interests of the country. The people of this country, let me say, are pretty intelligent and observing. It is not enough for them to know that a promise is made. What they are after is that the promise shall be kept, and they have to depend for such information upon the history of the individual or party to which they propose to intrust such interest. Now, is not that the best kind of sense? If a party promises to uphold the public credit, that party always having undertaken to destroy it, will you take such

a promise? If it promises to protect and care for our
American industries, when for thirty years it has sought to
paralyze and destroy them, will you accept such a promise?
[A voice—'No.'] Of course you won't. If it professes
and promises to take care of our financial interests, while
it has for years sought to destroy them, will you accept
such promises? I take it not.

"These are fair, square questions, which every one is
going to ask for himself, and to which he insists upon an
answer. What is the record of that old party? If this
hall was filled with Democrats, and very one of them solid
in the faith and firm in the belief, I could clear the hall in
three minutes by reading from the platform of 1868 and
1872. They have never made a promise in which the
interest of the country has been involved that they have
kept. [Cheers.] There has been no great measure of
public utility that the party has ever favored in all its
career of thirty years, and there is no good measure that
party has not opposed during that time. [Loud applause.]
Is there any one in this large and splendid audience, in this
old and splendid city of Boston, memorable for its history
and sanctified in the hearts of the people by the recollection of the revolution ; is there one of you, glorying in the
greatness of our country in the past, and with the hope
and promise of the future; is there one of you who can
point to anything in the last quarter of a century that the
Democratic party has done or attempted to do from which
you draw any pride, or from which the country would
have drawn any honor? Can you point to any great event
in history which makes up our patrimony and heritage
that it has not opposed? [Loud applause.] That is a
dreadful question, and a dreadful fact. Is there any one
such instance? The Republican party, whose advocate in
a simple way I am, has never made any great promises it

has not religiously performed. [Applause.] The promise
of to-day is the statute of to-morrow, and ripens into the
fundamental law of the land. In its brief career of
twenty-five years it has counted by its achievements 1,000
years of the grandest history. [Cheers.] It made our
territories all free, and elected Lincoln. [Great applause.]
By one supreme effort it lifted 4,000,000 people from the
position of African cattle to that of American citizenship.
[Applause.] It placed this great country in the midst of
prosperity unexampled in the world. [Cheers.]

"Gentlemen, I can never tire of speaking of the
achievements, or the non-achievements, of the Democratic
party. I make one honorable exception. Governor
Hoadly, of Ohio, visited Maine, where he spoke. He was
at one time a Republican, and, finding the need of a record, he furnished one to his friends there. The story he
told was like the old news from the Potomac —' Important
if true.' [Loud laughter.] There is no one here who
will mention what I am about to say. [Laughter.] Did
you ever see a washed-out Republican that had fallen into
the Democratic party that ever bragged about being a
Democrat? [Renewed laughter.] He is always proclaim-
ing that he has been something better — a Republican ;
that he has seen better days, like some of the gentlemen
in the old states [laughter and applause], a little raveled
out at the edge, and run down at the heel, but with here
and there marks to show that originally the goods were
valuable. [General laughter and applause.] He was an
abolitionist, he says, when Logan was voting the Democratic ticket. There is the place where the Democrats and
their allies agree. [Applause.] It is astonishing that
they speak about Logan voting the Democratic ticket.
Hendricks voted that ticket once. [Laughter.] But is
it, after all, the real question when a man began to be an

apostle half as much as how long he holds out? [Laughter and applause.] Who began first? Judas or Saul of Tarsus? Judas, I think. But think about him running around in that Democratic region of his, jingling those 30 pieces of silver he got from the Democratic committee of that day as his price for his joining the party of purity and reform, and claiming that he was a Christian long before the scales fell from the eyes of Saul of Tarsus. [Vociferous applause and laughter.] Logan did vote the Democratic ticket, but the first shot at Fort Sumter drove from him every spark of the Democratic faith, and in the flame and thunder of battle he made himself the peerless soldier of the war for the Union. [Renewed applause.] Take from the history of the country for the last twenty-five years the solid achievements of John A. Logan, and you make a chasm [applause] ; but take from the same time the achievements of his detractors, and there is no abrasion on the surface. [Renewed applause.]

"The hour is so late, however—[Voice — 'Go on.'] I am willing to go on. [Loud applause.] I was about to say the hour is so late it seems to be an outrage on the understanding of so fine an audience. But let's be fair about it. The night is hot, and while you suffer in listening, I suffer in talking, and so, in the good, old-fashioned way, let us bear one another's burdens. [Applause.] The life of man is limited to about seventy years, and you cannot expect me to spend all of it in going into the crimes and follies of the Democratic party. [Laughter and applause.] It seems to me a waste of time and timber. I was reading the Chicago *Tribune* the other day, and I saw a missionary had been sent from Boston to Chicago to organize the independent movement, which is a kind of 'go-as-you-please' affair, and requires a good deal of nursing. [Laughter.] There was a grand rally, and the whole five were present, some with Mr. Gladstone's last speeches, others with essays from the Cobden Club, others carrying their canes in the middle, and all appearing like three-story-and-mansard-roof patriots. [Laughter.] They were at the Palmer House, and one said Massachusetts was going to give Cleveland an overwhelming majority. He was an independent, and one of the better class of that party. [Laughter.] Of course, the statement was not false, was it? Not an extreme economy of the truth? [Laughter.] I have to be a little delicate about my language.

"I have been somewhat dazed at what seems to be the revolving and somewhat contradictory position the independent movement has taken. It is like the trip of the blind ass in a park. Very much walking and very little getting ahead. [Laughter.] They say to the Democrats: 'I will support your candidate on moral considerations alone. [Laughter.] I will vote your ticket; I will march under your banner; wear your uniform; take orders from your leaders; I will discharge my guns into the faces of my own friends from your ranks, but I must not be considered of you. I still claim the privilege of attending the councils of the army I have just deserted [loud applause] as well as yours, and, while I explode my batteries in the breasts of my old friends, I will, with a magnanimity, the like of which was never recorded in history, consent to draw rations from both armies.' [Loud laughter and applause.] The independent movement may have a basis somewhere. Can you see it? In the state of Massachusetts they issued a ringing address, signed by sixteen gentlemen, in which they arraigned the party for the misdeeds committed when they were members of that body. They said vice-President Colfax had been guilty of corrupt practices, as well as Belknap and ex-Attorney-

General Williams, and that Robeson had violated his trust. They then referred to the whisky ring and Star Route frauds, but the Republican party, as a party, could not be responsible for these, if there were such. [Applause.] I advise these gentlemen not to go to Indiana, where Colfax has an honored name, and where thousands respect him, and tell such things. [Applause.] It would not be prudent.

"But Schuyler Colfax has dropped out of public life. Belknap was impeached, and Robeson investigated by a hostile committee, while ex-Attorney-General Williams dropped from office and has never been honored since. [Cheers.] The last time I saw him was at the Republican convention in 1880, joining with these independents to oppose General Grant on the ground of morals in politics. [Loud applause.] What was done in the Star Route was in the administration of president Hayes, and was brought to light in the first weeks of Garfield, and both administrations these people indorsed. [Applause.] The Star Route was brought to trial under Arthur [cheers], prosecuted by Republican officials, backed by the party, but they were acquitted by a Democratic jury [applause], at the head of which was Dickson, who was a delegate at the Democratic convention, and voted for Cleveland, and is to-day supporting him with the sixteen gentlemen who signed that address on the ground of moral considerations. [Laughter and applause.] Now, gentlemen, as to the personal character of Mr. Blaine it becomes me to say nothing. The people of the state where he lives have passed on his character. [Tremendous applause.] For twenty-five years he has stood in the full front and blaze of the sun, one of the leading and most prominent figures in American history. [Applause.] We don't take our leaders from obscurities [laughter], nor from men conspicuous to the extent that they are not known. That has not been the policy of our party. [Cheers.] The Democrats prefer their armies shall be led by a skulker they have awakened up from under the band-wagon, because he shows no scars. [Laughter and applause.] Mr. Blaine has a tattoo of 16,000 majority. [Great applause.]

"There is only one other question. I did want to say something about the tariff, but as I sat in the quiet of my room to-day I felt I might subject myself in this vicinity to imminent peril by doing so, for, when such a man as Senator Hoar, who, in the West we had supposed was an honorable man — fair and honest — is crushed down by the rhetoric of David A. Wells, a private like me may take alarm. [Laughter.] This is to be a campaign, as I understand, where decorous language is to be used, and the practices of Fontenoy are to be observed. 'Gentlemen, please fire first!' Mr. Wells says Mr. Hoar knows nothing about the tariff, but many of the sophomores of Harvard are capable to give the instruction required. We are much obliged, for we know where to go for information, and when the question comes up as to the duty on scrap iron, we will leave Mr. Wells and go to Harvard. When we speak of steel rails we will go to Harvard. [Laughter.] In the club I came across the essay of the Cobden Club for 1871 and 1872 and it was one of eighty pages, written by Mr. David A. Wells, who was elected an honorary member in 1870. I wonder whether he had been withholding it from his own people and giving it to the British public. At page 536 he says 'so excessive and costly is the manufacture of steel rails that it would be better to burn up the shops.' He gives as a reason that steel rails could then be bought for sixty-two dollars a ton. Since then the manufacture has increased to 1,600,000 tons per annum, and the price has decreased to twenty-six or twenty-seven dollars per ton, and that is much better than the British manufacturer ever dreamed of. This is the class of men who now support Grover Cleveland. In that same article he declared that before 1881 we should have no protective legislation.

"The fact is all the other way. I have said we are all the sons and daughters of New England, and we are proud to come and show you what we have achieved while around the firesides of New England, God bless her! [Cheers.] The Republican party has made our country free. [Applause.] We have effaced the inscriptions of the bad old times, and the Dred-Scott decision no longer lives. The story of escaping slaves is no longer heard, but radiant as a planet is the story of a republic beneath whose banner every human being is free to think and vote as he pleases. [Cheers.] And we have the spirit of a mighty free empire caring for the poorest of her citizens, and on this account I shall vote for Blaine and Logan."

The above is an almost inimitable type of the catchy, spontaneous oratory of Mr. Storrs; but for a carefully prepared comparison of the two contending armies of voters, for a speech argumentative and in a stately recourse, a splendid example was given by Mr. Storrs at Cleveland, the night of October 6, immediately prior to the Ohio state election. In this masterly speech he spoke as follows:

"The reforms of this world rarely come from the skies down, but almost always from the ground up. This is especially true of reforms which are at all moral in their nature. The bloody pages of martyrdom required the self-sacrifice for opinion's sake of but few scholars, but by thousands and by tens of thousands the plain, honest people have willingly perished in dungeon, on the scaffold and at the stake for opinion's sake.

"We must deal, after all, with the great, grave questions of the hour. The two great parties to-day stand confronting each other, both seeking the indorsement of the people, both making promises for good behavior in the future. The essential inquiry is not which is the most vehement promise, but which of the parties promising is the most likely to perform. I might admit for the purposes of argument that the Democratic party in its platform of the present campaign promises all that we can ask, and yet refuse to act upon it, for the simple reason that its history renders it utterly impossible that it will perform any promise looking to the honor or prosperity of the country which, under the stress of a great emergency, it may see fit to make. For nearly a quarter of a century before the war it sought not only the degradation but the practical destruction of the dignity of free labor in this country, and why should I take its promise now that it will promote and elevate it? It refused to recognize the public judgment in the election of Abraham Lincoln, and sought the dismemberment of the nation for that reason. Why should I accept to-day its promise to strengthen and extend our national integrity? It opposed every measure to which our patriotic people were compelled to resort for the prosecution of the war to save the Union. Why should I now accept its assurances that it was all the time in favor of the preservation of the Union? It denounced as unconstitutional and void all schemes for the establishment of a national currency, and why should I now place the custody of that currency in its hands? It sought to prevent the enactment of all laws by which the ballot throughout the boundaries of the Republic should be made free and fair and equal, and why should I take its promise to make that ballot free and fair and equal in the future? It has steadily opposed every scheme to further the protection of

American industry, down even until to-day, and why should I accept its promise to care for and protect American industries in the future? Its history is opposed to its promises. I decline to place the nation in the hands of a party which sought to destroy it. I decline to place the custody of our currency in the hands of a party which believes it to be unconstitutional. I decline to intrust our industries to a party which has steadily and consistently sought their overthrow.

"These statements of the position of the Democratic party are not mere random assertions. There is not a line of legislation in our history for the last twenty-five years redounding to the honor or prosperity of the nation which the Democratic party has not bitterly opposed. Why should I intrust the national honor to the party which sought its destruction only sixteen years ago by a declaration in national convention demanding the practical repudiation of the public debt? I understand the anxiety of the Democratic party to be rid of its history — its anxiety that a profound silence should be maintained as to its past record. It has a record which it does not dare to read; it has a candidate whom it does not dare to exhibit; and the strongest evidence that we have that there is still some foundation to work upon for the reform of that party is that it is so profoundly ashamed of its past history, for where there is no shame for a misdeed there can be no conversion.

"Feeling this very keenly, patriotic Democrats — and there are thousands and tens of thousands of such — seek to claim some share in all the glories of our history since 1861. Mr. Hynes, of the city of Chicago, a most estimable gentleman, a very able and a thoroughly patriotic man, in a speech delivered at Fostoria a few nights since claims that the Democratic party is entitled to as much credit for

the resumption of specie payments as is the Republican
party. But in this Mr. Hynes is surely mistaken. Doubtless Mr. Hynes, during the time of the agitation of those
questions, was in favor of a sound and honest currency,
but surely his party was not. The trouble with Mr. Hynes,
and with thousands of others of excellent Democrats, is that
they have been wearing for many years the wrong label.
They have been carrying around a Democratic trade-mark
without really entertaining a single Democratic principle.
This is astonishing, but it is true. It is remarkable that a
man should mark silk goods down to a calico price, but
this Mr. Hynes and others have done.

" Now, what are the facts in regard to our currency ?
The Democratic platform of 1868 called for the payment
of the public debt in greenbacks, and demanded, in this
exact language, ' equal taxation of every species of property according to its real value, including government
bonds and other public securities.' It was deemed necessary in 1869, as a preliminary to bringing our currency
back to a solid basis, to assure the whole world that we
intended honestly to pay our public debt, and therefore
the public credit bill was originated by the Republican
party pledging the nation to the payment of its debt in
coin, and this bill was opposed in Congress, as Mr. Hynes
will find, by the practically solid vote of the Democratic
party, including James R. Doolittle, who was at that time
wavering between the lines. The Democratic party by a
practically solid vote opposed the resumption bill. Finding, in 1876, however, that it was necessary to nominate
Mr. Tilden, their jesuitical platform declared for honest
money, but, to satisfy the rank and file of the party,
denounced the Republican party for hindering resumption.
In January, 1876, the bill to repeal the resumption act
received 112 votes, all Democrats but one. In June, 1876,

as a rider to the civil appropriation bill, an amendment
repealing the resumption act received solid Democratic
support. The party was not converted by its double-
headed platform ; for on the 5th of August, 1876, a measure to repeal the fixing of the time for resumption received
in the house 106 votes, all Democratic but three, and the
platforms of the Democratic party, almost throughout the
Union, demanded in explicit terms the immediate repeal of
the specie resumption act. The contest was not closed
until 1878, when the Democratic party as a party solidly
favored the heresy of fiat money, at which time James G.
Blaine visited the West and was the leader in the great
final battle for honest money ; and in the state of Illinois
that heresy was buried under a majority of 40,000. That
for the time closed the contest. Specie payments were
resumed, and the efforts of the Democratic party in that
direction ceased only because they could not repeal an
accomplished fact, any more than they could repeal yesterday's sunrise.

"Equally hollow is it for Democratic orators to
claim that the Democratic party is in favor of a free
ballot. They called for it, it is true, in 1880, and they
demanded it again in their platform of 1884, but the solid
Democracy in Congress opposed the registry laws, and has
again and again sought their repeal. It has repealed registry legislation in this state and in New York, and the
party which professes to be in favor of a free ballot and a
fair count shows this extraordinary record : In 1872 the
Republican vote of Alabama was 90,272 ; in 1878 it was
nothing. In 1872 the Republican vote of Arkansas was
41,373 ; in 1878 it was 115. In 1872 the Republican vote
of Mississippi was 82,175 ; in 1878 it was 1,168. These
instances, in the main, hold good through the entire South.
In 1876 the Republican vote in South Carolina was 91,870 ;

in 1878 only 213 Republican votes were counted. In 1876 the Republican majority in Louisiana was over 20,000; two years later the vote disappeared from the election returns.

"These facts, which are the shame of our present history, are of record. No language can exaggerate their importance, nor the stupendous crime which makes such a condition of things a possibility.

"While, in the main, the people of this country do not require a change, in these respects they loudly demand a change, and insist upon it that the guaranty of a free ballot and a fair count, of equality, of political privileges, embodied in the constitution, shall be religiously performed. This is American policy, and it is typified in the persons of Blaine and Logan.

"For man years the Democrats have been vehement in demanding a change, but for just what reason they require it they have always been and still are unable satisfactorily to state. Certain changes we will have and do have. We will have a change from one Republican administration to another. We had a change from Grant to Hayes, and from Hayes to Garfield, whose untimely death made a change to Arthur, and we are about to have a change from the cleanly and patriotic and thoroughly upright administration of Chester A. Arthur to the thorough and cleanly and patriotic administration of James G. Blaine. We will change administrations, but we decline to change policies. We are willing to exchange one Union-saver for another Union-saver, one friend of American industries for another friend of American industries; but the poorest Union-saver is better than the best Union-hater, and the commonest friend of American industries is better than the most thoroughly accomplished enemy of our labor and its prosperity.

" When the country most needed a change, in 1860, the Democratic party was opposed to it. In 1860 our national wealth was $14,000,000. In 1880, under the influences of Republican policy, it had increased to $44,000,000,000 — an increase of over $125,000,000 per month, equal to one-third the daily accumulations of mankind.

" In 1860 our manufactures amounted in value to $1,-885,000,000. Then the Democratic party did not desire a change. In 1883 they amounted to $5,300,000,000, and now it demands a change. In 1860 the productions of our coal mines were 14,000,000 tons. The Democratic party was satisfied.

" In 1883 the production of our coal mines was 96,000,-000 tons, and now it demands a change. We to-day import one-tenth as much cotton as we imported in 1860, and we now export 150,000,000 yards per year. But the Democratic party, dissatisfied with the present situation, demands a change. We import no more silk now than we did in 1860, but we produce six times as much ; and still the Democratic party demands a change. Our wool production in 1880 was four times as large as in 1860, and the prices were higher than in 1860, and yet the Democratic party demands a change. In 1860 our productions of iron ore were 900,000 tons. This satisfied the Democratic party. But in 1883 the productions were over 8,000,000 tons, and hence it demands a change. In 1860 we had 30,000 miles of railroad. This suited the conservative Democracy. In 1884 we have 100,000 miles; and it demands a change. In 1868 our freight charges to New York from Chicago were 42 cents per bushel. In 1883 they were 16 cents per bushel. And Democracy now demands a change. Down to 1861, covering the entire period of our national history, the value of our exports had been $9,000,000,000; with this the conservative Democracy was content. But since 1861, a period of only twenty-three years, the value of our exports has been $12,000,000,000. This is not satisfactory, and the conservative Democrat demands a change.

"I am aware that Democratic orators claim that these marvelous exhibitions of prosperity are due to the fertility of our soil, favoring conditions of climate, and our great territorial extent. But the satisfactory answer to this is that the skies were just as blue, the soil was just as fertile, before 1861, as they have been since, and that this colossal development has occurred under what is to-day Republican policy in government. [Applause.] There is nothing impossible with the Almighty, but he would never undertake to make this country prosperous, even if the skies were of the bluest, the soil the most fertile, and our fields groaning under harvests, if running alongside them were a debased and shifting currency, an impaired national credit, and an unrestricted competition with the cheap and pauperized labor of the old world.

"So far as the question of protection to our industries is concerned, notwithstanding the asseverations of certain Democratic orators to the contrary, the policy of the Democratic party has been steadily against protection and in favor of free-trade. This a very hurried reference to its record will demonstrate. In 1876 the Democratic platform demanded that all custom house taxation should be 'for revenue only.' The Democratic platform of 1880 demanded a 'tariff for revenue only.' The policy of the party is entirely harmonious with that of the Southern Confederacy; for by the constitution of the Southern Confederacy it was provided, 'No bounty shall be granted from the treasury, nor shall any duties be laid to promote or foster any branch of industry.' The attitude of the Democratic party, therefore, during all these years, was

entirely that of the Southern Confederacy. A fair inter-
pretation of its platform of 1884 leads to precisely the
same result. Its language is, 'We therefore denounce the
abuses of the existing tariff.' But it is to be observed
that it does not enumerate these abuses. Further, 'We
demand that Federal taxation shall be exclusively for
public purposes and shall not exceed the needs of the
government economically administered.' This is somewhat obscure, but its meaning is not difficult to reach.
'Federal taxation' means the tariff; 'exclusively' means
'only,' and 'public purposes' can have no meaning but
'revenue,' and therefore, reduced to our every-day vernac-
ular, it reads, 'We demand that the tariff shall be only
for revenue,' so that its present position is entirely in
harmony with its past.

"In what I have thus far said with regard to the record
of the Democratic party, it is entirely fair for me to say
that its candidates stand upon its records so far as we are
able to ascertain. In his letter of acceptance, Governor
Cleveland says, 'I have carefully considered the platform
adopted by the convention and cordially approve the same.'
The attitude of Mr. Hendricks has been too well known to
require comment. So that the position of the Democratic
party being clearly ascertained, we have only to inquire,
Are we in favor of it?

"There is no abler exponent of the free-trade Democratic doctrine in this country, perhaps, than Mr. David
A. Wells. A Democratic philosopher and a philosophic
Democrat, a member of the Cobden Club, he looks upon
free-trade as the means by which a millennium among the
nations is to be secured, and the estimate in which he
holds our policy of protection is clearly indicated by an
essay written by him for the Cobden Club, and published
in its collection of essays in 1871, in which, referring to

the tariff of twenty-eight dollars per ton upon steel rails, he says that the tariff is 'so excessive and costly that it would be more profitable for the country at large to buy and burn up all the existing establishments and pension all the workmen, rather than continue the business under existing arrangements.' Mr. Wells proceeds to state in the same essay that in the event this tariff had not been imposed, steel rails could have been laid down in New York for sixty-two dollars a ton ; and he cheers and gratifies his English brethren at the close of his essay by saying : 'It is safe to predict that ten years will not elapse before every vestige of restrictive and discriminating legislation will be struck from the national statute book.'

"The advocates of protection have always insisted that such a spirit of competition grows up from it as not to enhance but rather to cheapen the product, and this has steadily been denied by the free-trader. How greatly Mr. Wells was at fault the experience of the years since 1871, when this remarkable essay was written, has demonstrated. At that time this great industry was practically in its infancy in this country ; but encouraged and stimulated by protection, it has developed to such an extent that our capacity is greater than that of any other country on the face of the earth, and steel rails manufactured by our own people are to-day for sale in the American market at the rate of $27 per ton. Had the advice of Mr. Wells been followed the thousands and the tens and hundreds of thousands of men engaged in these establishments would have found no employment ; the tens of thousands of men engaged in the various branches of industry collateral to this would have found no employment. Our own steel rail manufactories would have been destroyed by the influx of the English product, and the instant that result was accomplished prices would have been advanced and the transportation interests of this country would have been chained to the car of the English manufacturer.

"I do not need in this presence to descant upon nor argue the case of protection as against free-trade. It is enough, I apprehend, for me to show what the attitude of our parties really is. The figures which I have already given demonstrate that every interest is promoted by protection. The price of labor is advanced and it has been the policy of the Republican party from the beginning so to legislate that there might be an honest day's wages for an honest day's toil paid in honest money. Mr. Blaine uses this emphatic language, and covers not only the ground of protecting the manufactured article, but protecting the laborer himself: 'The Republican party has protected the free labor of America so that its compensation is larger than is realized in any other country, and it has guarded our people against the unfair competition of contract labor from China, and may be called upon to prohibit the growth of a similar evil from Europe. It is obviously unfair to permit capitalists to make contracts for cheap labor in foreign countries to the hurt and disparagement of the labor of American citizens.' This is the doctrine of our candidate. It covers the whole ground of the controversy. And on this great vital question, in which the hearths and homes of hundreds of thousands of industrious citizens throughout this country are involved, Grover Cleveland has not one word to say, and, so far as we know, has never had a thought.

"The exhibit that I have made of the wonderful growth of our country since 1860 encounters one extraordinary exception, viz., our shipping interests, and with reference to those Mr. Hendricks says that the obituary of our merchant marine is written in our tariff and shipping laws. If Mr. Hendricks does not know that this statement is false he is not nearly so well versed in the history of his country and of that great interest as a candidate for vice-president surely ought to be. Now, what are the facts, and where shall we seek the explanation of this decline in our shipping interests? First it is important to mention that from 1855 to 1861 there was a relative decrease, for reasons surely not attributable to the Republican party, of over 16 per cent. In 1848 the value of the total imports and exports in American ships was about $240,000,000 against about $71,000,000 in foreign ships, and the British government then paid $3,250.000 annually as subsidies. From that time she at once began increasing her subsidies, and at the breaking out of the war in 1861 they were nearly five million dollars, while our tonnage had run down from five hundred millions in 1860 to three hundred and eighty-one millions in 1861. In the years 1870 and 1871, in response to the Pacific Mail subsidy, Great Britain ran her subsidies up to over six millions. So that in 1882, by this policy, she had reduced the value of our imports and exports under our flag to two hundred and forty-two millions, and had increased hers to one billion three hundred millions. It is idle to talk of the individual shipbuilder competing not only against the British shipbuilder, but the British government as well. The policy pursued by the British government has been wise. The value of the English fleet is to-day $1,000,000,000, and of this $900,000,000 has been expended for labor. This policy has given employment to 240,000 men regularly and 220,000 more to run the ships. The gross earnings of this fleet have been $330,000,000. Our country pays $100,000,000 for the service of these ships, and now the clamor is for free ships. Free ships will not relieve us. Great Britain might present to us five hundred vessels free of charge, and yet as the case now stands we could not successfully encounter the competition; for behind the English ship-owner and builder and master stands, as I have said, the British treasury, and until the treasury of the United States, which has granted hundreds of millions of subsidies to railroads, shall hold its shield over and stand behind the American ship-owner and builder it is idle to look for a change in the present condition of affairs. Does not this demonstrate that we need an American policy?"

This political campaign of 1884—the last one he was destined to adorn—ended with the defeat of the Republican party, but throughout its months of close contest the oratorical powers of Mr. Storrs won victory after victory. He had earnestly advocated, both prior to the Republican convention and as a delegate, the renomination of Chester A. Arthur, whose presidential career had reflected dignity and honor upon his party; but, true to his often-repeated expression that the will of the majority should rule in politics, upon the selection of Blaine and Logan he championed their cause most valiantly and untiringly. As he said at Boston, he recognized "no purgatorial politics, no halting, half-way station between heaven and hell."

IX.

THE TARIFF ISSUE.

THE economic policy of the administration is with us an open question, upon which men of both the great political parties are divided in opinion. The historic issues which make an impassable gulf between the parties will always remain as a reason for distinct party existence, even though a temporary coalition on the tariff question should decide the event of one presidential election.

In 1870 there was a state of affairs in this country exactly parallel to that which presents itself for consideration to-day. There was a needless surplus of over one hundred millions of dollars in the Treasury, and the people generally were crying out for a reduction of the heavy burdens of taxation imposed for the purpose of carrying on the war, and to which they had patriotically consented as a necessary war measure. These taxes were raised by means of the most oppressive prohibitive tariff on foreign goods, resulting in a correspondingly high tax on the consumer of goods of domestic manufacture; and now that the war was ended, and the government had an enormous surplus of one hundred millions of dollars in the Treasury, men of all shades of political opinion naturally thought the time had come for a substantial measure of relief.

Mr. Storrs addressed a convention at Springfield, Ill., which was largely made up of agricultural repre-sentatives, and proved that by his power of lucid expo-sition and happy illustration he could make even an economic question interesting. His address was a mas-terly exposition of the injustice of the existing tariff, and of the protectionist fallacies which were then every-where being brought forward in favor of its continuance. In later years he saw reason to modify his opinions, under circumstances which require to be stated in order to make his later utterance on this question intelligible. His free-trade manifesto in 1870 was as follows:

"The grave political questions arising during the prog-ress of the rebellion, and the questions resulting from the war, as affecting the restoration of the seceding States, are so far settled at least as to justify the direction of public attention to, and the discussion of, questions of a financial character, which are, whether we would have it so or not, pressing for decision.

"It may quite safely be said that no attempt at all serious in its character will be made by any political party to re-open the questions settled by the war. The right of secession from the Union was conclusively denied at Appo-matox Court House. The freedom of the slave is an accom-plished fact. The repudiation of the national debt has received its quietus at the hands of the people and in Con-gress; and although there are wide differences of opinion still existing as to the manner in which the debt shall be paid, it is quite safe to say that all parties are agreed that it shall be paid.

"During the prosecution of the war, it was deemed necessary, in order to enable the government to meet the gigantic expenses which its prosecution entailed, to impose upon every conceivable product of human use, wear or consumption heavier tariffs than had ever before been known in our our history. Taxes were also levied upon nearly everything that we ate or drank or wore, upon the product of our industry, upon the articles which we manufactured, and upon the incomes which are derived from the prosecution of our business, whatever that business might be. But little complaint was made against these tariffs and taxes while the war was pending. They were regarded by the great mass of the people as war measures, and to cease when the war itself ceased. Moreover, as every form of industry and almost every character of business was stimulated to a feverish activity by the vast requirements of the government, aided in no small degree by a paper currency, these taxes, onerous as they were, were easily paid, and hence, during that period of time, public complaints were not frequent. But the war finally ended. The vast demands of the government upon the industry of the country ceased. Nearly a million of men who had been engaged in the armies, relieved from those duties, returned quietly but suddenly to their ordinary pursuits. As the currency was contracted and appreciated in value, prices began to shrink, and under such a change of circumstances the burdens of taxation began at once to be felt, and the desire in some measure to be relieved of those burdens came to be almost universally expressed, and the necessity for some such relief is urgent and undeniable.

"I have said that the imposition of the heavy tariff during the war, and the general scheme of taxation then adopted, were generally regarded as war measures to be dispensed with when the war itself should cease. The war ceased four years ago; but the tariffs have not ceased, nor have they even been lessened. Nay, they have been increased since the close of the war.

"The requirements of the government are certainly not as great as they were five years ago. Its expenses have been, during the short period of time that General Grant has been President, reduced many millions. A vast amount of the national debt has already been paid, and in the midst of general business depression the over-burdened public are curiously enough confronted by a surplus which will, during the year 1869–70, reach at least one hundred millions, and probably one hundred and twenty-five millions of dollars. A surplus so gigantic demonstrates, better than any argument could possibly do, that taxation is unnecessarily high. The fact that the government will have, during the current year, from one hundred to one hundred and twenty-five millions of dollars beyond its actual wants and necessities, is of the greatest significance when placed by the side of the other universally conceded fact that taxes and tariffs are seriously burdening the industry and the prosperity of the people.

"A demand to reduce the tariff to something like its former proportions can not be met by the answer that the necessities of the government, in the payment of the principal or interest of the public debt, require that the present rate or tariffs shall be maintained, for the government is certain to have, during the current year, one hundred and twenty-five million dollars more than it will require for the payment of all its expenses, including the maturing interest upon its public debt. However desirable the speedy payment of the national debt may be regarded, there are probably but very few men who would deem it wise or prudent to attempt its entire payment within a period of ten or fifteen years, nor would the people readily consent that from one hundred millions of dollars to one hundred and twenty-five millions of dollars over and above the interest upon the debt and the ordinary expenses of the government should be yearly raised by taxation and tariffs, even were that sum to be religiously appropriated toward such payment.

"That the people are under a serious and oppressive burden of taxation is a fact so conspicuous that it can not be denied. How shall that burden be lightened? is a question now being asked in language so emphatic that some satisfactory answer must be made to it. The present administration has achieved much by the steady reduction of the national expenses and by increased efficiency in the collection of the revenue; but still there stands, in a time of profound peace, an enormous tariff, the effect of which is felt in every department of business, and the maintenance of which enhances the cost of living of every man in the land. Why should that tariff be continued? The fact of the surplus to which I have referred demonstrates that it is not necessary for the support of the government, and so those who are interested in maintaining it are compelled to place their demands upon what they call the 'protection of American industry.'

" I propose this evening to discuss a few general principles affecting the theory of protection. It will be quite impossible to enter very largely, if indeed at all, into detail. And first I will inquire precisely what is meant by protecting American industry? Against what, or against whom, is American industry to be protected? Who attacks, or proposes to attack, American industry? How is the attack made? Is American industry so feeble that it can not, without assistance from the government, protect itself?

"These are all vital questions. If no one is attacking American industry, it needs no protection. If it is able to

defend itself, it should call for no protection. The forms
of American industry are wonderfully diversified. The
great body of the farmers of the country constitute a
large element of what may be called American industry,
and I know of no attack upon them so serious in its character as that made by the tariff; and if the farmers need
protection against anything, it is against protection.
There are thousands of printers in the country; who
attacks or proposes to attack them? No one, except it be
the tariff, which enhances the cost of the material with
which their industry is carried on; of the clothes which they
wear; of the coal which they burn; of the lumber with
which their homes are built; of the salt which they consume, and of the books which they read. There are thousands fo ship-builders in the country; who attacks them
and their interests, and from what enemy do they need to
be protected? The deserted ship-yards of the East answer
this question—they need to be protected against protection,
and that is all the protection they need. The thousands
and hundreds of thousands of carpenters and joiners, boot
and shoe makers, blacksmiths, and the daily toilers with
their hands, upon the land or upon the sea, are threatened
with no attack against which, for their own protection, the
intervention of the government is necessary.

"The fundamental principle of American politics is
'the greatest good to the greatest number.' As a member
of the Republican party, I at the organization of that party
believed that the institution of slavery was a special interest. I was willing to say of it, 'if it can stand up and sustain itself against the sharp and eager competition of free
labor, let it it stand. If it can not, let it fall. I am
opposed to protecting it, for the protection of that interest
is a war upon all other interests.' I deny that the imposition of heavy tariffs upon particular articles of manufacture

is protection. It is a burden instead of a protection; a burden upon all those who use or consume such articles; a bounty to the persons manufacturing them, that bounty being paid by the consumer; and if the consumers are more numerous than the manufacturers, the fundamental idea of our politics is at once violated, government then being administered, not for the greatest good of the greatest number, but for the greatest good to the least number, and the least good to the greater number. Moreover it is not the policy of our government to confer special privileges upon any special classes of men. Our theory is that of individual development, of leaving each man the architect of his own fortunes. All that our government, or indeed any government, should do is to see to it that in the race each man starts, before the law, even with his neighbor. In such a race, to place extra weights upon the swift-footed and the strong-lunged man is not, in fact, protection to the weak-kneed and the narrow-chested man. He runs no faster, nor will his legs or lungs hold out any longer, by reason of the weights which are put upon his competitor. He may, under such circumstances, win in the race; but the purpose of government is that the swiftest, and not that the slowest man, shall win. Who would dream of calling such a policy 'the protection of American speed, wind and bottom'? In such a race I would prefer to see the iron manufacturer and the farmer start even; but, if the farmer is to be loaded down with heavy heavy weights of taxation, and not only that, shall be compelled to stop and lift his competitor over all the rough places which he may encounter on the route, I should call it a very unfair race, and would never think, were it not suggested by the iron manufacturer himself, that I had all the time been protecting American industry. Reason and refine upon it as we may, protection to any manufacturing

interest means simply such legislation as enables the manufacturer to sell his manufactured article for a higher price
than he otherwise could obtain, and which compels the
consumer to pay for such article a higher price than he
would otherwise be compelled to pay.   If it does not mean
this, it means nothing.   If the tariff which is imposed for
the purpose of protection does not enable the manufacturer
to sell his wares at a higher price than they would command without the tariff, of what use is the tariff to him?
For the only way in which he can be benefited is by the
enhanced price.   This enhanced price the consumer is
obliged to pay, not to the government, but to the manufacturer; and thus one kind of industry is compelled to
pay tribute to another.   A special class is privileged and
enriched at the expense and to the impoverishment of
another class.   The home manufacturer is completely protected only when he succeeds in shutting out and exclud-
ing from competition with him the wares of the foreign
manufacturer.   When that is accomplished, revenue ceases;
and in precisely the same proportion that a tariff operates
as a protection to the home manufacturer does it operate
to reduce the revenues of the government.

"Not only does the so-called protection system offend
in the particulars which I have named, but it is also a
direct violation of the liberty of the citizen to sell where
he pleases, and to buy where he can buy cheapest.   Every
man should be permitted to sell his labor where he can get
the highest price for it.   The question is not, after all, how
many dollars does the laboring man receive for a day's
work, but how much of what he must consume will his
day's labor purchase?   If a day's labor at $3 per day will
purchase for the laboring man his hat, or his boots, or the
blanket which he needs, he is receiving better pay than when
he gets $5 per day; but his boots, or his hat, or his blanket

costs him $10. The laborer should be permitted to take his labor or its products to the market, where, in exchange for those commodities which he needs, he can get the most of such commodities. But to compel the farmer to exchange one day's labor for one yard of cloth manufactured in New England, when he might exchange the same amount of labor for two yards of cloth manufactured in Old England, is merely a system of legalized plunder of the farmer, instead of protection to American industry.

"I apprehend that, should the government levy a direct tax upon all the property of the country, to be paid over directly to the iron manufacturers, so that they might be enabled to hold their own against the competition of the foreign manufacturers, but few would be found who would justify such an exercise of the power of taxation. If there is any difference between such a plan and a tariff for protection, the difference is against the tariff. When reduced to its exact practical operations, the protection of American industry, so called, is simply the forcible taking from the consumer of a portion of his earnings, and handing it over to the manufacturer. The proposition to the consumer is simply this: We, the government, will take from you 10 or 15 or 20 per cent of your earnings, and give it to the manufacturer, and he will spend it so much more judiciously than you would, that ultimately, and in the process of time, it will in some curious and circuitous manner, which we haven't the time to explain now, rebound more greatly to your advantage than it would had you spent it yourself and for yourself.

"We are all now in favor of free speech, free thought, free soil, free labor; what is there about trade that it should not be free? If I am permitted to attend church where I please; to think upon all political and religious subjects as I please, why should I not be permitted to buy and sell where I please? Why should I be compelled to make my exchange of coin for woolen and cotton goods in New England, my exchange of my wheat for iron goods in Pennsylvania, my pork and beef for salt at Syracuse or Saginaw? Am I, thus compulsorily driven to a particular market, a free man? So far as my corn and wheat and pork and beef are concerned, I have to come in competition with the world. The prices which I secure for them are fixed by the markets of the world. I am compelled to sell, giving to the purchaser all the benefits of the largest competition, but am compelled to purchase in a restricted market. This, we are assured, protects American industry.

"The evils resulting from the protective system being so direct and immediate, so plain and so easily understood, we are naturally led to inquire, 'What compensation does the system furnish for the many evils which flow from it? It will hardly do to answer this inquiry by saying that the system fosters and encourages American industry, for if the entire agricultural interests are compelled to pay tribute to the manufacturing, certainly the former are not thereby fostered and encouraged in following agricultural pursuits. The ship-builder it not fostered and encouraged in building ships so long as, through the operation of a tariff, he is compelled to pay so high a price for almost every article which enters into the construction of a ship that it costs him nearly twice as much to build a ship here as it costs the Englishman to build one in his own ports. So long as that difference exists in the cost of ship-building, those who desire ships will have them built where they can be built the cheapest, and the industry of our home ship-builder, so far from being fostered and encouraged, is destroyed, and he is driven from that employment.

" But we are assured that by the protection of home industry we furnish a home market for our own products.

It requires some argument, and pretty close attention, to the statement of the argument, to clearly perceive how the farmer, in being compelled by a protective tariff to pay for his reapers and threshers, his hoes and his spades, his wagons and his harness, his clothing and his salt, anywhere from 15 to 20 per cent more than he otherwise would be compelled, receives an adequate compensation from the fact that the persons to whom these prices are paid reside at Pittsburgh and Lowell, instead of at Sheffield and Manchester. It is quite true that the man who employs his entire time in manufacturing iron will not be able to till the soil, but this is quite as true of the artisan in England as in Pennsylvania. In order to enhance the price of grain, the general demand for it must be increased. Our grain market responds as readily to the state of the English harvests as to the condition of our own. If to-day one half the laborers in the fields in England should be withdrawn from that form of industry, that vacancy not being supplied, and at once transferred to the mill and the workshop, the effect would as readily be felt here as should the same transfer be made from our own fields. Unless the system of protection decreases the number of grain producers, I fail to see how it is to affect the prices of grain advantageously. It is not, I believe, claimed that protection actually increases the population. The system creates no additional mouths, and unless it be demonstrated that the worker in an iron mill or in a cotton factory eats more,— is from the nature of his pursuits a hungrier man than other kinds of laborers,— I fail to see how, by the protective system, the grain market is improved.

"We are also assured that the protective system keeps gold at home; that, inasmuch as it is not expended for foreign manufactures, it is retained in the country, and we are thereby made the richer for such retention. Even

if that result were certain to follow from the protective
system, it would by no means furnish a substantial argument in its favor.   If my gold will buy me more of what
I need by expending it abroad than at home, the actual
wealth of the country is lessened by compelling me to spend
it at home.   If I receive for my labor five dollars per day,
in gold, and with that gold can buy one blanket in New
England and two blankets in Old England, I am a loser,
and the country is a loser, in compelling me to buy my
blankets in New England.   I am worth, under such a
system, just one blanket less than I would be without it.
The gold which I receive represents my day's labor, and
the more of what I need to consume I am enabled to get
with my day's labor, the better I am off.

"Another point strenuously urged by the advocates of
protection is that it diversifies American industry.   I do
not believe that industry can be diversified by legislation.
I do not believe that the natural tendencies of mankind,
particularly in this country, set so strongly towards the
tilling of the soil and rural lives, that an act of Congress
is necessary to check them.   The necessities and wants of
men are all the provocatives needed to diversify labor.
This has been shown to be so from the beginning of the
world; it will probably continue so to the end.   Our first
parents were, in their first and happiest condition, engaged in purely rural pursuits and pleasures.   After their
expulsion from Paradise, Adam was compelled to manufacture either a hoe or a spade, before he could dig the soil.
Eve also manufactured an apron.   Tubal Cain was a blacksmith.   Abel was a wool grower.   Noah was at one time a
ship-builder, and after the flood manufactured wines from
grapes grown in his own vineyard, and, as we are informed,
was on one occasion at least a very liberal consumer of his
own products.   We do not all raise wheat and corn,

although we all consume bread. But the farmer needs something besides bread. He needs clothing, and the manufacturer supplies it to him. His horses must be shod—the blacksmith does it for him. His grain must reach a market—the carrier takes it to the market for him. He must have a house to shelter himself—the mechanic builds it for him. His children must be taught—the schoolmaster teaches them for him. He must have books and papers to read—the printer and publisher furnish them. The manufacturer of clothes, the blacksmith, the carrier, the mechanic, the teacher, the printer, and the publisher, by the various articles which they furnish the farmer, supply themselves with bread. The very structure of civilized society is rested upon this variety of wants and necessities, and the consequent variety and diversity of employments by which they may be supplied.

" But I insist that the natural result of the protective policy is not to diversify labor, but to commit it to some particular channels. For if, through the intervention of the government, the manufacturers of iron goods and woolen goods receive particular benefits and advantages at the expense of other forms of industry, the industry which is pursued without these adventitious aids will certainly desire to change its form and adopt the kind thus specially favored. When the farmer and the printer, the shipbuilder and the carpenter, find that the government leaves them to take care of themselves, and compels them to pay tribute to the iron manufacturer and the cotton or woolen manufacturer, they will abandon their former pursuits and seek the more favored one, just as certainly as the night succeeds the day. The attempt to diversify labor by legislation is like an attempt to diversify the character of our garments by a statute. We will probably wear light goods when the heats of summer are upon us, and heavier and thicker ones when the frosts of winter are about us. We diversify our wearing apparel to meet the diversities of climate; we will just as naturally diversify our labor to meet the diversities of our wants, necessities, and tastes.

"Another favorite argument of the protectionists is that it is unjust to submit our industry to competition with what they call the pauper labor of Europe. This argument, if it may be called an argument, answers itself. The price of the manufactured article naturally depends in a great measure on the price of labor employed in its manufacture. The price of that labor depends necessarily upon the relation between the supply of such labor and the demand for it. If, by a protective tariff, the production of cotton goods is largely and unnaturally increased, the demand for that kind of labor will also be increased; the supply will meet that demand; industry will be deviated from other channels, and the very fact that a feverish and unnatural demand for that kind of labor is created, tends inevitably to the lessening of the wages of the operative. An artificial stimulus given to the manufacturing interests in this country brings to our shores what is called the pauper labor of Europe. With that labor our own industry must be brought into competition, and there is no method more positively certain of bringing the prices of labor down to m e factory rates than by making the country one vast factory. The jingling phrase, 'American prices for American labor,' means nothing, unless it be a fact that American prices are better and larger than any other prices. If English prices for labor are higher than American prices, then I am in favor of English prices for American labor. The fact is when we take into account the difference between our currency and gold, and the difference in price of living in this country and in the old world, the prices paid to the skilled artisan in England, in

France, and in Belgium are greater than are paid in this country.

"Legislation can not regulate prices any more than it can change the rotation of the seasons. A policy which looks to a rapid and artificial increase in the number of laborers in any branch of industry can have but one consequence, and that is a reduction in the rewards of each laborer. Unless all natural laws have ceased to operate, such must be the result. The old manufacturers of the Damascus blade needed no protection. The superior quality of the steel, and the superior skill of the artisans engaged in the manufacture, furnished all the protection that was needed. Demosthenes needed no protection against the competition of foreign orators; nor did Pericles or Phidias seek a discriminating tariff to aid them in their appeals to Athenian taste and culture against the competition of the foreign sculptor or painter. Socrates and Plato for success with their countrymen needed no tariff upon philosophy to give them precedence over all competitors, but the vigor of their understandings and the marvelous skill with which they gave expression to their ideas adequately protected them against any and all competition. Great skill and great genius protect themselves. They carry always with them a shield which renders them absolutely secure against all attacks, save those made by greater skill and greater genius; and before such attacks they ought to be subdued; they will be overcome, and all the legislative art and legerdemain on earth can not long postpone such result.

"We are also assured that the country is new and young, and that we must have a protective tariff for the benefit of our infant manufacturers. When, I ask, will the country be old? When will our manufactures pass the adolescent period, and reach the quality of manhood? If to-day there were carved out of the British Isles another

empire, the empire thus newly created, as a distinct
national existence, would be new, but in every other sense
it would be as old as the original empire from which it was
taken.   Nations are not new or old, dating merely from
the commencement of their national existence, but from
the experience with which the history of the world has
supplied them.   This young Republic of ours, almost the
newest born among the nations, is vastly older than the
old Assyrians, who flourished hundreds of years, and then
fell, thousands of years ago.   It is older in the experiences
of the world than the Egyptians, whose unriddled sphinxes
lie half buried in the desert sands, and whose mighty pyramids, records of which are lost in the early morning of
this world's history, in the midst of utter barrenness, rear
their colossal forms against the sky.   All that past art, or
science, or skill, or thought, or study, has taught, is ours.
Reckoning the age of a people by its possessions, we are
the oldest people in the world.   There is no infancy in
our national life.   It is the bone and gristle of manhood.
That our territorial extent is great, and as yet undeveloped,
is true; but a protective tariff will neither lessen its territorial extent nor assist in the rescue from the native wild-
ness of the prairie or the forest, the portions which the
industry of man has not yet touched.   In the sense in
which it is said that our country is new, it will remain so
just as long as it has not the same amount of population
to the square mile as England, and France, and Belgium.
A protective tariff will not hasten that increase of population; nor would the immediate doubling of the laboring
interests materially benefit those who are already here.

"But what about our infant manufactures ?   If I
were plundered of my possessions, it would be but a sorry
consolation to be told that an infant had done it.   Certainly I should not approve a policy which looked to the

increase of the strength and plundering capacity of the infant. I should be apt to say, 'He may be an infant in years, but he is a giant in strength.' Hercules, when he strangled the serpents and vanquished the Nemean lion, was an infant, but among serpents and lions an exceedingly dangerous and uncomfortable infant; and had it been left to the vote of the serpents and the lions, I doubt not there would have been an unanimous expression of opinion against their being compelled to contribute to the increase of his strength on the ground of his infancy. In all those essentials which ordinarily characterize infancy, have our manufacturing interests any of the marks of infancy about them ? If their present pecuniary strength and power is infancy, God deliver us from their youth and their manhood ! Abundantly able to go alone, I insist that they now shall go alone, and that neither the government shall of itself help them, nor compel me to help them.

" But the laborer himself is not assisted by a protective tariff. The proprietor derives all the benefits from it, and the profits all go to him. Not only that, but protection is the ultimate ruin of our manufactures. It stimulates an unnatural and artificial production; it withdraws capital and labor from pursuits in which they are naturally employed, and, under a delusive prospect of larger profits, inveigles them into the protected manufacture or pursuit. Thus an extortionate tariff upon iron will greatly stimulate its production until the market is glutted, and ruin follows. Cotton mills are even now closed. The tariff on wool led thousands into wool-growing who would not otherwise engaged in it, and the wool-grower now knows that, so far from conferring any substantial benefits upon him, the protective tariff is a delusion and a snare.

" It ruins the inventive genius of the people, by rendering its exercise unnecessary. In the affairs of this world

skill must meet skill. Natural obstacles in the way of
competition must be overcome by greater ingenuity in
mechanical appliances. The manufacturer of pig iron can
slumber, and run his mills upon the old plans, and by the
old methods of machinery. The bounties which the government compels the public to pay him render it unnecessary for him to do more than to suffer things to run as they
are. When necessity drove the inventive genius of the
people in that direction, the sewing machine was one of its
results, and with those machines we now supply the world.
Our vast fields presented, for the reaping of our grains,
the preparation of the soil, planting of the seeds, and the
harvesting of the ripened crops, new problems; and,
turned by necessity in those directions, the genius of the
people brought forth the patent drill, the reaper, the
thresher, the cultivator, and the harvester. Without a
navy when the rebellion began, and with three thousand
miles of sea coast to blockade, the necessities of the situation turned in that direction the inventive genius of the
people, and one bright morning at Hampton Roads the
sudden offspring of that ingenuity, the Monitor, revolutionized the naval architecture of the world, and rendered
the old wooden walls as useless and as worthless as mere
fabrics of pasteboard.

"Let us not distrust ourselves. The shoemakers of
Lynn need no protection. The wonderful skill of their
machinery places foreign competition out of the question.
Open the door to competition. Let it be known that in
any branch of industry there is a necessity that American
ingenuity should exhibit itself, and it will certainly do so.
In its presence all natural difficulties and obstacles will be
overcome, and it will assuredly triumph.

" Protection destroys our carrying trade, and thereby
drives our vessels from the seas. I have already shown

that, as a regular pursuit, ship-building in this country
has substantially ceased. The tariffs upon the materials
which enter into the construction of a ship are so enormous,
and the cost is thereby so greatly enhanced, that competition with foreign ship-builders is simply impossible. But
the trouble does not cease here. Before the tariff, a large
and profitable trade was carried on with South American
ports, where our calico and sheetings, and other products
of our labor, were exchanged for their wools. This trade
gave employment to the ship-builder and ship-owner, and
to the sailor. It opened a market for our own products,
and gave thereby employment to our own labor. Our own
wares were sold at profitable prices. We were supplied
with cheap and fine wools. Every one was benefited.
But the protective tariff laid its hand upon wool, and all
these interests perished as if they had been blighted with
a mildew. On the shores of the Mediterranean the
Almighty has seen fit to confer warmer suns and more
genial heats than shine upon the salt marshes of Syracuse
or Saginaw. Congress has sought to correct this order of
Providence, and to protect the Onondaga and the Saginaw
salt, manufactured by mechanical heats and appliances,
against that perfected by the cheaper agencies of solar
heat. We bring in our vessels no more salt from the shores
and the islands of the Mediterranean. We get poorer salt,
and at a higher price than formerly; but be assured, Providence will win.

"Even though their culture be protected by an act of
Congress, oranges will not grow so luxuriantly in Vermont
as in Portugal. The sun still shines as warm in Southern
Europe, and as coyly and as coldly in New York and
Michigan, as before Congress undertook to decree that it
should be otherwise; and the benefits and blessings of God's
sunshine we must have, come from whatever source they
may.

"We have an enormous tariff on coal. As well might you attempt to impose a tax upon one of the elemental forces of nature as upon coal. It is the power which moves all our machinery, and the use of which enters directly or indirectly into every article of human wants, necessities, comforts or luxuries. Yet we are obliged to pay tribute for the use of that power which drives our machinery and which heats our houses. As well might you tax the sunshine. The tariff on iron not only enhances the price of every article into which it enters, and which we are obliged to use, but it swallows up the hard labor of the farmer in the cost of transportation of his products to a market. The cost of railroad construction is thereby enhanced, and an advance in rates of transportation follows as a necessity. In its practical operations, our present tariff is simply a nuisance. Of about 4,000 articles subject to the tariff, twenty furnish half the revenue, and the balance are purely mischievous.

"A gentleman of the name of Spaulding prepares glue and sells it for a good price under the name of 'Spaulding's Prepared Glue.' His is American industry, and hence is protected. Last year the government received by way of revenue from the tariff on glue the magnificent sum of $17. Our hens are protected; and in 1868 the government received $6.90 from duties on ostrich eggs; and yet I believe that, even thus protected, the native hen will never succeed—so far at least as the size of the egg is concerned—in competition with the ostrich. Sauerkraut is protected, and the protection yielded a revenue to the government of $6. Apple sauce is also protected, and in 1868 yielded a revenue to the government of $300. We are also protected against Spanish flies and Brazilian bugs. Our native flies and bugs are in their infancy, and must be protected.

" Finally, what is a tariff ? It is a tax. It is nothing less than, and nothing but, a tax. It is a tax which we do not pay to the government, but to the manufacturer for his private enrichment; for where protection begins revenue ceases. The consumer is impoverished, the government is not aided. Shall this system be continued ? The question we must answer. We may dodge it and evade it for a time; but the millions of men who protected the nation in the hour of its sore peril, and with their lives, demand that this question be answered. I am, for myself, prepared to answer it. My answer is: Our soil is free, our men are free, our thought is free, our speech is free, our trade shall be free."

Circumstances altered Mr. Storrs' economic opinions. He was engaged by the iron and steel interests to present their case before the House Committee of Ways and Means in 1880, in opposition to a proposed reduction of the tariff on steel rails. The reduction was advocated by Hon. James F. Wilson of Iowa in the interest of the agricultural West, and the eloquence of Mr. Storrs was put in requisition to oppose it. He was successful, and not only convinced the committee, but himself, that in certain cases protection was a proper thing. The ground of his argument for the iron and steel men was that they had paid $800,000,000 for the use of the Bessemer patent in the United States, and that it would be mere robbery to permit the English manufacturers of Bessemer steel to introduce their goods in the market of the United States on terms which would make their competition hurtful to American manufacturers. His argument prevailed, but having once turned his attention to a "favored industry," he opened his mind to the whole question of protection,

and we have now to place before the reader an utterance radically different from the foregoing. The
economic philosopher loses himself in the advocate, and
builds up untenable theories to help him out to extrava-
gant conclusions. It must be remembered, in reading
the speech we have now to introduce, that it was
spoken to men in the employ of the steel ring, and is
to be considered as the utterance of an advocate. The
speech of 1870, without doubt, conveyed Mr. Storrs' real
opinions:

"I am satisfied that there is no necessity to make any
speech on the subject of the tariff here to-night for the
purpose of convincing anybody who is present of the necessity, the propriety, and wisdom of the protective system.
You have the most conclusive proofs of the wisdom of the
tariff policy in your own experience, in your occupation,
and in your lives. There is no proof in this world quite
so satisfactory and demonstrative as that which a man gets
from his actual living condition; and the man who has a
full stomach and a comfortable home, is well housed, and
his children and his family are well educated and well
clad, knows it; and there is no amount of collegiate
theorizing nor fine spun theories in the world that is going
to change that condition which he knows he may be en-
joying. There is no man with an empty stomach that is
ever going to have it filled by an argument. The experiment has been tried over and over again by all free-trade
orators in America. There is no man whose children and
whose family are badly clothed and inadequately fed that
is going to have them kept warm by Professor Sumner's
theories.

"I do not speak for any class here to-night. There
are 50,000,000 of people in this country, pretty nearly

that — 50,000,000 of citizens. Out of that 50,000,000 of citizens there are probably about 45,000,000 who may be called laborers. These laborers constitute the great body of American citizenship, and the capitalists and the college professors and the preachers cut a very small figure numerically when they are compared with the whole body of citizenship. I am talking in favor to-night, therefore, of the great body of American citizenship, which is affected either for good or for ill by the tariff system.

" And when I speak in favor of the laboring classes of this country, I talk in favor of the whole country. The very useful and the very excellent class to which I belong, that of lawyers [laughter], might all die to-night; it would be a great loss to their families and to their friends, but the country would go right on to-morrow as usual. The postmasters might all die to-night and the members of Congress [laughter], and the preachers and the editors, and we would gather ourselves together and go right on quite comfortably day after to-morrow.

" But the laboring interests of this country are its spinal column. You can take the natural man, and cut off his fingers and his hands, or his arms or his legs, and he will struggle along ; but a very slight wound in that spinal column destroys absolutely the individual.

Now, when I speak to you laboring men I do not speak to you men who work in mills, for I take an exceedingly broad view of this tariff question. I hold that the man on the farm is quite as much benefited by the enforcement of the protective system as the man in the mill. Now there is no mistake about it, for if you should turn loose on all the farms and into the fields as cultivators and tillers of the soil all the men who are engaged to-day in workshops, factories, foundries, furnaces and mills, there would be such an impairment of the general prosperity of the agricultural

interests of the country as I can not command any language
adequately to describe. For the success of any sort of
labor requires two things : first, an intelligent and well-
paid laborer who produces, and next a provident and a
prosperous purchaser and consumer ; and there can not be
any such thing as prosperity among our agricultural classes
unless it is accompanied by prosperity among manufacturing classes, that they may be able to buy what comes out
of the ground, and so that the farmer may be able to buy
what comes out of the mill.

"God in His infinite wisdom is, I think, wiser than the
free-trader. About the first thing that God did after He
made Adam and Eve was to diversify industry. He didn't
set them all to tilling the Garden of Eden, but they went
into the iron business, as I understand it, at a very early
day.

"I have said we have 50,000,000 people here. I remember some few month since, in discussing this complicated
tariff question, a gentleman asked me what I considered to
be the best evidence of general prosperity — real prosperity, not that which was apparent and fictitious, but the real
genuine article. Now it is a favorite trick with free-trade
orators and scholars to say of all prosperity which exists
under the protective system, that it is delusive, deceptive,
and fictitious. The result of their logic is that there is
nothing genuine but want; that there is nothing really
prosperous but pauperism, and that there is nothing really
solid except the poor-house. I am inclined to the opinion
that a full stomach is just as much a reality as an empty
one. I have tried both. I am fully convinced that when
the sunshine of hope and contentment shines over all your
hearthstones, and you go home and find your table well
supplied and your little children well fed and well clad,
that that is just exactly as genuine as to see them driven

by necessity and want, beggared and tattered, into the streets. I answered this man, that, given a sound currency (which we have), the surest earthly evidence that any one could furnish of real prosperity was well-paid labor. I have read a great deal of political economy, and you may read it till you become, as I have become, dizzy in its contemplation; but there is in all this world no indication of prosperity so sure, so certain, as that.

"Now, laying the tariff at one side, why am I in favor of the protective system as I am? I will tell you very briefly. This country never was prosperous except when labor was adequately rewarded — and in this country labor was never adequately rewarded except when we had a protective tariff.

"The other day a gentleman said to me, 'Why, sir, they tried free trade in England, and have for years. Isn't it prosperous? If England prospers under free trade why should not we prosper under the same doctrine?' I said: 'That depends — that depends. What you call England I don't call the United States of America.'

"England, or the British Empire, has 30,000,000 of people or thereabout, and of those 30,000,000 there are not 5,000,000 who can be called financially prosperous. When writers speak of the prosperity of England, they mean simply the prosperity of the land-owner, the capitalist, the banker, and the commercial interests of that empire.

"England, I am told, is prosperous, but there is one pauper out of every thirty-five of its subjects; in this country there is one pauper out of every 278. England, I am told, is prosperous. You can't go into a manufacturing town in England anywhere and take from their mills anywhere, or their factories anywhere, an audience of workingmen such as I see here to-night, who have their own homes, educate their children, clothe them comfortably, are well housed, themselves well clad and as well dressed as I see this audience to-night — you can't find it in all England. You may go all over that empire and such a spectacle can not be presented. Now, why is that? It is because their labor, for purposes which we want to make the citizen in this country, is inadequately rewarded. The citizen here is one thing; the subject in Great Britain is quite another thing. The citizen here is a component part of the government, and the prosperity of the government and its strength depend upon the happiness and contentment and prosperity of the citizen. The object of this government is to make a happy and contented individual [Hear! hear!] ; and the object of their government is to make good pig-iron, no matter what happens to the man. In that government the product is elevated above the worker; in this country the worker is superior to anything that he makes. We would rather pay more for our iron and have the man who made it happy and more prosperous; they want their iron cheap so they can sell it in competition with the world, no matter what happens to the man who makes it.

"England is not free trade, and never was, and never will be. There never on the face of the earth was a country so thoroughly and efficiently protective of its manufacturing interests as Great Britain to-day. The beginning of their alleged free-trade system was with the abolition and repeal of the corn laws. Why were they repealed? It was to reduce the price of labor and manufacture so that they could carry on this competition with the world, and their whole struggle has been to reduce the cost of production, including the reduction of the wages of the laborer, so that they may compete with the world in the articles which they manufacture. They protect their manufacturing interest by lowering the laborer — taxing his reward;

we protect our manufacturing interest by increasing his wages and keeping our competition within ourselves.

"They don't plow the sea with their ships on anything like an even competition There is no disguise in the way in which they protect their merchant marine. They don't do it through the indirect and guarded agency of the tariff, but they do it by the payment to their merchant marine of enormous sums of money by way of subsidy directly, so that there is no people on the face of the earth that can manage to keep up a competition with them.

"Now, then, the question comes right home to us. 'What is our duty as American citizens?' I am not a humanitarian in its very largest sense. It is enough for my humanity to be circumscribed within the boundaries of this continent. I am in favor of all politics which will contribute to the interests of the citizens of this country, and it is to the American citizens' interest that I am, in the first instance, compelled to look. I know, for the history of this country has taught us, that there has never been a time when we have taken away the protection from our own industries that our labor has not been universally paralyzed and a reign of terror and financial bankruptcy extended over the whole country, embracing not merely our manufacturing interests within its baleful effect, but bringing down the commercial, mercantile, financial and agricultural interests with it as well, in one common and universal ruin. I know that ruin has followed, from the organization of the government down to this moment, every attempt to put into practical operation the theories of free trade; and I know full well — the history of this country teaches it to me, and there is no gainsaying and denying it — that prosperity of the largest and most satisfactory character has always attended adequate, honest, and judicious protection of American industries.

"What the industries of this country require is steadiness. We want not only a tariff to-day, we want to know what it is going to be to-morrow and the next day and the next year. The time has come in our politics when we know no longer any color lines, and when it is for our interests to look after our interest and the interest of no other country. I am willing to take care of England when I am through taking care of the United States of America, and the time is coming when our political action must be guided and determined by what we know to be not only our individual but the national interest. The time is coming when we should no longer be deceived by political trade-marks and labels, but when every man who looks to, and regards, and is a well-wisher for the prosperity of, the great laboring interest in this country will give his support and his ballot to no man that would in the slightest degree imperil or put in jeopardy these great interests. Now the man who is in favor of free trade is opposed to your interest; and I don't care by what political name he is designated, the man who is in favor of constant tinkering with our tariff, rendering large investments insecure and uncertain, rendering your tenure of place insecure and uncertain,— such a man is not either your personal nor political friend, and it behooves you when you understand the situation to act upon it. You are masters of the situation, and can emphasize your views in such a manner that your selected rulers will be compelled to observe them.

"Gentlemen, I said when I started that there was no necessity of our arguing about the tariff to you. A few illustrations of its workings — and working on a limited scale—perhaps furnish the best sort of argument that we can possibly command.

"I am opposed to putting the American laborer in field or farm or factory or furnace or mill or shop on an even competition with any man who doesn't live as well as he does. Now that is a very fair way to state it. I am opposed to having the American laborer, who clothes his children and eats meat, compelled to work in competition with a man who throws his children upon the town and never eats meat. [Applause.] The competition is not a fair one, and such competition means this: Under its influence both laborers will by and by leave their children in rags, and neither will eat meat. Suppose you had two foundries here side by side. In one foundry there was not a man in it who furnished a single article of clothing to his family, paid a dollar for their education, ever had a fire in his home, and ever had meat upon his table. And suppose in the other, honest and intelligent workingmen thought it was their duty to clothe and educate their children and keep themselves well. Now, gentlemen, do you suppose that for any length and period of time the well-fed, public-spirited laborers could sustain a competition with the others? Why, they could work for 25 cents a day and make money where you was losing it on $1.50. They would have no expenses.

"Take it where it was illustrated in San Francisco. Now the proposition of the free-trader is simply this: It is to throw down the barriers and place every laborer in America in active competition with every laborer everywhere else all over the world, barring the mere question of transportation. You are brought into direct competition with the English, with the French, with the German and with the Chinese laborer. Now, take it in San Francisco. This whole problem of free trade has been wonderfully worked out there, for free trade means nothing under heaven but a competition of the American laborer with the underpaid laborer of the old world. From 1870 to 1880 every city in the United States had gained in population except San Francisco. From 1875 to 1880 every city in the United States had gained in its business interests except San Francisco. During those five years of time every city in the United States had increased its taxable wealth except San Francisco. Every city was prosperous in 1880 except San Francisco. Every city in the United States from 1875 to 1880 had gained in the number of its laboring men and in the amount of their accumulation except San Francisco. What was the trouble? The free-trader tells us that the elysium of free trade is a cheap product. Isn't that it? He says to the farmer, 'Let us abolish all this infernal tariff, and everything will be cheap.' As if the beauty of heaven was that everything was cheap there! Your clothes will all be cheap, and all work will be done for you cheap. Your furniture will all be cheap — everything you need for supplying all human wants and necessities will be cheap. Well, what if it is? Suppose it is cheap, that isn't heaven. In this free-trade elysium that ruled in San Francisco, laundry was cheaper than anywhere in the world. There were about 30,000 Chinamen there, and with that competition, why the white washer of clothes stood no sort of chance. Cigars were cheaper there than anywhere else in America. Why? Because the China-man had gone into making cigars, and the white laborer who clothed himself and fed himself could hold no sort of competition with him. In the manufacture of tinware and wooden-ware the white labor was driven out of the markets of San Francisco and all the state, and those goods were never so cheap, and San Francisco was never so utterly wretched. What was the trouble? You had merely transferred from China just a mere speck of population, a mere drop, put it into a locality and brought the intelligent laborer into competition with it, and down the intelligent American laborer went. Why? Why the article with which he was then compelled to compete had had its stomach adjusted to famine by 3,000 years of experience. What could the American laborer with his notions of comfortable and decent living do in competition with the man who dined off rice and supped off rats?

" Now, then, if— and I want you to answer this question for yourselves— if placing that little trifle of competition down by the side of the American laborer produces that result; if bringing but one-hundred-thousandth part of China over here to compete with us destroys the prosperity of a great city, what will it do when the barriers are all thrown down and you compete with 300,000,000 of Chinamen? What will it do when the barriers are all thrown down — and the repeal of the protective system is the overthrow of these barriers, every one of them — when you not only compete with this labor, but with the degraded labor all the world? This is the proposition of which the free-trader loses sight. He loses sight of the purpose of this government. He never seems to conceive why it was organized. He doesn't seem to be able to understand or comprehend the great idea that lies at its foundations. The object of this government, the mission which it is to perform, is the ennobling of the citizens and the elevation and dignifying of humanity. It is too big an idea — altogether too big an idea — for the free-trader to grasp. But that man never was dignified, and that individual never was ennobled, that labor never was prosperous, and that citizenship never was great, that had to depend, in the race for success in this world, upon competition with cold firesides, desolate homes, hungry children, the poor-house in the near distance, illiteracy and want.

" I expect to see this country great. This country will be great, not because its prairies are vast nor its streams long and running, bearing the soil of thousands of miles on their

bosoms to the ocean; not because the mountains are high—
that is not what makes this country great; but this
country is the greatest missionary of all the world, from all
the ages and to all the ages, because it is the first country
upon which the sun, in all its revolving course, ever shone,
that puts the individual above the government, and that
says that all that government was made for was simply to
furnish the machinery by which the man might develop
the largest manhood that was in him. When labor prospers this is done. I am in favor of protecting our industries, not because I am a mechanic, or ever was, but because
down in the bottom of my heart, with a love as deep as I
have felt for wife or parent, I love this country, I believe
in its future, and I know that it is the hope of all the ages,
to be answered only by the prosperity of the average citizen.

www.ingramcontent.com/pod-product-compliance
Lightning Source LLC
Chambersburg PA
CBHW020505270326
41926CB00008B/752

* 9 7 8 3 3 3 7 0 6 8 6 9 1 *